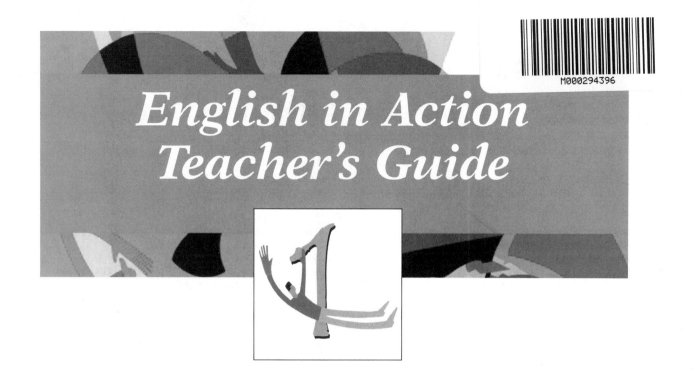

English in Action
Teacher's Guide

Barbara H. Foley

Elizabeth R. Neblett

John Chapman

THOMSON
™
HEINLE

Australia • Canada • Mexico • Singapore • Spain • United Kingdom • United States

English in Action 1, Teacher's Guide
by Barbara H. Foley, Elizabeth R. Neblett, and John Chapman

Publisher, Adult and Academic ESL: *James W. Brown*
Acquisitions Editor: *Sherrise Roehr*
Senior Development Editor: *Jill Korey O'Sullivan*
Development Editor: *Sarah Barnicle*
Editorial Assistant: *Audra Longert*
Marketing Manager: *Eric Bredenberg*
Director, Global ESL Training &
  Development: *Evelyn Nelson*
Senior Production Editor: *Maryellen Killeen*
Senior Frontlist Buyer: *Mary Beth Hennebury*
Project Manager: *Tünde A. Dewey*

Compositor: *Pre-Press Co., Inc.*
Text Printer/Binder: *Edwards Brothers Printing*
Text Designer: *Sue Gerald*
Cover Designer: *Gina Petti/Rotunda Design House*
Photo Researcher: *Claudine Corey*
Unit Opener Art: *Zita Asbaghi*
Illustrators: *Scott MacNeill; Ray Medici Glen Giron, Roger*
  Acaya, Ibarra Cristostomo, Leo Cultura of
  Raketshop Design Studio, Philippines
Cover Art: *Zita Asbaghi*

International Division List

ASIA
Thomson Learning
5 Shenton Way
#01-01 UIC Building
Singapore 068808
Tel: 65-6410-1200
Fax: 65-6410-1208

AUSTRALIA / NEW ZEALAND
Nelson Thomson Learning
102 Dodds Street
South Melbourne
Victoria 3205
Australia
Tel: 61-(0)3-9685-4111
Fax: 61-(0)3-9685-4199

BRAZIL
Thomson Pioneira Ltda
Rua Traipú, 114-3° Andar
Perdizes
01235-000 - São Paulo - SP
Brasil
Tel: 55 11 3665-9900
Fax: 55 11 3665-9901

CANADA
Nelson Thomson Learning
1120 Birchmount Road
Scarborough,
Ontario M1K 5G4
Canada
Tel: 416-752-9448
Fax: 416-752-8102

JAPAN
Thomson Learning
Nihonjisyo Brooks Bldg. 3-F
1-4-1 Kudankita
Chiyoda-ku
Tokyo 102-0073
Japan
Tel: 81-3-3511-4390
Fax: 81-3-3511-4391

KOREA
Thomson Learning
Suite 301 Richemont Building
114-5 Sung San-Dong Mapo-ku
Seoul 121-250
Korea
Tel: 82-2-322-4926
Fax: 82-2-322-4927

LATIN AMERICA
Thomson Learning
Séneca 53
Colonia Polanco
11560 México D.F.
México
Tel: 52-55-5281-2906
Fax: 52-55-5281-2656

SPAIN / PORTUGAL
Paraninfo Thomson Learning
Calle Magallanes 25
28015 – Madrid
España
Tel: 34-(0)91-446-3350
Fax: 34-(0)91-445-6218

TAIWAN
Thomson Learning
12F, No. 10 Heng Yang Road
Taipei, Taiwan, R.O.C.
Tel: 886-2-2375-1118
Fax: 886-2-2375-1119

EUROPE / MIDDLE EAST/AFRICA
Thomson Learning
High Holborn House
50 / 51 Bedford Row
London WC1R 4LR
United Kingdom
Tel: 44-20-7067-2500
Fax: 44-20-7067-2600

Acknowledgments

We would like to acknowledge the many individuals who helped, encouraged, and supported us during the writing and production of this series. In keeping with an open-ended format, we would like to offer a matching exercise. Please be advised, there is more than one correct "match" for each person. Thank you all!

Jim Brown	• for your creative eye for art and design.
Anita Raducanu	• for your enthusiasm and support.
Eric Bredenberg	• for your support, patience, and humor while guiding this project.
Sherrise Roehr	• for your faith in the authors.
Maryellen Killeen	• for your smiles and your stories.
Jill Korey O'Sullivan	• for your encouragement, comments, and suggestions.
Sarah Barnicle	• for putting up with us!
Audra Longert	• for your understanding of the needs of teachers and programs.
Tünde A. Dewey	• for your keeping us all on schedule.
All the Heinle sales reps	• for your help with research.
The students at Union County College	
The faculty and staff at UCC	
Our families	

The authors and publisher would like to thank the following reviewers and consultants:

Linda Boice
Elk Grove Unified School District, Sacramento, CA

Kathleen Newton
New York City Board of Education, Bronx, NY

Rocio Castiblanco
Seminole Community College, Sanford, FL

Alberto Panizo
Miami-Dade Community College, Miami, FL

Jared Erfle
Antelope Valley High School, Lancaster, CA

Eric Rosenbaum
Bronx Community College, Bronx, NY

Rob Kustusch
Triton Community College, River Grove, IL

Michaela Safadi
South Gate Community, South Gate, CA

Patricia Long
Old Marshall Adult School, Sacramento, CA

Armando Valdez
Huantes Learning and Leadership Development Center, San Antonio, TX

Contents

Contents

Many years ago, I attended an ESL workshop in which the presenter asked a full audience, "How many of you read the **To the Teacher** at the front of the text?" Two participants raised their hands. Since that time, I have begged my publishers to release me from this responsibility, but have always been overruled.

As a teacher, you can form a clear first impression of this book. Flip through the pages. Will the format appeal to your students? Look carefully through the table of contents. Are most of the structures and contexts that your program has established included in the text? Thumb carefully through a few units. Will the activities and exercises, the support, the pace be appropriate for your students? If you wish, you can even read the rest of **To the Teacher** below.

English in Action is a four-level core language series for ESL/EFL students. It is a comprehensive revision and expansion of *The New Grammar in Action*. The popularity of the original edition delighted us, but we heard the same requests over and over: "Please include more readings and pronunciation," and "Could you add a workbook?" In planning the revision, our publisher threw budgetary concerns to the wind and decided to produce a four color, redesigned version. The revision also allowed us, the authors, an opportunity to refine the text. We are writers, but we are also teachers. We wrote a unit, then immediately tried it out in the classroom. Activities, tasks, and exercises were added, deleted, and changed in an on-going process. Students provided daily and honest feedback.

This first book is designed for students who have had little exposure to English, including new arrivals or adults who have lived in the United States for many years, but never formally studied English. The text assumes that students are literate in their native language.

The units in Book 1 branch from self to school, family, home, jobs, and community. The contexts are everyday places and situations. The units build gradually, giving students the vocabulary, the grammar, and the expressions to talk about the situations and themselves. Students see, hear, and practice the language of everyday life in a great variety of exercises and activities. Because this is the first book and students are unsure of themselves, there is ever-present support in the form of grammar notes, examples, vocabulary boxes, and so on. By the end of Book 1, students should feel comfortable talking, reading, and writing about their lives using basic English phrases and sentences.

Each unit will take between five and seven hours of classroom time. If you have less time, you may need to choose the exercises you feel are the most appropriate for your students. You can assign some of the activities for homework. For example, after previewing **Writing Our Stories**, students can write their own stories at home, instead of in class. The short descriptions that follow give you an idea of the sections in each unit.

Finally, the book comes with an audio component. You need the audio program! The listening activities in the units are motivating and interesting. They provide other voices than that of the teacher. We have encouraged our adult students to buy the book/audio package. They tell us that they listen to the audio at home and in the car.

Dictionary

Each unit opens with a one- or two-page illustrated **Dictionary**. Students are asked to listen and repeat each item. All teachers realize that one repetition of vocabulary words does not produce mastery. Ask students to sit in groups and study the words together. Stage spelling bees. Play word bingo. Look for the same items in the classroom or school environment. Vocabulary instruction should take fifteen to thirty minutes. Students must also study the words at home.

Active Grammar

Three to six pages of structured exercises present and practice the grammar of the unit. This first book integrates the new vocabulary and the grammar throughout all the activities in the unit. At this level, grammar mastery is not the goal, but rather an introduction to the basic structures of English and a feeling of comfort and security in the new language. As students progress through this section, they will find a variety of supportive features. Artwork and photos illustrate the context clearly. Answer boxes show the verbs or nouns to use in the answers. For many of the exercises, the entire class will be working together with your direction and explanations. Other exercises have a pairwork icon — students can try these with a partner. You can walk around the classroom, listening to students and answering their questions. Expect to spend about three hours with this section, with pair and group activities taking up the bulk of the time.

Pronunciation

Within the **Active Grammar** section is an exercise that focuses on pronunciation. These are specific pronunciation points that complement the grammar or vocabulary of the lesson, such as plural *s*, contractions, numbers, and syllables.

Working Together

For these one to two pages, students work in groups, trying out their new language with cooperative tasks, such as writing directions to the local hospital, interviewing partners, writing conversations, or arranging a person's daily schedule. Be prepared—students will make lots of mistakes during the practice. Allow about an hour for this exploration of the language, as students gain comfort and fluency in English. If your students represent several different languages, group students with classmates who speak a language other than their own.

The Big Picture

Do not rush through our favorite section, **the Big Picture**, that integrates listening, vocabulary, and structure. A large, lively picture shows a particular setting, such as a restaurant, a doctor's office, or an electronics store. Students listen to a short story or conversation, and then answer questions about the story, fill in exercises, review structures, or write conversations. You could limit time on this page to forty minutes, but teachers may wish to extend the time by developing vocabulary.

Reading

A short reading expands the context of the lesson. We did not manipulate a selection so that every sentence fits into the structure presented in the unit! There are new vocabulary words and structures. Teachers can help ESL readers learn that understanding the main idea is primary. They can then go back over the material to find the details that are interesting or relevant. If students can find the information they need, it is not necessary to master or look up every word. Plan about thirty minutes for this section.

Writing Our Stories

In this writing section, students first read a paragraph written by an ESL student or teacher. By using checklists or fill-in sentences, students are directed to brainstorm about their own schools, families, jobs, etc. Students then have an opportunity to write about themselves. Several teachers have told us about the creative ways they share student writing, including publishing student magazines, designing a class Web page, and displaying stories and photos taken by their students. If you are running low on time, introduce the writing section and ask students to write stories at home. If class time permits, students should write in class.

Practicing on Your Own

This is simple: it's a homework section. Some teachers ask students to do the exercises in class. Another suggestion for homework is the audio component. Ask students to listen to it three or four more times, reviewing the vocabulary and the exercises they did in class. Our students tell us that they often write the story from **The Big Picture** as a dictation activity.

Looking at . . . .

We can't claim any pedagogical theory for this section. We found it a convenient place for forms, math problems, or interesting information we located about the topic as we were writing the units.

Grammar Summary

Some teachers wanted this summary at the beginning of the unit; others were pleased to see it at the end. Use this section if and when you wish. Some students like to see the grammar up front, having a clear map of the developing grammar. We have found, though, that many of our students at this beginning level are confused with a clump of grammar explanations at the beginning of a unit. There are small grammar charts as needed throughout the unit. The ending summary brings them together.

Teacher's Guide

We have developed the *English in Action 1 Teacher's Guide* to be a support to teachers of all levels of experience. New teachers will benefit from the clear, step-by-step instructions on using the Student Book, while more experienced teachers will find creative and fun ideas for expanding on the Student Book material. Each **Teacher's Guide** page includes a reduced Student Book page, along with guidelines for effectively teaching and expanding on the activities on that page. At the bottom of many of the **Teacher's Guide** pages are audio scripts for the listening activities on that page. These audio scripts are for listening activities that do not already appear on the Student Book page. The audio scripts are also included at the end of the Student Book. The audio scripts allow teachers who do not have access to the audio to read aloud to their students the audio portion of the listening activities.

The **Teacher's Guide** also features a helpful grammar section in the appendices. This section, the **Grammar Summary Expansion**, is designed to give teachers more information about the grammatical structures and points taught in each Student Book unit.

I am sure we will be revising the text again in three or four years. We will be gathering your input during that time. You can always e-mail us at **www.heinle.com** with your comments, complaints, and suggestions.

About the Authors

Liz and I both work at Union County College in Elizabeth, New Jersey. We teach at the Institute for Intensive English, a large English as a Second Language program. Students from over 70 different countries study in our classes. Between us, Liz and I have been teaching at the college for over 40 years! When Liz isn't writing, she spends her time traveling, taking pictures, and watching her favorite baseball team, the New York Mets. Liz took many of the pictures in the texts, for which our students eagerly posed. In the warm weather, I can't start my day without a 15- or 20-mile bicycle ride. My idea of a good time always involves the outdoors: hiking, kayaking, or simply working in my garden.

Barbara H. Foley
Elizabeth R. Neblett

Photo Credits

All photos courtesy of Elizabeth R. Neblett with the following exceptions:

p.33 Courtesy of Anita Raducanu, Tony Arruuza/CORBIS, Owen Franken/CORBIS, Bohemian Nomad Picturemakers/CORBIS;

p.79 Amos Nachoum/CORBIS;

p.81 Gail Mooney/ CORBIS;

p.84 Mike Segar/Reuters New Media/CORBIS, Kelly-Mooney/CORBIS, Mark E. Gibson/CORBIS;

p.86 Dan Larmont/Corbis;

p.120 Pablo Corral/CORBIS, Jules T. Allen/CORBIS, Steve Raymer/CORBIS, Leif Skoogfors/ CORBIS, Dave Bartruff/CORBIS, Owen Franken/CORBIS, Jacques M. Chenet/CORBIS, Bob Rowan/Progressive Image/CORBIS, Roger Ressmeyer/CORBIS;

p.121 Catherine Karnow/CORBIS, Kelly-Mooney/CORBIS, Mark E. Gibson at CLM/CORBIS OUTLINE;

p.126 Owen Franken/CORBIS;

p.127 Richard T. Nowitz/CORBIS, Catherine Karnow/CORBIS;

p.132 Pablo Corral V/CORBIS, Willie Hill Jr./Index Stock Imagery;

p.141 SW Production/Index Stock Imagery;

p.144 Duomo/CORBIS, Layne Kennedy/CORBIS, Index Stock Imagery, Bill Bachmahn/Index Stock Imagery;

p.154 Doug Mazell/Index Stock Imagery;

p.194 Reuters New Media Inc./CORBIS;

p.210 Wallace Garrison/Index Stock Imagery;

p.211 Spike and Ethel/Index Stock Imagery;

p.227 Anthony James/ Index Stock Imagery.

Unit 1
Hello

Discuss the person swinging on the unit number. Ask:

• *What is the man doing?*
(He's swinging/hanging from a big number 1.)

☀Dictionary:
One to Ten

 A. Listen and repeat.
(CD1, Track 1)

• Play the audio or read the words under each photo two times. The first time, have students just listen as you point to each picture. The second time, have students repeat the words. Repeat this activity until students feel comfortable pronouncing the words.

• Point to pictures at random and call on different students to say the words that correspond to the pictures.

Suggestion

Ask students to stand. Guide them to form groups of two, three, four, and so forth, around the room. Then point to each group and call on a student to say the words that describe that group. Change the numbers in each group and repeat the activity.

Hello

Dictionary: One to Ten

A. **Listen and repeat.**

one student

two students

three students

four students

five students

six students

seven students

eight students

nine students

ten students

Active Grammar: Present Tense: *Be*

A. Listen.

B. Pair practice. (Answers will vary.)

A: Hello. My name is _____ .

B: Hi. I'm _____ .

A: Nice to meet you.

B: Nice to meet you, too.

| I am = I'm |

C. Complete. (Answers will vary.)

My first name is _____ .

My last name is _____ .

Ana Santos
First name: Ana
Last name: Santos

☀Active Grammar: Present Tense: *Be*

Teacher Note

You can wait until the Grammar Summary on page 17 before discussing the verb *be* in this unit. Students will understand how to use *am* and *is* here through sentence context.

A. Listen. (CD1, Track 2)

Point to the two people in the picture. Ask students who the people are and what they are doing. Have students listen as you play the audio. Then play the audio again. Pause the audio after each line of the dialogue and have students repeat.

B. Pair practice.

Ask two students to act out the dialogue using their own names. Then have students introduce themselves to people sitting nearby.

C. Complete.

• Point to the two sentences and complete them using your own first and last names. Say the sentences again.

• Point to the picture at the right and explain the meaning of *first name* and *last name*.

• Ask students to complete the two sentences using their own names. Ask several students to read their sentences to the class.

Audio Script

A. Listen. (CD1, Track 2)

A. Hello. My name is Ana.
B. Hi. I'm Carlos.
A. Nice to meet you.
B. Nice to meet you, too.

☀ The Alphabet

 A. Listen. (CD1, Track 3)

> Have students listen to the audio as they look at the chart.

⊪ B. Listen again and repeat.

> Play the audio several times and have students repeat the letters.

Suggestion

Write any letters students are having difficulty pronouncing on the board. Provide intensive practice with these letters. If you know the student's native language, you might contrast the pronunciation of the letter in English to that in the student's native language.

C. Write.

> Point out that the lowercase letter in each pair only comes up to the dotted middle line and that all capital letters reach to the top line. Then have students copy the pairs of letters in the space provided beside each set of lowercase and capital letters.

The Alphabet

⊪ A. Listen.

Aa	Bb	Cc	Dd	Ee	Ff	Gg
Hh	Ii	Jj	Kk	Ll	Mm	Nn
Oo	Pp	Qq	Rr	Ss	Tt	Uu
Vv	Ww	Xx	Yy	Zz		

⊪ B. Listen again and repeat.

C. Write.

A = capital letter
a = lowercase letter

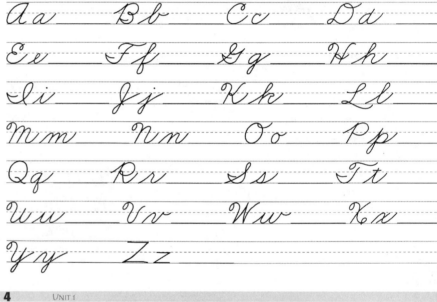

Please spell that.

A. Read.

A: What's your first name?

B: Ana.

A: What's your last name?

B: Santos.

A: Please spell that.

B: S – A – N – T – O – S.

B. Ask five students. Complete. (Answers will vary.)

What's your
first name?

What's your
last name?

Carlos.

Moreno.

Helpful Expressions
Please spell that.
Please repeat.

What's your first name?	What's your last name?
Carlos	Moreno
1.	
2.	
3.	
4.	
5.	

Writing Note
Names begin with capital letters: Carlos, Ana.

☀ Please spell that.

Suggestion

Write your name on the board using capital and lowercase letters. Then point to and say each letter of your name. For the name *Carl* you would say: *c-a-r-l*. Write a student's name on the board and repeat the naming activity. Point out that names begin with capital letters.

A. Read.

First, ask students to follow along in their books as you read the whole dialogue. Then read each line and ask students to repeat. Finally, have pairs of students read the dialogue to the class.

Suggestion

Point out the Helpful Expressions and ask students to explain or demonstrate what each one means.

B. Ask five students.

• Have two students read the sample dialogue to the class. Then have the class stand. Tell students to move around the room and use the questions to find out the first and last names of five classmates. Have students write the information in the chart.

• After they finish, invite some students to point to the classmates they talked to and introduce them using their first and last names. For example: *That's Carlos Moreno.*

Teacher Note

Students sometimes become upset when their names are mispronounced. Ask the class to take the time to learn how to say each other's names correctly. This may require some students to say their names several times to help others with the pronunciation.

☀ My Classmates

A. Read.

• Point out the three people. As you read *My name is Sandra*, point to yourself. For the *his* and *her* statements, point to the appropriate picture as you say the statement.

• Ask two male and two female students to stand in front of the class. Prompt them to make statements about each other using *His name is . . .* and *Her name is . . . .* Repeat each statement and ask the class to repeat after you.

B. Say your classmates' names.

Point to different students and call on a volunteer to name the selected student using *his* or *her*.

☀ Where are you from?

A. Complete.

Write the incomplete statements on the board. Then demonstrate the activity with your own information. Fill in your name and country.

Suggestion

Write the word *Countries* on the board. Ask students to tell where they come from. List all the countries on the board. Say the names of the countries and ask students to repeat.

B. Read.

Have students practice the dialogues in pairs. Then ask volunteers to take turns reading one of the dialogues to the class.

My Classmates

A. Read.

My name is Sandra.

His name is Tuan.

Her name is Erica.

B. Say your classmates' names.

His name is Boris.

Her name is Jessica.

Where are you from?

A. Complete. (Answers will vary.)

What's your name?   My name is _____.

Where are you from?   I'm from _____.

B. Read.

What's her name?

Her name is Ana.

Where is she from?

She is from Mexico.

What's his name?

His name is Luis.

Where is he from?

He is from Colombia.

C. Match.

1. What's his name? — Her name is Roya.
2. Where is he from? — His name is Carlos.
3. What's her name? — She is from India.
4. Where is she from? — He is from Colombia.

 D. Pair practice. Ask about each person's name and country.

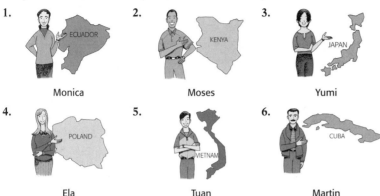

1. Monica (ECUADOR)
2. Moses (KENYA)
3. Yumi (JAPAN)
4. Ela (POLAND)
5. Tuan (VIETNAM)
6. Martin (CUBA)

 E. Pronunciation: Contractions. Listen and repeat.

1. (He is from Mexico.)   He's from Mexico.
2. She is from Vietnam.   (She's from Vietnam.)
3. I am from Russia.   (I'm from Russia.)
4. He is from China.   (He's from China.)
5. (I am from Haiti.)   I'm from Haiti.
6. (She is from Peru.)   She's from Peru.
7. He is from Cuba.   (He's from Cuba.)
8. She is from Egypt.   (She's from Egypt.)

F. Listen to Exercise E again. (Circle) the sentence you hear.

Hello **7**

C. Match.

Ask students to complete the activity on their own. Then have students practice asking and answering the questions in pairs.

Suggestion

Display a world map. Invite volunteers to point to their countries and say: *My name is _____. I'm from _____.*

D. Pair practice.

• Model the pronunciation of each country's name and ask students to repeat.

• Invite a pair of students to do item 1 as the class listens. Remind students that we use *his* for a man and *her* for a woman. Students can then do the exercise in pairs.

E. Pronunciation: Contractions. (CD1, Track 4)

Point out the differences in pronunciation between some of the long forms and contractions in the sentences. Introduce and practice the pronunciation of any countries students are seeing for the first time. Then play the audio and have students listen and repeat.

F. Listen to Exercise E again. (CD1, Track 5)

Have students listen to the audio and circle the sentences they hear. Play the first sentence as an example.

Audio Script

F. Listen to Exercise E again.
   Circle the sentence you hear.
   (CD1, Track 5)

1. He is from Mexico.
2. She's from Vietnam.
3. I'm from Russia.
4. He's from China.
5. I am from Haiti.
6. She is from Peru.
7. He's from Cuba.
8. She's from Egypt.

☀ Numbers 1–20

🔊 A. Listen. (CD1, Track 6)

Have students point to each number as you play the audio.

🔊 B. Listen and repeat. (CD1, Track 6)

Play the audio again. This time have students repeat each number. Monitor students' pronunciation and provide focused practice with any problem numbers. Point out that the syllables with -teen get heavy stress. For example: SevenTEEN, not SEVenteen.

Suggestion

Before doing Exercise C, review the spelling of the numbers one through ten on page 2. Then introduce the written words eleven through twenty. For practice, list the words on the board. Ask different students to come to the board and point to the words as you say them in random order. Then ask students to write the correct numeral after each word.

C. Write.

Ask students to fill in the numerals in their books on their own.

🔊 D. Listen and circle. (CD1, Track 7)

Have students listen to the audio and circle the numbers they hear.

Numbers 1–20

🔊 A. Listen.

0	1	2	3	4	5	6	7	8	9	10
	11	12	13	14	15	16	17	18	19	20

🔊 B. Listen and repeat.

C. Write.

a. ten   __10__   g. twelve   __12__

b. six   __6__   h. eighteen   __18__

c. eleven   __11__   i. twenty   __20__

d. three   __3__   j. seven   __7__

e. zero   __0__   k. fourteen   __14__

f. four   __4__   l. nineteen   __19__

🔊 D. Listen and circle.

a. 0   (1)   3   g. 10   (20)   12

b. 3   4   (8)   h. (6)   7   17

c. 2   3   (10)   i. 3   (13)   15

d. (0)   1   11   j. (2)   3   13

e. 3   5   (7)   k. 11   (12)   13

f. 4   (14)   15   l. 8   18   (19)

8   UNIT 1

Audio Script

D. Listen and circle. (CD1, Track 7)

a. 1   g. 20

b. 8   h. 6

c. 10   i. 13

d. 0   j. 2

e. 7   k. 12

f. 14   l. 19

What's your telephone number?

A. Read.

A: What's your name?

B: Ana Santos.

A: And your telephone number?

B: 301-555-1796.

A: 301-555-1796?

B: Yes.

A: Thank you.

Culture Note
In a telephone number, say each number separately.

B. Listen and write.

a. 5 5 5 - 3 2 3 1

b. 5 5 5 - 3 6 9 2

c. 5 5 5 - 7 5 4 8

d. 5 5 5 - 3 0 8 0

e. 2 0 1 - 5 5 5 - 4 4 1 3

f. 8 0 0 - 5 5 5 - 4 2 4 2

g. 6 1 9 - 5 5 5 - 7 0 4 2

h. 8 1 3 - 5 5 5 - 1 6 2 4

C. Pair practice. Say these telephone numbers with a partner.

a. 555-8320

b. 555-2390

c. 555-5636

d. 555-8124

e. 908-555-9932

f. 201-555-3452

g. 617-555-9898

h. 212-555-7335

☀ What's your telephone number?

Suggestion

Before doing Exercise A, point out and discuss the Culture Note. Explain that the word *separately* means *one by one*.

A. Read.

- Ask students to read the conversation. Answer any questions they have.
- Have pairs read the conversation together. Ask students to pay special attention to the pronunciation of the numbers.

B. Listen and write.
(CD1, Track 8)

Students listen to the audio and write the telephone numbers they hear. Play the audio more than once if appropriate for your class.

C. Pair practice.

Model the pronunciation of one or two of the telephone numbers and ask students to repeat. Then have students practice saying the numbers to a partner. Move around the room monitoring the pair work and correcting pronunciation as needed.

Suggestion

Have a few students go to the board. Dictate several telephone numbers and ask the students to write the numbers on the board.

Audio Script

B. Listen and write. **(CD1, Track 8)**

a. 555-3231

b. 555-3692

c. 555-7548

d. 555-3080

e. 201-555-4413

f. 800-555-4242

g. 619-555-7042

h. 813-555-1624

A. Ask five students these questions.

- Have two students read the sample dialogue to the class. Point out the Helpful Expressions and review how these expressions are used.
- Have the class stand. Tell students to move around the room and use the questions in the sample dialogue to find out the names of five classmates and the countries they come from. Have students write the information in the chart.
- After they finish, invite some students to point to people they talked to and to say each person's name and country. For example: *That's Sun-Hi Young. She's from Korea.*

B. Write about the students in Exercise A.

Review the example and have students complete the activity on their own.

Suggestion

Before having students fill in the blanks, ask them to practice the sentences orally with a partner. The two students should take turns pointing to an item in Exercise A and giving the information orally.

Working Together

A. Ask five students these questions. Complete. (Answers will vary.)

Helpful Expressions
Please repeat.
Please spell that.

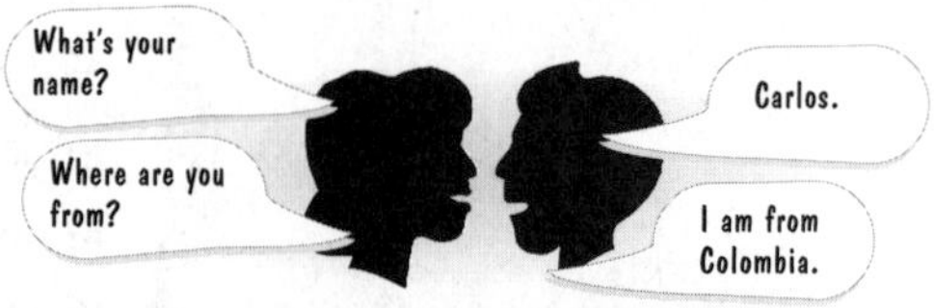

What's your name?
Where are you from?

Carlos.
I am from Colombia.

Name	Country
Carlos	Colombia
1.	
2.	
3.	
4.	
5.	

B. Write about the students in Exercise A. (Answers will vary.)

1. _____Carlos_____ is from _____Colombia_____.
2. _____ is from _____.
3. _____ is from _____.
4. _____ is from _____.
5. _____ is from _____.
6. _____ is from _____.

The Big Picture: My Classmates

A. Listen.

Tomas   Jenny   Erica   Hiro   Marie

Peru   Hong Kong   Mexico   Japan   Haiti

B. Listen again and write the correct name on each person.

Tomas	Hiro	Erica	Marie	Jenny

C. Complete with *He* or *She* and the name of the country.

1. This is Jenny. _____She_____ is from _____Hong Kong_____ .
2. This is Erica. _____She_____ is from _____Mexico_____ .
3. This is Hiro. _____He_____ is from _____Japan_____ .
4. This is Marie. _____She_____ is from _____Haiti_____ .
5. This is _____Tomas_____ . _____He_____ is from _____Peru_____ .

D. Listen. Write the number next to the answer.

  __4__ He is from Japan.
  __2__ I'm from Peru.
  __3__ His name is Hiro.
  __5__ Her name is Marie.
  __1__ My name is Tomas.
  __6__ She's from Haiti.

Hello   **11**

The Big Picture: My Classmates

A. Listen. (CD1, Track 9)

Point to and say the country names under the pictures and ask students to repeat. Then play the audio and ask students to listen only.

B. Listen again and write the correct name on each person.
(CD1, Track 9)

Point to the names of the five people and ask students to repeat. Then play the audio again and ask students to write the correct name on each person in the picture.

Teacher Note

Most students will not understand everything on the audio. Assure them that the best way to understand rapid spoken English is to focus on the key information they need and let the rest go. Suggest that here they listen only for the students' names and their countries of origin.

C. Complete with *He* or *She* and the name of the country.

Remind students to look back at their answers for Exercise B as they complete the sentences.

D. Listen. (CD1, Track 10)

Explain that students will hear a question on the audio and that they will pick out the answer that fits that question. Play or read the first question (*What's your name?*) and point out the related answer (*My name is Tomas.*) in the book.

Audio Script

The Big Picture: My Classmates

A. Listen. (CD1, Track 9)

Hi. My name is Tomas. I'm a student in English 1. I'm in class now. Here are four students in my class. This is Hiro. He's from Japan. This is Erica. She's from Mexico. This is Marie. She's from Haiti. This is Jenny. She's from Hong Kong. And this is me. I'm from Peru.

D. Listen. Write the number next to the answer. (CD1, Track 10)

1. What's your name?
2. Where are you from?
3. What's his name?
4. Where is he from?
5. What's her name?
6. Where is she from?

A. Before You Read.

• Ask students to locate the nine countries on the map as you read the names aloud. Then ask: *Do most people in _____ speak English?*

• Ask students to read the story on their own. Explain that they won't understand everything. Suggest that as they read they just try to note the countries where most people speak English. Then read the story aloud to the students.

Suggestion

You can help students understand the story by following these steps:

• Read the story to the class.
• Ask: *Do you understand the story? Read me a sentence you understand.*
• Ask students to point out sentences they do not understand. Help with these sentences.
• Read the story again.

B. Write four words you know.

Students can write any four words and sentences they know. Invite volunteers to read their sentences to the class.

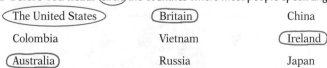
Reading: English

A. Before You Read. (Circle) the countries where most people speak English.

(The United States)   (Britain)   China

Colombia   Vietnam   (Ireland)

(Australia)   Russia   Japan

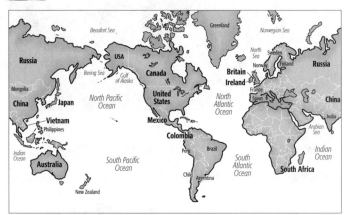

People in the United States speak English. People in Canada, Britain, Australia, and Ireland speak English. Almost 500,000,000 people speak English.

You can speak some English, too. You know words like *car, man, woman,* and *money*. You know sentences like *I'm a student* and *I'm from Mexico.*

For you, English is a new language with new words and new grammar. It will take time to learn. Many people speak English. You will, too.

B. Write four words you know. Write four sentences you know. (Answers will vary.)

Words	Sentences
telephone	Nice to meet you.

Writing Our Stories: All About Me

A. Read.

My name is Antonio.
I am from Mexico.
I am studying English.
I am a student at
Bayside Adult School.
My teacher is
Ms. Johnson.

B. Write. (Answers will vary.)

My name is _____. I am from

_____. I am studying English. I am a student at

_____. My teacher is _____.

A. Read.

Read the story aloud to the class. Then ask some simple questions about the story, such as:

What is his name?
Where is he from?
What is he studying?

B. Write.

• Students can use Exercise A as a model as they complete this activity.
• Invite some students to read their stories aloud to the class.

Suggestion

Talk about how capital letters are used. Ask students to underline all the capital letters in the story. Then ask students to write their story again in their notebooks. Move around the room as they work, reminding them to use capital letters where appropriate.

A. Complete.

Ask students to look at the
driver's license and ID card.
If necessary, explain (or have
a student explain) the meaning of *middle initial* and *ID
number*. Have students fill in
the answers on their own.

Suggestion

Pair less fluent students with more
fluent students and have them
complete the activity together. The
less fluent students benefit from
the guidance they receive. The
more fluent students get a valuable
review as well as extra practice
speaking English.

B. Match.

Have students complete the
matching activity on their own.
Review the answers by calling
on one student to read the question and another to read the
correct answer.

Suggestion

For oral language practice, have
students practice saying the questions and answers in pairs.

Practicing on Your Own

A. Complete.

1. His first name is __Tuan__.
2. His middle initial is __B__.
3. __His__ last name is __Vo__.

4. Her first name is __Luisa__.
5. Her middle initial is __P__.
6. __Her__ last name is __Reyes__.
7. __Her__ student ID number is __443887__.
8. Luisa is a student at __Edison School__.

B. Match.

1. What's his name? — Her name is Imelda.
2. Where is he from? — He is from Mexico.
3. What's her name? — His name is Hector.
4. Where is she from? — I'm from Poland.
5. What's your name? — She is from the Philippines.
6. Where are you from? — My name is Dorota.

14 Unit 1

C. Complete.
(Answers will vary.)

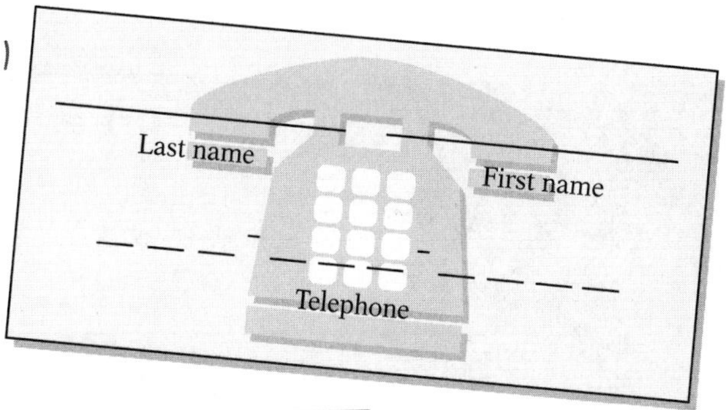

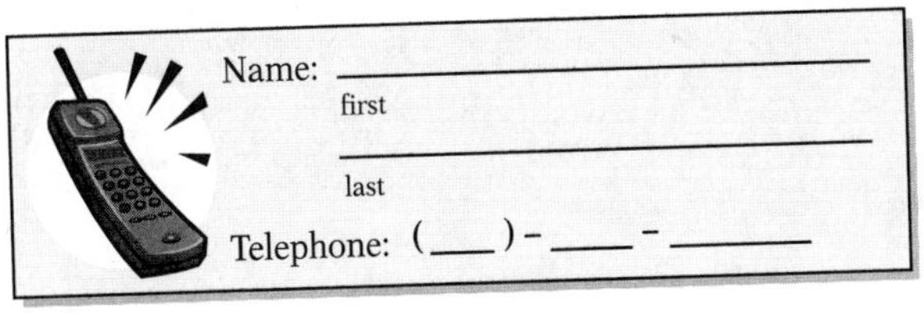

Last name _____ First name _____

_ _ _ _ _ _ _ _ _ _ _ _
Telephone

Name: _____
      first
      _____
      last
Telephone: (___) - ____ - _____

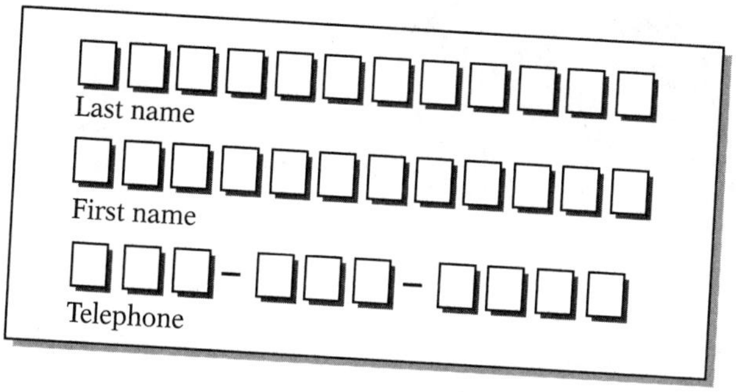

□□□□□□□□□□□□
Last name

□□□□□□□□□□□□
First name

□□□- □□□- □□□□
Telephone

Name: [   ] [   ]
      first   initial

      last
      Telephone:
      (_____) - _____ - _____

C. Complete.

Ask students to fill in information about themselves.

Suggestion

Ask students to bring to class other forms they need to fill out. Have students help each other fill out the forms.

☀ Good-bye

Good-bye

▀ A. Listen. (CD1, Track 11)

Play the audio twice. The first time through, have students listen as you point to the two people in the picture. The second time, have students repeat each phrase. Pause the audio after each person speaks to give students time to repeat. Repeat the second activity until students feel comfortable pronouncing the phrases.

B. Pair practice.

Have students practice the dialogue with partners. Invite volunteer pairs to perform the dialogue for the class.

▀ A. Listen.

B. Pair practice. (Answers will vary.)

    A: Good-bye, _____.

    B: Good-bye, _____.

    A: See you tomorrow.

    B: Have a nice day.

16   UNIT 1

Audio Script

A. Listen. (CD1, Track 11)

    a. Good-bye, Ana.
    b. Good-bye, Carlos.
    a. See you tomorrow.
    b. Have a nice day.

When I don't understand, I say, "Excuse me?" (Answers will vary.)
or I say, "I don't understand."

☐ I like this idea.
☐ I don't like this idea.
☐ I'm going to try this idea.

Excuse me?

Grammar Summary

▶ 1. Statements: *be*	Contractions
I **am** a student.	I**'m** a student.
He **is** a student.	He**'s** a student.
She **is** a student.	She**'s** a student.
▶ 2. Possessive adjectives	
My name is Ana.	
His name is Dan.	
Her name is Maria.	
▶ 3. *Wh-* questions	
What's your name?	My name is Carlos.
Where are you from?	I'm from Colombia.

Discuss the Learning Tip with students. Ask them to repeat the two sentences. Then read and explain the meaning of the three choices. Have students check the one that applies to them.

Grammar Summary

• Review the summary with the class. Invite students to make up alternate sentences for each example in the chart. For example, in place of *I am a student,* a man might say *I am a man.* In place of *My name is Ana,* a student might say *My name is Esin.*

• See the Grammar Summary Expansion on page 230 for a more complete explanation of these grammar points.

Unit 2
The Classroom

Discuss the person next to the unit number. Ask:

• *Who is next to the number 2?* (A man)

• *What is he doing?* (He's writing with a giant pencil.)

 ## Dictionary: Classroom Objects

A. Listen and repeat.
(CD1, Track 12)

• Ask students to describe the picture. Ask:

Who is in the picture?
Where are they?

• Have students listen as you play the audio or say the words and point to the items in the picture. The second time through, have students repeat the words.

• Repeat the second activity until students feel comfortable pronouncing the words. Then point to different items in the picture at random and call on different students to say the words.

Suggestion

Ask students to study the words at home. During the next class, have students give each other spelling tests on the words. Have them take turns saying and writing the words.

Dictionary: Classroom Objects

 A. Listen and repeat.

B. Listen and repeat.

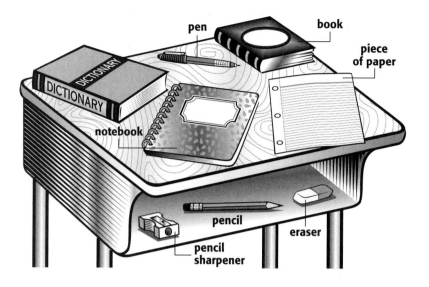

pen

book

piece of paper

DICTIONARY

notebook

pencil

eraser

pencil sharpener

C. Check (✔) the items in *your* classroom. Add to this list. (Answers will vary.)

> **a/an**
> Use **a** or **an** for the singular.
> a book   an eraser

_____ a table

_____ a chair

_____ desks

_____ a map of the United States

_____ a map of the world

_____ a clock

_____ a computer

_____ a pencil sharpener

_____ a board

_____ a piece of chalk

_____ an eraser

_____ _____

_____ _____

_____ _____

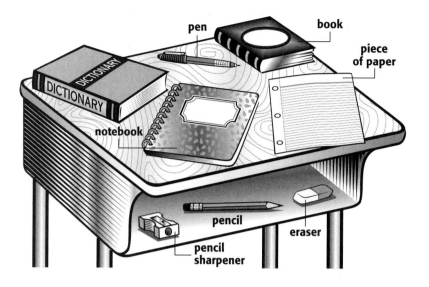

A. Listen and repeat.
(CD1, Track 13)

- Have students listen as you play the audio and point to the items in the picture. The second time through, have students repeat the words.
- Repeat the second activity until students feel comfortable pronouncing the words. Then point to different items in the picture at random and call on different students to say the words.

Suggestion

Collect an example of each item in the picture from students. Display the items where all students can see them. Then pick up one at a time and ask students to name it in unison.

C. Check the items in your classroom.

- Have students complete the check-off activity on their own and then review their answers with a partner.
- Ask volunteers to point to and name additional objects in the classroom. Repeat the word, correcting pronunciation as necessary. Write the word on the board and have students copy it into their books.

Teacher Note

Point out that *a* and *an* mean *one*.

Suggestion

Have a competition using all the vocabulary words learned so far. Divide the class into two teams. The first person on Team A holds up or points to an item. The first person on Team B has five seconds to identify the item. Continue until all students have had a chance to point to or identify items.

☀ Active Grammar:
Yes/No Questions

📶 A. Listen. (CD1, Track 14)

- Point out the sample conversation in the box and read it aloud.
- Ask students to identify each of the three objects. Explain that students will hear conversations that match the objects.
- Play the audio. The first time students only listen. Play the audio a second time and have students mark their answers.

📶 B. Listen and complete.
(CD1, Track 15)

Tell students they will hear five different conversations. Explain that they must fill in the missing words. Point out the choices in the box at the right.

Suggestion

Review the correct answers with the class by calling on different pairs to read one dialogue each.

👥 C. Pair practice.

Have students practice the conversations in the speech bubbles using the four numbered items at the bottom of the page.

Active Grammar: Yes/No Questions

📶 A. Listen. Number the conversations.

1. ___3___   2. ___1___   3. ___2___

> Is this your book?
> Yes, it is.
> No, it isn't.

📶 B. Listen and complete.

		pen
1. Is this your ____dictionary____ ?
   Yes, it is. Thank you.
2. Is this your __pen__ ?
   Yes, it is. Thank you.
3. Is this your __pencil sharpener__ ?
   No, it isn't.
4. Is this your __paper__ ?
   Yes, __it__ __is__ . Thank you.
5. Is this your __notebook__ ?
   No, __it__ __isn't__ .

> pen
> paper
> ✓ dictionary
> notebook
> pencil sharpener

👥 C. Pair practice.

> Is this your ____ ?

> Yes it is. Thank you.

> Is this your ____ ?

> No,

1.   2.   3.   4.   Dictionary

Audio Script

A. Listen. Number the conversations.
(CD1, Track 14)

Conversation 1
A: Is this your book?
B: Yes, it is. Thank you.
Conversation 2
A: Is this your eraser?
B: Yes, it is. Thank you.
Conversation 3
A: Is this your pencil?
B: No, it isn't.

B. Listen and complete.
(CD1, Track 15)

1. Is this your dictionary?
   Yes, it is. Thank you.
2. Is this your pen?
   Yes, it is. Thank you.
3. Is this your pencil sharpener?
   No, it isn't.
4. Is this your paper?
   Yes, it is. Thank you.
5. Is this your notebook?
   No, it isn't.

Singular and Plural Nouns

☀ Singular and Plural Nouns

A. Listen and repeat.

1.

a book   books

2.

a pencil   pencils

3.

a student   students

4.

a man   men

5.

a woman   women

6.

a child   children

B. Circle.

1.

a table   (tables)

2.

(a clock)   clocks

3.

an eraser   (erasers)

4.

(a student)   students

5.

a woman   (women)

6.

a man   (men)

☀ Singular and Plural Nouns

A. Listen and repeat.
(CD1, Track 16)

Ask students to listen as you point to the pictures and play the audio. Then have them repeat each singular/plural pair several times.

Teacher Note

Take time with each word pair. Say one of the words and ask students to point to the correct picture. Pay special attention to the pronunciation of *man/men* and *woman/women*. You may need to go over these pairs several times.

B. Circle.

Have students complete the activity individually and check their answers with a partner.

Suggestion

Ask students to point out and say the names of any of these items they see in the classroom. Confirm each response: *That's right. Those are tables.*

☼ A pencil—pencils

🔊 A. Pronunciation: Plural nouns.

(CD1, Track 17)

Call on different students to read aloud the pairs of words. Then play the audio and have students circle the word they hear for each pair. Play the audio a second time so students can check their answers.

👥 Sit with a partner.

Have students practice the singular and plural noun word pairs together.

B. Write.

Have students complete the activity independently. Invite volunteers to write their answers on the board. Review the correct answers with the class.

A pencil—pencils

🔊 A. Pronunciation: Plural nouns. Listen and (circle.)

1. (a pencil)   pencils
2. a student   (students)
3. a teacher   (teachers)
4. a man   (men)
5. (a map)   maps
6. (a dictionary)   dictionaries
7. (an eraser)   erasers
8. a notebook   (notebooks)
9. a classroom   (classrooms)
10. (a woman)   women

👥 Sit with a partner. Say the words above.

B. Write.

1.
   pencils

5.
   books

2.
   a map

6.
   a pencil sharpener

3.
   pens

7.
   students

4.
   a woman

8.
   a man

Audio Script

A. Pronunciation: Plural nouns.
Listen and circle.
(CD1, Track 17)

1. a pencil
2. students
3. teachers
4. men
5. a map
6. a dictionary
7. an eraser
8. notebooks
9. classrooms
10. a woman

Numbers 1–1000

A. Listen and repeat.

1	2	3	4	5	6	7	8	9	10
one	two	three	four	five	six	seven	eight	nine	ten
11	12	13	14	15	16	17	18	19	20
eleven	twelve	thirteen	fourteen	fifteen	sixteen	seventeen	eighteen	nineteen	twenty
21	22	23	24	25	26	27	28	29	30
twenty-one	twenty-two	twenty-three	twenty-four	twenty-five	twenty-six	twenty-seven	twenty-eight	twenty-nine	thirty

10	20	30	40	50	60	70	80	90	100	1,000
ten	twenty	thirty	forty	fifty	sixty	seventy	eighty	ninety	one hundred	one thousand

B. Listen and circle.

a. 4   15   (17)   e. 22   (27)   29   i. 43   44   (45)

b. (7)   17   27   f. 24   25   (26)   j. (56)   66   76

c. 14   15   (16)   g. 13   23   (33)   k. 62   67   (76)

d. (8)   9   18   h. 11   (12)   20   l. 84   94   (89)

C. Write the number.

a. 6 _____ six _____   f. 37 _____ thirty-seven _____

b. 13 _____ thirteen _____   g. 52 _____ fifty-two _____

c. 18 _____ eighteen _____   h. 70 _____ seventy _____

d. 24 _____ twenty-four _____   i. 85 _____ eighty-five _____

e. 27 _____ twenty-seven _____   j. 99 _____ ninety-nine _____

The Classroom **23**

☀ Numbers 1–1000

A. Listen and repeat.
(CD1, Track 18)

Have students follow along and listen as you play the audio. Play the audio again, this time pausing the audio as students repeat each number. Do the activity several times, giving special attention to the numbers that are difficult for your students.

Suggestion

Say pairs of numbers that are either the same or that sound similar. For example: *sixteen/sixteen, fourteen/forty.* After saying each pair, ask students to tell you whether the numbers in the pair are the same or different.

B. Listen and circle.
(CD1, Track 19)

Have students listen to the audio and circle the numbers they hear.

Suggestion

Before doing Exercise C, review the written forms of the numbers in Exercise A. You might have students study the words and give each other spelling tests.

C. Write the number.

Ask students to write each number on their own.

Audio Script

B. Listen and circle.
(CD1, Track 19)

a. 17   e. 27   i. 45
b. 7   f. 26   j. 56
c. 16   g. 33   k. 76
d. 8   h. 12   l. 89

☀ There is—There are

A. Listen.
(CD1, Track 20)

• Point to each item in the picture and say its name. Then ask students to hold up or point to identical objects in the classroom.

• Have students listen as you point to the items as they are mentioned on the audio. Repeat this activity several times.

B. Look at the desk above.

Have students complete the sentences individually. Review the answers orally with the class.

C. Complete about *your* class.

Ask students to complete the sentences and check their answers with a partner.

👥 Suggestion

After students complete the activity, have them close their books. Then ask them to work in pairs. One partner says the name of an object in the classroom and the other makes a statement about it using *There is . . .* or *There are . . .*
For example:
S1: *Desks.*
S2: *There are fourteen desks in our classroom.*

There is—There are

A. Listen.

B. Look at the desk above. Complete.

1. There is a __dictionary/notebook__ on the desk.
2. There is a piece of __paper__ on the desk.
3. There is an __eraser__ on the desk.
4. There are two __pens__ on the desk.
5. There are three __pencils__ on the desk.
6. There are five __books__ on the desk.
7. There isn't a __(Answers may vary.)__ on the desk.

C. Complete about *your* class. Use *is* or *are* and the number.

1. There __is__ __one__ teacher in our classroom.
2. There __are__ __(Answers may vary.)__ chairs in our classroom.
3. There __are__ __(Answers may vary.)__ desks in our classroom.
4. There __is__ __one__ pencil sharpener in our classroom.
5. There __are__ __(Answers may vary.)__ students in our class.
6. There __are__ __(Answers may vary.)__ men in our class.
7. There __are__ __(Answers may vary.)__ women in our class.

Audio Script

A. Listen. (CD1, Track 20)

There is a dictionary on the desk.
There's a piece of paper on the desk.
There are two pens on the desk.
There are three pencils on the desk.
There are five books on the desk.
There's an eraser on the desk.
There's a notebook on the desk.

Working Together: My Classroom

A. Try this! Put two or three items from each student on a desk.

Student 1: Is this your cell phone?

Student 2: No, it isn't.

Student 1: Is this your cell phone?

Student 3: No, it isn't.

Student 1: Is this your cell phone?

Student 4: Yes, it is.

B. Interview two students. Circle their answers. (Answers will vary.)

	Partner 1		Partner 2	
	_____		_____	
Do you have a dictionary?	Yes, I do.	No, I don't.	Yes, I do.	No, I don't.
Do you have an eraser?	Yes, I do.	No, I don't.	Yes, I do.	No, I don't.
Do you have a piece of paper?	Yes, I do.	No, I don't.	Yes, I do.	No, I don't.
Do you have a pencil sharpener?	Yes, I do.	No, I don't.	Yes, I do.	No, I don't.
Do you have a pen?	Yes, I do.	No, I don't.	Yes, I do.	No, I don't.
Do you have a pencil?	Yes, I do.	No, I don't.	Yes, I do.	No, I don't.

C. Draw a *large* picture of your classroom. Label everything! (Answers will vary.)

☀ Working Together: My Classroom

A. Try this!

• Ask students to follow along in their books as you read the dialogue. Then read each line and ask students to repeat. Have a group of four students read the dialogue to the class.

• Ask a group of four students to come to the front of the room. Have each student bring one possession and place it on a table where the rest of the students can see it. Guide students as they take turns asking and answering questions about the objects. Then divide the class into small groups and have them continue the activity.

B. Interview two students.

Ask two different students the first question. Hold up your book and circle the answers they give. Then have each student ask two different partners the questions. Instruct them to write the person's name in the blank and circle his or her responses under the name.

C. Draw a *large* picture of your classroom.

Have students draw and label as many classroom objects as they can.

Suggestion

Use large pieces of poster paper. Have pairs of students work together to make a single large drawing. You can show them different symbols for furniture, such as a square for student desks and a rectangle for the teacher's desk. Ask students to label as many parts of their drawings as they can. Display the pictures around the classroom.

☀ The Big Picture:
The Classroom

A. Circle the things you see in this classroom.

Ask students to describe the picture. You might use questions like these to get started:

Who is this?
What is he/she doing?
What's this?
What is the room number?
What time is it?

Ask students to talk about the picture using *there is* and *there are*. You can also ask *how many* questions:

Are there any maps in the room?
How many maps are there in the room?

B. Listen. (CD1, Track 21)

Play the audio and ask simple comprehension questions. Play the audio several times if appropriate for your class.

The Big Picture: The Classroom

A. **the things you see in this classroom.**

a computer	(a clock)	(a map of the United States)
(a board)	(a book)	(desks)
(a table)	(a door)	(a window)
a pencil sharpener	(a pencil)	(a man)
(a woman)	(a teacher)	a child

B. Listen.

Audio Script

☀ The Big Picture:
The Classroom

B. Listen. (CD1, Track 21)

I am a student in English 1. My classroom is on the second floor in Room 204. There are ten students in my class. There are four men and six women. We are from many different countries. There are five students from Mexico. There are two students from Vietnam. There is one student from El Salvador, one from India, and one from the Philippines.

Our room is small. There is a big table in the front for the teacher. There are twelve desks for the students. There is a chalkboard on the wall. There are two maps on the wall, one of the United States and one of the world.

Our teacher is Mr. Wilson. We like our teacher, and we like our class.

C. Listen and circle.

1. Yes	(No)	6. Yes	(No)
2. Yes	(No)	7. (Yes)	No
3. Yes	(No)	8. (Yes)	No
4. (Yes)	No	9. (Yes)	No
5. Yes	(No)	10. (Yes)	No

D. Complete. Write *is* or *are* and the number.

1. There ___are___ ___ten___ students in this class.

2. There ___are___ ___four___ men and ___six___ women.

3. There ___is___ ___one___ teacher, Mr. Wilson.

4. There ___are___ ___twelve___ desks.

5. There ___are___ ___two___ maps on the wall.

6. There ___is___ ___one___ clock on the wall.

> **There is/There are**
> | There | is | one |
> |---|---|---|
> | | are | two |
> | | | three |

E. Complete.

clock	clocks	student	students
map	✓maps	man	men
woman	women	desk	desks

1. There are two ___maps___ on the wall.

2. There is a ___map___ of the world.

3. There are ten ___students___ in the class.

4. There are four ___men___ and six ___women___.

5. There is one ___student___ from India.

6. There are twelve ___desks___ in the room.

7. There is a ___clock___ on the wall.

The Classroom **27**

C. Listen and circle.
(CD1, Track 22)

• Point to the picture on page 26 and play the audio for Exercise B again. Then play the audio for Exercise C and ask students to circle the right answers.

• Check the answers by playing the audio again, pausing after each statement and calling on a student to give the answer.

D. Complete.

Point out the sample language in the box next to this exercise. Ask students to complete the sentences on their own.

E. Complete.

Have students complete the sentences in pairs.

Suggestion

Ask each student to write a statement about the picture on page 26. It can be true (*There is a book on the desk.*) or false (*There are 12 students in the room.*). Have students copy their statements on the board. Ask the class to help you correct any errors. Then read the sentences aloud and call on students to tell whether each statement is true or false.

Audio Script

C. Listen and circle. (CD1, Track 22)

1. The classroom is in Room 208.
2. There are twelve students in this class.
3. There are ten men in this class.
4. There are six women in this class.
5. There are four children in this class.
6. There are five students from India.
7. There is one student from El Salvador.
8. The room is small.
9. There are two maps on the wall.
10. We like our class.

A. Read these school signs.

Ask students to discuss the signs in pairs. Explain any of the signs students don't understand.

Teacher Note

Point out the icons and drawings used on some of the signs. Explain that these are very helpful in figuring out the meanings of the words. For example, the books might indicate a bookstore, classroom, or library. Knowing this might help the student recognize the word *library* if he or she has heard the word before, but not seen it in written form.

B. Walk around the school.

Encourage students to find signs they don't understand as well as ones they do. Have students draw all the signs on the board. Discuss what each one means.

Suggestion

Encourage students to bring in drawings of different signs they encounter outside of school for the next class meeting. Discuss the signs that each student brings in.

Reading

A. Read these school signs. Ask your teacher about any signs you don't understand.

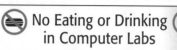

B. Walk around the school. Copy three signs that you see. Put your signs on the board. (Answers will vary.)

Writing Our Stories: My English Class

A. Read.

I study English at the English Adult School. My class is large. It's very large. There are 30 students in my class. We are from 20 different countries. We speak ten different languages.

Our classroom is small. There are 30 small desks. Our teacher, Mrs. Garcia, has a large desk for her books and her papers. We have many pencils, but we don't have a pencil sharpener. We are from many countries, but we don't have a map on the wall.

We need a larger classroom with a pencil sharpener and a map.

Writing Note
Use a period at the end of a sentence.

B. Write. Complete this story about your class.
(Answers will vary.)

I study English at _____.

There are _____ students in my class. We are from

_____ different countries. We speak _____ different languages.

Our classroom is _____. There are _____

_____

_____

_____

Writing Our Stories: My English Class

A. Read.

Have students read silently. Then, read the passage aloud to the class. Ask:

Do you understand the story? Are there any new words you don't understand?

Suggestion

Before starting Exercise B, ask students to look through the writing activity and note what information is provided. For example:

How many students are there in the class?
How many different countries do they come from?
How many different languages do they speak?
How many desks are there in the classroom?

Help students find the answers to these questions before they start writing.

B. Write.

• Students can use Exercise A as a model for this activity.
• Invite some students to read their stories aloud to the class.

Suggestion

Make a typed copy of one student's composition, leaving out all the singular and plural nouns or all the uses of *There is* and *There are*. Make class copies and ask students to fill in the blanks.

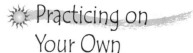

Practicing on Your Own

A. Write.

Have students do the activity individually and check their answers with a partner.

B. Complete.

Have students complete the activity on their own.

Suggestion

Ask students to work in pairs. Have them take turns asking each other the questions and replacing the answers in their books with true answers.

C. Complete with *There is* or *There are.*

Have students complete the sentences on their own.

Suggestion

Read each sentence aloud. Ask students whether the sentence is true about their own class. For each sentence that is not true, work together to create a sentence that is true about the class.

Practicing on Your Own

A. Write.

1. 10 _____ten_____
2. 14 _____fourteen_____
3. 18 _____eighteen_____
4. 19 _____nineteen_____
5. 20 _____twenty_____

6. 22 _____twenty-two_____
7. 35 _____thirty-five_____
8. 47 _____forty-seven_____
9. 69 _____sixty-nine_____
10. 100 _____one hundred_____

B. Complete.

1. Is this your pencil?   Yes, it _____is_____.
2. Is this your dictionary? No, _____it_____ _____isn't_____.
3. Is this your computer?   Yes, _____it_____ _____is_____.
4. Is this your classroom?   Yes, _____it_____ _____is_____.
5. _____Is_____ this your notebook?   _____(Answers will vary.)_____
6. _____ _____ your _____? _____ _____ _____.
7. _____ _____ your _____? _____ _____ _____.

> Is this your book?
> Yes, it is.
> No, it isn't.

C. Complete with *There is* or *There are.*

1. _____There_____ _____are_____ twenty students in our class.
2. _____There_____ _____are_____ twelve students from my country.
3. _____There_____ _____is_____ one student from China.
4. _____There_____ _____is_____ a map of the world on the wall.
5. _____There_____ _____are_____ two doors in our classroom.
6. _____There_____ _____is_____ a large table in the classroom.
7. _____There_____ _____is_____ a computer on the table.
8. _____There_____ _____is_____ a chalkboard on the wall.
9. _____There_____ _____are_____ two erasers on the chalkboard.

30   UNIT 2

Looking at Forms: School Registration

A. Complete. (Answers will vary.)

SCHOOL REGISTRATION

Last Name: _____   First Name: _____
Student is registered for:

Class: _____   Room: _____

Teacher: _____   Date: _____

Grammar Summary

1. Yes / No questions	
Is this your book?　　Yes, it **is.**　No, it **isn't.**	
2. Singular and plural nouns	
Regular　　　　　　*Irregular*	
book　　book**s**　　　man　　m**en**	
map　　map**s**　　　wom**a**n　wom**en**	
student　student**s**　child　child**ren**	
3. There is / There are	
There is a book on the table.	
There are three books on the table.	

☀ Looking at Forms: School Registration

A. Complete.

Ask students to fill in the form as if they were registering for the class they are in right now.

Grammar Summary

• Review the summary with the class. Invite students to say other statements, questions, and noun pairs that might appear in each of the three sections of the summary.

• See the Grammar Summary Expansion on page 231 for a more complete explanation of these grammar points.

Unit 3
The Family

Discuss the people next to the unit number. Ask:

- *Who is standing next to the number 3?* (A mother and child)
- *What are they doing?* (The mother and the child are holding a flower.)

 Dictionary: The Family

 A. Listen and repeat.
(CD1, Track 23)

- Play the audio. Have students point to each word as they hear it. Do the activity again, this time pausing for students to repeat each word.
- Draw a large version of the family tree on the board. Then point to and name pairs of people and tell how they are related to each other. For example: *Edwin and Rosa—husband and wife*, or *Edwin and Sylvia—father and daughter*. Ask students just to listen as you describe all the relationships. Then do it a second time and have students repeat.

Suggestion
Point to pairs of people on the family tree and call on individuals to name the relationships. Introduce the expression *family tree*.

B. Complete.

Have students complete the answers on their own or with a partner.

Suggestion
Play a game with the words in the boxes. Say one of the words. If the word is for a female, the women stand up or raise their hands. If the name is for a male, only the men respond. If it is a word used for both sexes (such as *parents*), both men and women respond.

Teacher Note
Students will need to bring family photos to class to do some of the exercises in this unit.

Dictionary: The Family

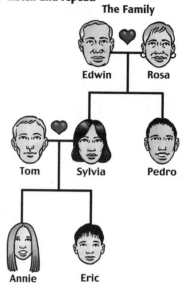 A. Listen and repeat.

The Family

Edwin   Rosa

Tom   Sylvia   Pedro

Annie   Eric

husband
wife
father
mother
son
daughter
brother
sister
grandfather
grandmother
grandson
granddaughter
uncle
aunt
nephew
niece

father + mother = parents

B. Complete.

1. Eric and Annie: __brother and sister__
2. Edwin and Rosa: __husband and wife__
3. Rosa and Sylvia: __mother and daughter__
4. Edwin and Pedro: __father and son__
5. Pedro and Eric: __uncle and nephew__
6. Pedro and Annie: __uncle and niece__
7. Rosa and Annie: __grandmother and granddaughters__
8. Edwin and Eric: __grandfather and grandson__

Culture Note
Mom = mother
Dad = father

Active Grammar: *How old* Questions

A. Read.

How old is he?
He's 7.

Margaret:	This is my son, Nicholas.
Kathy:	How old is he?
Margaret:	He's 7. And this is my daughter, Alexa.
Kathy:	How old is she?
Margaret:	She's 3.
Kathy:	You have a beautiful family.

B. Family photographs. Listen to the conversations. Number the photographs.

1

3

2

Relationship	Age
daughter	35
grandson	4

Relationship	Age
daughter	25
son-in-law	28

Relationship	Age
son	3
daughter	6

Listen again and write the relationships and ages.

The Family   **33**

Audio Script

B. Family photographs. Listen to the conversations. Number the photographs.
(CD1, Track 24)

Conversation 1
A: This is my daughter, Lana, and her little boy. His name is Michael, and he's four years old. He's our first grandchild.
B: How old is Lana?
A: She's 35.

Conversation 2
A: This is my son, Brian. He's three. And this is our daughter, Erica.
B: How old is Erica?
A: She's six.
B: That's a beautiful picture.

Conversation 3
A: This is my daughter, Silvia. She's 25. And this is her husband, Carlos. He's 28. They live in Florida.
B: Do they have any children?
A: No, they don't.

Active Grammar:
How old Questions

A. Read.

• Ask: *Who are the boy and girl in the picture?* Then read the conversation with a student.

• Ask students who have children about their children:

  Who has a son?
  What's his name?
  How old is he?
  Who has a daughter?
  What's her name?
  How old is she?

B. Family photographs.
(CD1, Track 24)

• Play the audio. Answer any questions students may have about the people in the pictures.

• Present the dialogues again and have students number the photographs.

• Present the dialogues a third time and have students write the relationships and ages.

Suggestion

Invite pairs of students to make up short conversations using the pictures and the relationship and age information they have written below each picture. They can use the dialogue in Exercise A as a model. For example:

A: *This is my daughter, Lana.*
B: *How old is she?*
A: *She's 35. And this is my grandson, Michael.*
B: *How old is he?*
A: *He's 4.*

 Adjectives

 Adjectives

 A. Listen and repeat.
(CD1, Track 25)

Point to each person as you play the audio. Have students listen once all the way through. The second time through, pause and have them repeat each sentence.

Suggestion

Ask students to point out people in the class who fit the descriptions on this page. Ask them to make statements about these students such as, *He's tall. She has curly hair.* Talk about the descriptive words that may be considered negative (*heavy, old, bald, short*) to other students in the class.

Alternatively, have students turn to other pages in the student book and ask them to describe the people on that page. (Try pages 29 and 33.)

Suggestion

Write on the board pairs of sentences from the middle of the page. Then replace the adjectives and nouns with blank lines.

> *Her _____ is _____.*
> *She has _____ _____.*

Ask students to make up sentences about students in the class.

 A. Listen and repeat.

 He's tall.   He's short.   She's heavy. She's thin.

 He's young.   He's old.

Her hair is long.
She has long hair.   Her hair is short.
She has short hair.

 Her hair is straight.
She has straight hair.   Her hair is curly.
She has curly hair.   Her hair is wavy.
She has wavy hair.

 He has a beard.   He has a moustache.   He's bald.

B. Complete about yourself. (Answers will vary.)

1. I am **tall / short / medium height**.
2. I am **thin / heavy / average weight**.
3. I am **young / old / middle aged**.
4. My hair is _____.
   color
5. I have **short / long / medium-length** hair.
6. My hair is **straight / wavy / curly**.

C. Describe. (Answers will vary.)

1. Describe the president of the United States.
2. Describe a famous athlete.
3. Describe a movie actor or actress.

D. Answer.

blond

brown

black

red

gray

| Yes, she is. | Yes, it is. |
| No, she isn't. | No, it isn't. |

1. Is she tall? _No, she isn't._
2. Is she heavy? _No, she isn't._
3. Is she old? _No, she isn't._
4. What color is her hair? Her hair is _black_ .
5. Is it curly? _No, it isn't._

| Yes, he is. | Yes, it is. |
| No, he isn't. | No, it isn't. |

6. Is he tall? _Yes, he is._
7. Is he thin? _Yes, he is._
8. Is he old? _No, he isn't._
9. What color is his hair? His hair is _black_ .
10. Is it long? _No, it isn't._

The Family   **35**

B. Complete about yourself.

Have students circle the words that describe themselves.

C. Describe.

• Point to the pictures showing hair color on the right side of the page. Say each word, and ask students to repeat.
• Ask: *Who is the president of the United States? Let's describe him.* Write student responses on the board, correcting any errors. Repeat this activity for a famous athlete and a movie actor or actress.

Suggestion

Tape pictures of ten famous people to the board. Let students take turns describing one of the people in the pictures. The rest of the class guesses which person the student is describing.

D. Answer.

• Tell students to answer the questions with a short answer from the box above the questions.
• Ask students to answer the questions individually and check their answers with a partner.

What's your date of birth?

A. Listen and repeat.
(CD1, Track 26)

Play the audio and have students listen and repeat. Then ask some questions that can be answered with a month or day such as, *What month is it? What day is today?*

B. Listen and repeat.
(CD1, Track 27)

Point out the ordinal numbers (*first, second, third,* etc.) at the bottom of each day in the calendar. Play the audio. Then point to Tuesday the first and say: *It's the first day of the month. It's Tuesday the first.*

C. Listen.
(CD1, Track 28)

Play the audio and have students listen and write in the dates on their own. To check the answers, have different students write their answers on the board.

Sit with a partner.

Have students say the dates they have written to a partner.

What's your date of birth?

A. Listen and repeat.

Months: January, February, March, April, May, June, July, August, September, October, November, December

Days: Sunday, Monday, Tuesday, Wednesday, Thursday, Friday, Saturday

B. Listen and repeat.

Sunday	Monday	Tuesday	Wednesday	Thursday	Friday	Saturday
		1 first	2 second	3 third	4 fourth	5 fifth
6 sixth	7 seventh	8 eighth	9 ninth	10 tenth	11 eleventh	12 twelfth
13 thirteenth	14 fourteenth	15 fifteenth	16 sixteenth	17 seventeenth	18 eighteenth	19 nineteenth
20 twentieth	21 twenty-first	22 twenty-second	23 twenty-third	24 twenty-fourth	25 twenty-fifth	26 twenty-sixth
27 twenty-seventh	28 twenty-eighth	29 twenty-ninth	30 thirtieth	31 thirty-first		

C. Listen. Write the date.

1. January 4, 2003
2. February 11, 1982
3. April 17, 1976
4. July 25,1990
5. August 18, 2005
6. September 7, 1964
7. November 30, 1999
8. December 25, 2000

Writing Note
Months begin with a capital letter.
January February

Sit with a partner. Say the dates above.

Audio Script

C. Listen. Write the date.
(CD1, Track 28)

1. January 4, 2003
2. February 11, 1982
3. April 17, 1976
4. July 25, 1990
5. August 18, 2005
6. September 7, 1964
7. November 30, 1999
8. December 25, 2000

D. Read and complete.

Date of birth: __9__ / __14__ / __75__
Month   Day   Year

A: What's your date of birth?

B: September 14, 1975.

Birth date: | 0 | 3 | 0 | 3 | 8 | 0 |
Month Day Year

A: What's your birth date?

B: March 3, 1980.

Looking at Forms

married

single

divorced

A. Complete. (Answers will vary.)

Name: _____ _____ _____
                   first   last   middle initial

Status: single married divorced   **Sex:** male female

Telephone: (   ) _____

Date of Birth: _____ _____ _____
               month   day   year

NAME (Last, First, Middle)

MARITAL STATUS	SEX
Single Married Divorced	☐ Male ☐ Female
TELEPHONE NUMBER (include Area Code) ( )	BIRTH DATE Month / Day / Year _____ / _____ / _____

D. Read and complete.

- Ask students to read the dialogue.
- Point out to students that the first date of birth mentioned in the dialogue has been filled out on the top form.
- Fill in the second date of birth mentioned in the dialogue on the bottom form together. (Point out that when using numbers in some forms it is necessary to add a zero before the numbers 1 to 9.)

Looking at Forms

Suggestion

Before doing Exercise A, introduce the words *married, single,* and *divorced.* Ask students to repeat the words and explain what each one means. Also introduce the words *male* and *female.* Check students' understanding by saying words for family members (*mother, uncle,* etc.) and asking the class to call out *male* or *female.*

A. Complete.

Have students complete the forms with their own information. Ask pairs of students to check each other's work.

Working Together:
My Family Tree

A. Draw your family tree.

• Draw your own family tree on the board, with names and faces representing your family members.

• Ask students to draw their family trees. For more help, students can refer to the family tree on page 32 as they work. Walk around the room and ask questions such as:

Who's this?
What's her name?
How many sisters do you have?
Are your parents here or in your home country?

B. Explain your family tree to a partner.

• Have students read the examples.

• Ask students to explain their family tree to a partner. Students should name all the family relationships shown in their family tree.

Working Together: My Family Tree

A. Draw your family tree. Complete this family tree. Show your parents, your husband or wife, your children, and your brothers and sisters. Add more circles if you need to. Write each person's name. *(Answers will vary.)*

 father mother

 you

_____

B. Explain your family tree to a partner.

Examples:

This is my mother. Her name is Manisha. She has five children.

This is my son. His name is Raj. He's six years old.

C. Family photographs. Bring in two or three photographs of your family. Tell your group about your family.

That's a nice picture. Is this you?

Your son is good-looking. He's tall!

Your son looks like you.

D. Write about a student in your class. Do not use the name. Write *he* or *she*.
(Answers will vary.)

_____

_____

_____

_____

_____

Read your description to the class. Can they guess the student?

E. Figure it out!

1. My daughter's son is my _____grandson_____.

2. My brother's daughter is my _____niece_____.

3. My brother's son is my _____nephew_____.

4. My mother's brother is my _____uncle_____.

5. My mother's sister is my _____aunt_____.

*6. My daughter's husband is my _____son-in-law_____.

*7. My sister's husband is my _____brother-in-law_____.

*8. My wife's father is my _____father-in-law_____.

> *in-laws
> mother-in-law
> father-in-law
> sister-in-law
> brother-in-law
> son-in-law
> daughter-in-law

C. Family photographs.

Have students work in groups. Encourage students to give a lot of information about their own photos and to ask many questions about other group members' photos. Walk around the classroom and ask questions such as:

> Who's this?
> Where are you?
> How old is he?
> Is this here or in your home country?

D. Write about a student in your class.

Ask each student to write a description of another student in the class. Have volunteers read their descriptions aloud to the class. Ask others to guess who is being described.

Suggestion

Before doing Exercise E, introduce the words used to describe *in-laws*. Say and have students repeat the words in the box next to Exercise E. Use the family tree on page 32 or the students' own family trees to point out and name these relationships.

E. Figure it out!

Have students complete the activity and check their answers with a partner.

The Big Picture: A Family Photo

A. Look at the family photo.

- Invite students to describe the people in the picture and make guesses about who they are. For example, *This is Linda's mother. She's a grandmother. She's tall. She has dark hair.*
- Have students write two adjectives about each person.

B. Listen. (CD1, Track 29)

Play the audio several times and have students write the names of the other people in the picture.

C. Listen again.
(CD1, Track 29)

Have students write each person's age above his or her name.

The Big Picture: A Family Photo

A. Look at the family photo. Write two adjectives for each person. (Answers will vary.)

Bob: <u>tall, bald</u>

Sarah: _____

Linda: _____

Steve: _____

B. Listen. Write these names on the picture.

| Emily | Kim | Joanne | Mary | Andy |

C. Listen again. Write the ages that you hear.

Audio Script

The Big Picture: A Family Photo

B. Listen. Write these names on the picture. (CD1, Track 29)

A: I have the pictures from the party last week.

B: Oh, yes, your mom's birthday party. Let me see.

A: Here's a picture of everyone.

B: Oh, that's you and Steve. And your two little girls. Which one is Emily and which one is Kim?

A: Emily is five. She has long hair. And Kim is six. She has short hair.

B: Now, that's your mom and dad. Right? In the middle?

A: Yes. That's mom. It's her birthday. She's 55 years old. And that's dad, next to her.

B: Oh, your dad has a moustache!

A: Yes. He has a moustache. At one time, he had curly hair, but now he's bald.

B: Who's this?

A: These are my sisters. I have two sisters. This is my sister Joanne. She's 21. And next to her, that's my sister Mary. She's 23.

B: Joanne and Mary look a lot alike.

A: I know. They're tall and they both have dark, curly hair. But Joanne is a little heavy, and Mary is very thin.

B: Are your sisters married?

A: No, I'm the only one who is married.

B: And who's this?

A: That's my brother, Andy.

B: Oh, you have a brother?

A: Yes, I have a brother. Andy is the baby of the family. He's 18.

B: He looks like your dad.

A: Hmm. You're right.

B: That's a great picture.

D. Complete.

1. _____**Mary**_____ is tall and thin. She has short, curly hair.
2. _____**Bob**_____ has a moustache, and he's bald.
3. _____**Emily**_____ is five years old. She has long hair.
4. _____**Steve**_____ is short and heavy. He has blond hair.
5. _____**Linda**_____ is short and thin. She has short, straight hair.
6. _____**Andy**_____ is tall and thin. He has wavy hair.
7. _____**Joanne**_____ is tall and heavy. She has short, curly hair.

E. Answer.

Andy

1. How old is Andy?
   He is 18.
2. Is he short?
   No, he is tall.
3. Is he heavy?
   No, he is thin.
4. What color is his hair?
   His hair is black.
5. Is it curly?
   Yes, it is.

Mary

1. How old is Mary?
   She is 23.
2. Is she single?
   Yes, she is.
3. Is she tall?
   Yes, she is.
4. What color is her hair?
   Her hair is black.
5. Is it long?
   No, it isn't.

 Ask and answer questions about other people in this family.

F. Pronunciation. Listen and repeat.

Statements

He is tall.
She is short.
It is curly.

Questions

Is he tall?
Is she short?
Is it curly?

Listen and complete. Then put a period (.) or a question mark (?) at the end of each sentence.

1. __**She**__ __**is**__ old.
2. __**Is**__ __**he**__ young?
3. __**Is**__ __**it**__ heavy?
4. __**It**__ __**is**__ tall.
5. __**She**__ __**is**__ thin.
6. __**Is**__ __**he**__ tall?
7. __**Is**__ __**she**__ short?
8. __**He**__ __**is**__ heavy.

Practice the sentences above with a partner.

The Family   **41**

Audio Script

F. Pronunciation. Listen and repeat.
(CD1, Track 30)

He is tall.   Is he tall?
She is short.   Is she short?
It is curly.   Is it curly?

Listen and complete.

1. She is old.   5. She is thin.
2. Is he young?   6. Is he tall?
3. Is it heavy?   7. Is she short?
4. It is tall.   8. He is heavy.

D. Complete.

Have students complete the sentences individually. Review the answers orally with the class.

E. Answer.

- Let a different student answer each of the questions.
- Have students work with a partner to create new questions and answers about the family members. Move around the room to offer students help as needed.

F. Pronunciation.
(CD1, Track 30)

- As you play the audio, direct students' attention to the rising and falling intonations used with the statements and questions. Play the audio again and have students repeat the statements and questions, copying the intonation as they repeat.

Statements (Falling intonation)

He is tall.

Questions (Rising intonation)

Is he tall?

- Have students listen to the audio, fill in the blanks, and add a period or question mark to the end of each sentence.
- Invite students to practice saying the sentences with a partner.

☀Reading:
I Miss My Family

A. Before You Read.

- Invite several different students to answer the questions. Encourage them to add information. For example: *I call my family once a week. I don't like to write letters.*
- Ask students to read the stories to themselves. When they finish, invite them to ask questions about anything they don't understand. Also invite them to add their comments about the readings.

B. Check.

- Ask different students to read the statements aloud. Point to the word *e-mail* in statement 1. Ask them to point out the word *e-mail* in the story. Repeat the activity for other words in statements 2–6 such as *photographs, computer,* and *cell phone.*
- Have students complete the activity on their own.

Teacher Note

Remind students that scanning involves looking for a specific piece of information in a reading while ignoring everything else.

C. Discuss.

Ask two or three different students to answer the questions. Then have students discuss the questions in small groups.

Reading: I Miss My Family

A. Before You Read.

1. Where do your brothers and sisters live? Where do your parents live?
2. Do you call them? Do you write them?

Donna

I have a computer. My brothers and my parents have computers, too. I e-mail everyone in my family. I write one e-mail and send it to everyone. We send photographs of the children, too!

Cecilia

My family is in the Philippines. My parents don't have a telephone. I write my parents once a month. I send them many photographs. They show the letters to my brothers and my sisters.

Gloria

I love to talk! I have a cell phone. My three sisters live in the United States, and I call them every week. My father lives in Colombia. I call him once a month. It's very expensive.

B. Check. (✓)

	Donna	Cecilia	Gloria
1. This person sends her family e-mail.	☑	☐	☐
2. This person sends photographs.	☑	☑	☐
3. This person calls her family a lot.	☐	☐	☑
4. This person has a computer.	☑	☐	☐
5. This person has a cell phone.	☐	☐	☑
6. This person writes letters.	☐	☑	☐

C. Discuss. (Answers will vary.)

1. Do you have a computer? Do you e-mail anyone?
2. Do you write letters? Who do you write?
3. Do you have a cell phone? Do you call your family a lot?

Writing Our Stories: My Family

A. Read.

My name is Liudmila. This is a photograph of my family. I am on the left. I have long, wavy hair. My eyes are brown. I am from Cuba. This is my husband, Carlos. He is 30 years old. Carlos is from Ecuador. He has black, curly hair. He is tall and handsome. He is hardworking. This is our son. His name is Jake. He is very active and friendly. He has brown hair and brown eyes. I think he looks like my husband.

B. Write about a photograph.
Bring in a photograph of your family. Write about your photograph. **(Answers will vary.)**

This is a picture of _____

_____

_____

_____

_____

_____

_____

_____

_____

_____

Writing Note
A name begins with a capital letter.

☀ Writing Our Stories: My Family

A. Read.

Read the story aloud or have students read it on their own. Then ask one student to read the sentences about Liudmila. Ask another to read the sentences about Carlos. Ask a third to read the sentences about Jake.

B. Write about a photograph.

• Explain to students that they should use the story at the top of the page as a model for their writing.

• Invite some students to show their family photos and read their stories aloud to the class.

Suggestion

Make suggestions for corrections on each story and have students make clean, revised copies. Number the stories and post them on a large bulletin board. Label each family photo with a letter and post them on another area of the bulletin board. Have students try to match each story with the correct photo.

A. Write the answer.

Have students do the activity
individually and check their
answers with a partner.

Suggestion

After finishing Exercise A, students
can work in pairs and use these
questions to ask and answer questions about people in their own
family photos.

B. Write the date.

Have students complete the
activity on their own.

Suggestion

Ask volunteers to come to the board
and write a date that is important
to them (such as a child's birthday
or a wedding anniversary) both
in numbers and in words. Ask the
other students to try to guess why
this date is important to the student. If no one guesses correctly,
ask the student to tell why the
date is important.

Practicing on Your Own

A. Write the answer.

No, she isn't. She's single.	She's 23.
He lives in New Jersey.	She lives in Texas.
✓ That's my brother.	His name is Shin Kim.
Her name is Erica.	He's 26.
Yes, he's married.	That's my sister.

1. Who's this? — That's my brother.
2. What's his name? — His name is Shin Kim.
3. How old is he? — He's 26.
4. Where does he live? — He lives in New Jersey.
5. Is he married? — Yes, he's married.

6. Who's this? — That's my sister.
7. What's her name? — Her name is Erica.
8. How old is she? — She's 23.
9. Where does she live? — She lives in Texas.
10. Is she married? — No, she isn't. She's single.

B. Write the date.

1. 1/3/03   January 3, 2003
2. 4/7/99   April 7, 1999
3. 3/21/86   March 21, 1986
4. 4/8/75   April 8, 1975
5. 9/6/68   September 6, 1968
6. 11/12/00 November 12, 2000
7. 12/25/05 December 25, 2005

Writing Note
Put a comma between the
day and the year.
January 3, 2003

> **I study with two classmates. We work together two days a week after class.**

☐ I like this idea.   (Answers will vary.)
☐ I don't like this idea.
☐ I'm going to try this idea.

Grammar Summary

1. *How old* questions	
How old is he?	He's 15.
How old is she?	She's 7.
2. Adjectives	
He's **tall.** He's **young.**	
He has **black** hair.	
3. Short questions and answers		
Is he tall?	Yes, he **is.**	No, he **isn't.**
Is she old?	Yes, she **is.**	No, she **isn't.**
Is his hair long?	Yes, it **is.**	No, it **isn't.**

☀ Learning Tip

Discuss the Learning Tip with students. Ask:

• *Do you study alone?*
• *Does anyone help you with your English?*
• *Do any of you study together?*
• *Where do you study?*
• *When do you study?*

Grammar Summary

• Review the summary with the class. Invite students to say other statements, questions, and answers that might appear in each of the three sections of the summary.
• See the Grammar Summary Expansion on page 232 for a more complete explanation of these grammar points.

Unit 4
Moving Day

Discuss the person next to the unit number. Ask:

• *Who is standing next to the number 4?* (A man)
• *What is he doing?* (He's pushing a cart loaded with boxes.)

☀ Dictionary: Rooms, Furniture, Locations

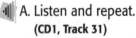

A. Listen and repeat.

(CD1, Track 31)

• Play the audio for the *Rooms* and *Furniture* sections on pages 46 and 47. Have students point to each word as they hear it. Do the activity again, this time pausing for students to repeat each word.
• Ask students to point to and say the names of any of these items they see in the classroom.

Suggestion

Ask students to study the words for rooms and furniture in pairs. Suggest that they take turns doing the following: one student covers a row of words with a pencil and points to the pictures in random order; the other student then supplies the correct words.

4 Moving Day

Dictionary: Rooms, Furniture, Locations

A. Listen and repeat.

Rooms

living room   dining room   kitchen

bathroom   bedroom

Furniture

sofa   armchair   TV   lamp

picture   bookcase   coffee table   end table

table   chair   rug   mirror

bed

dresser

desk

night table

stove

sink

microwave

refrigerator

sink

toilet

bathtub

shower

Locations

The book is on the chair.

The book is under the chair.

The book is next to the chair.

The book is between the chair and the desk.

The book is in the desk.

The picture is over the chair.

A. Listen and repeat.
(CD1, Track 31 *continued*)

• Now focus on the *Locations* section at the bottom of page 47. Play the audio and have students point to each word as they hear it. Do the activity again, this time pausing for students to repeat each word.

• Ask students to identify familiar objects in the room and tell where they are located. For example: *My backpack is next to my chair.*

Suggestion

Draw a picture of a book, a table, and a chair on the board. Then make up sentences using prepositions and have different students go to the board and draw the correct pictures. For example: *The book is on the table. The chair is next to the table.*

☀ Active Grammar: Prepositions

A. Read.

• Talk about the picture. Have students identify the rooms and the objects. Ask:

Where is the woman?
Who are the two men?
What are they doing?
What's happening in the picture?
Is this a house or an apartment?
What is she saying?
What is the first man carrying?
What is the second man carrying?
Where is the _____?
Where are the _____?

• Read the dialogue and ask students to point to the objects and locations. Then read each line and ask students to repeat.

Suggestion

Have a pair of students read the dialogue to the class.

B. Complete.

Ask students to complete the sentences individually and check their answers with a partner.

A. Read.

A: Where do you want this armchair?

B: Put it in the living room.

A: Where do you want this lamp?

B: Put it in the bedroom.

B. Complete.

1. Put the refrigerator in the _____ kitchen _____.
2. Put the bed in the _____ bedroom _____.
3. Put the coffee table in the _____ living room _____.
4. Put the dresser in the _____ bedroom _____.
5. Put the armchair in the _____ living room _____.
6. Put the table in the _____ dining room/kitchen _____.
7. Put the stove in the _____ kitchen _____.

C. Complete these sentences about the house.

1. The mirror is _____over_____ the bed.
2. The stereo is _____between_____ the boxes.
3. The telephone is _____on_____ the night table.
4. The pillows are _____on_____ the dresser.
5. The computer is _____on_____ the coffee table.
6. The night table is _____next to_____ the bed.
7. The end table is _____next to_____ the sofa.
8. The TV is _____on_____ the desk.
9. The armchair is _____next to_____ the desk.
10. The cat is _____under_____ the sofa.
11. The lamp is _____on_____ the coffee table.
12. The boxes are _____under_____ the window.

D. Ask and answer.

> Where is the TV?
> It's on the desk.

> Where are the books?
> They're next to the box.

1. Where is the computer? — It's on the coffee table.
2. Where is the mirror? — It's over the bed.
3. Where are the keys? — They're on the dresser.
4. Where is the cell phone? — It's on the bookcase.
5. Where are the movers? — They're in the living room.
6. Where is the desk chair? — It's in the living room.
7. Where is the desk? — It's next to the coffee table.
8. Where is the rug? — It's under the bed.

C. Complete these sentences about the house.

Have students look at the picture on page 48 and fill in the prepositions.

Suggestion

Before doing Exercise D, use the picture on page 48 to introduce the words *keys, cell phone,* and *movers.*

D. Ask and answer.

- Have students ask and answer the questions in pairs. Move around the room checking students' use of prepositions and monitoring pronunciation.
- Invite different pairs of students to ask and answer one of the questions for the class.

☀ Where is my cell phone?

Suggestion

Before doing Exercise A, use the picture to introduce the words *photos, printer,* and *remote.*

A. Answer.

- Ask general questions about the picture. Also, invite students to ask you questions. For example:

  Who are these two people?
  Where are they?
  What is the man saying?
  Where is the _____?
  Where are the _____?

- Read the eight questions aloud and call on individuals to answer.

Suggestion

Repeat the activity. This time ask students to tell where each object is. For example:

T: *Is the cell phone on the coffee table?*
S: *No, it isn't. It's next to the sofa.*

B. Look at the picture above and read the conversations.

- Ask students to read the conversations silently. Answer any questions they have. Point out the statements *Yes, here it is!* and *Yes, here they are!*
- Ask students to practice the conversations in pairs. Walk around the room offering help as needed.

C. Look at the picture above.

Ask students to locate each of the items in the picture. Then have students practice the conversations in Exercise B with a partner, using these items.

| Yes, it is. | Yes, they are. |
| No, it isn't. | No, they aren't. |

A. Answer.

1. Is the cell phone on the coffee table? **No, it isn't.**
2. Are the photos on the coffee table? **Yes, they are.**
3. Is the remote on the desk? **No, it isn't.**
4. Are the keys next to the computer? **Yes, they are.**
5. Are the pillows on the sofa? **Yes, they are.**
6. Is the printer next to the computer? **Yes, it is.**
7. Is the clock on the bookcase? **No, it isn't.**
8. Is the cat under the sofa? **No, it isn't.**

B. Look at the picture above and read the conversations.

Conversation 1

A: Where is my cell phone?
B: Is it on the coffee table?
A: No, it isn't.
B: Is it under the coffee table?
A: No, it isn't.
B: Is it on the floor?
A: Yes, here it is!

Conversation 2

A: Where are my glasses?
B: Are they next to the stereo?
A: No, they aren't.
B: Are they under the coffee table?
A: No, they aren't.
B: Are they on the armchair?
A: Yes, here they are!

C. Look at the picture above. Practice the conversations again with these items.

| clock | pillows | house keys |
| camera | CDs | remote |

Working Together

A. Sharing an apartment. You and a partner are sharing an apartment. Place all of these items in your living room. Where is each item? **(Answers will vary.)**

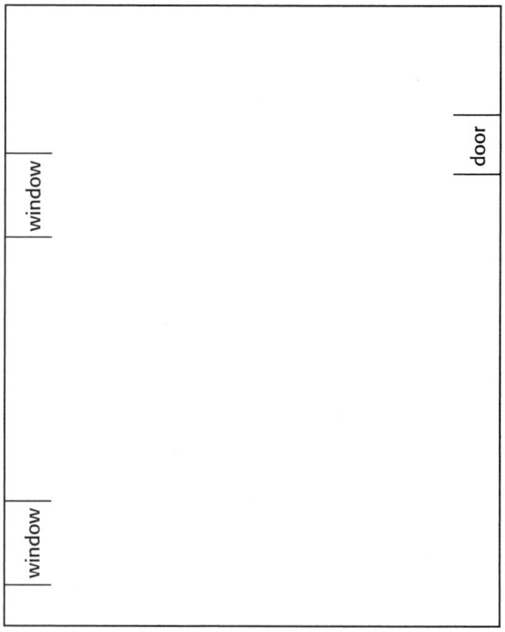

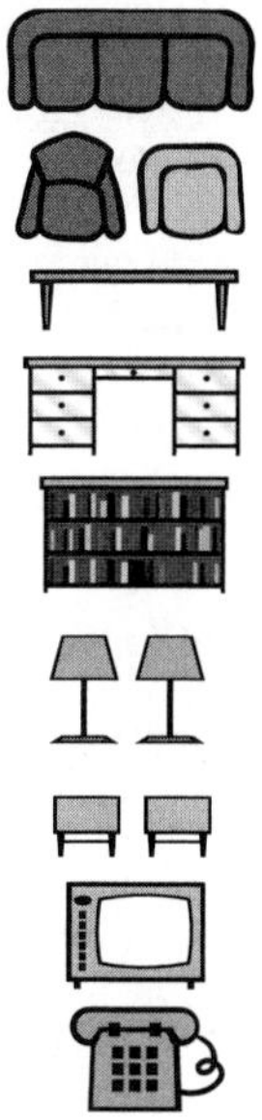

	the sofa
	two chairs
	the coffee table
	the desk
	the bookcase
	the lamps
	the end tables
	the TV
	the telephone

window

window

door

B. Look around your classroom. Write the locations of five items. (Answers will vary.)

1. _____ The clock is over the door. _____
2. _____
3. _____
4. _____
5. _____
6. _____

☀ Working Together

A. Sharing an apartment.

- Read and discuss the instructions. Explain to students that they will be working with a partner to decide where to put each item, and to draw the items on the blank outline of the room.
- Role-play one or two exchanges with a student. For example:

T: *Where do you want the sofa?*
S: *Between the windows. Where do you want the desk?*
T: *Next to the door.*

- Move around the room offering help as needed.

Suggestion

When students finish Exercise A, direct the pairs to ask and answer questions about where they have placed each item. For example:

T: *Where is the sofa?*
S: *It's between the windows.*

B. Look around your classroom.

Have students complete the activity on their own. Invite several students to write their sentences on the board.

☀ What's your address?

A. Read.

Ask students to read the dialogue silently. Then say each sentence and have students repeat. Answer any questions they have.

Suggestion

Point out that zip codes are usually pronounced one number at a time. Say: *07016 is oh-seven-oh-one-six, not oh-seventy-sixteen*. Also, explain how to say three- and four-digit street numbers such as 419 (*four nineteen*), 623 (*six twenty-three*), 1533 (*fifteen thirty-three*), and 2146 (*twenty-one forty-six*).

Suggestion

Ask students to give examples of local addresses. Write some of the addresses on the board and have students read them aloud.

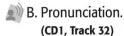 B. Pronunciation.

(CD1, Track 32)

Ask students to listen as you play the audio or say the street addresses. Then repeat the process once or twice more, having students repeat each address.

C. Listen. **(CD1, Track 33)**

• Ask students to listen to the audio and write in the addresses next to the street names. Play the audio again and have them check their work. Write the answers on the board as a final check.

Repeat the addresses above with a partner.

• Have students practice saying the addresses with a partner.

What's your address?

A. Read.

A: What's your new address?
B: 419 South Avenue.
A: What town?
B: Cranford.
A: And what's your zip code?
B: 07016.

B. Pronunciation: Street addresses. Listen and repeat.

a.    b.    c.

d.    e.    f.

C. Listen. Write the addresses.

1. ___73___ North Avenue
2. ___66___ Maple Street
3. ___143___ Central Avenue
4. ___861___ Park Avenue
5. ___9924___ First Street
6. ___3285___ Main Street

Repeat the addresses above with a partner.

Audio Script

C. Listen. Write the addresses.
(CD1, Track 33)

a. 73 North Avenue
b. 66 Maple Street
c. 143 Central Avenue
d. 861 Park Avenue
e. 9924 First Street
f. 3285 Main Street

Sending a letter

A. Interview three students. (Answers will vary.)

What's your name?	What's your address?	What's your zip code?
Pierre	349 Pine Place Santa Rosa	03402
1.		
2.		
3.		

B. Read.

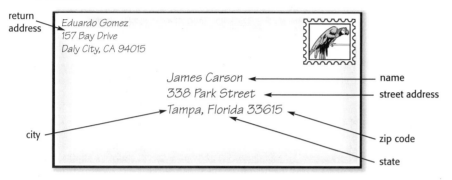

return address — Eduardo Gomez / 157 Bay Drive / Daly City, CA 94015

James Carson ← name
338 Park Street ← street address
Tampa, Florida 33615 → zip code

city → Tampa, Florida 33615 → state

C. Address this envelope to a friend. (Answers will vary.)

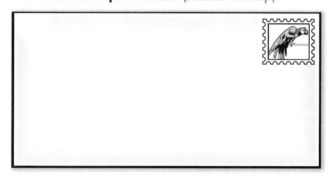

Teacher Note

Some students may not be comfortable giving their real addresses to their classmates. Before doing Exercise A, tell the class that it's OK to make up an address.

Suggestion

You may wish to review the Helpful Expressions on page 5 in Student Book Unit 1 (*Please spell that. Please repeat.*). This is also a good time to review the pronunciation of the letters of the alphabet on page 4.

A. Interview three students.

Have students repeat the three questions at the top of the chart. Then have them move around the room and ask three classmates these questions. Have students write down the answers their classmates give them.

B. Read.

Point out each part of the return address in the upper left corner of the envelope and of the mailing address in the lower right.

C. Address this envelope to a friend.

Suggest that students address their envelopes to a real friend or relative.

The Big Picture:
A Dorm Room

A. Write the name of each item on the picture.

- Ask students to write as many of the words on the picture as they can. Then have them work with partners to add more.
- Review the names and locations of all the items with the class.

Suggestion

Have students look at the picture for sixty seconds. Then ask them to close their books and name the items in the picture they remember.

Teacher Note

The audio story includes all the items that students labeled in Exercise A. As they listen, have students point to each item in the dorm room. If a student is having difficulty, have him/her sit next to a classmate who can follow the audio easily. The second student points out the correct items to the first student.

B. Listen to this conversation between Kathy and her father. (CD1, Track 34)

Review the three questions before students listen. Then play the audio and have students answer the questions.

The Big Picture: A Dorm Room

A. Write the name of each item on the picture.

| bed | CDs | dresser | computer | small table | printer |
| TV | clothes | desk | remote | stereo | telephone |

small table · CDs · stereo · dresser · printer · computer · desk · telephone · bed · remote · TV · clothes

B. Listen to this conversation between Kathy and her father.

1. Is Kathy at home? No, she isn't.
2. Where is Kathy? She is in her dorm room.
3. Is her room large or small? It's small.

Audio Script

The Big Picture:
A Dorm Room

B. Listen to this conversation between Kathy and her father. (CD1, Track 34)

F: Your dorm room is very small, Kathy.

K: I know. It is small. But everything is in my room now.

F: Tell me about your room. Where did you put everything?

K: Well, the bed is on the right. My pillow is under the window. The night table is at the end of my bed, and the TV is on the table.

F: Where's the dresser?

K: The dresser is on the left. I put the stereo on the dresser, and my CDs are next to the stereo.

F: Where's your desk?

K: It's next to my dresser. I put the small bookcase on my desk. The computer is on the desk, and the printer is next to the computer.

F: Where are your clothes?

K: Most of my clothes are in the closet.

F: And where's your telephone?

K: It's under the bed!

C. Complete.

1. The TV is _____on_____ the night table.
2. The pillow is _____under_____ the window.
3. The stereo is _____on_____ the dresser.
4. The CDs are _____next to_____ the stereo.
5. The computer is _____on_____ the desk.
6. The printer is _____next to_____ the computer.
7. Some clothes are _____in_____ the closet.
8. Some clothes are _____on_____ the floor.
9. The telephone is _____under_____ the bed.
10. Kathy is _____in_____ her dorm room.

D. Sit with a partner. Ask and answer these questions.

> Yes, it is.
> No, it isn't.

> Yes, they are.
> No, they aren't.

1. Is the bed on the right?
   Yes, it is.
2. Is the dresser on the left?
   Yes, it is.
3. Is the telephone under the bed?
   Yes, it is.
4. Is the bookcase on the desk?
   Yes, it is.
5. Is the stereo next to the computer?
   No, it isn't.
6. Is the TV on the dresser?
   No, it isn't.
7. Are the CDs next to the TV?
   No, they aren't.
8. Are the clothes on the bed?
   Yes, they are.
9. Is the remote on the TV?
   No, it isn't.
10. Is the pillow on the bed?
    Yes, it is.

E. Ask and answer questions about these items in Kathy's room.

> Where is the stereo?
> It's on the dresser.

> Where are the CDs?
> They're next to the stereo.

the computer   the books
the telephone   the TV
her boots   the shoes
the remote   the telephone

C. Complete.

Ask students to complete the sentences individually. Then have them check their answers with a partner.

Suggestion

Before doing Exercise D, introduce the phrases *on the right* and *on the left*. Write the two phrases on the board. Turn so that your back is to students and demonstrate the difference between the two phrases. Ask students to name some things in the classroom that are on the right and on the left.

D. Sit with a partner.

Point out the short answers and practice them with students. Then have pairs complete the activity together. Review the answers with the class.

E. Ask and answer questions about the items in Kathy's room.

Invite students to work with a partner to ask and answer questions about the items in Kathy's room.

Suggestion

Ask students to draw pictures of their own bedrooms. During the next class you can display the pictures and have students describe them to the class.

Reading: Classified Ads

Suggestion

Bring to class, or have students bring to class, copies of local newspapers that have classified sections. Display the papers and encourage students to look through them together before class.

A. Before You Read.

• Ask students to hold up local newspapers, say the name of the newspaper, and show where the classified ad section is.

• Have students read silently. Then read the paragraph about garage sales to them.

B. Scan these ads.

• Read the directions and demonstrate how to scan for information. Say, *I'm looking only for baby items.* Hold up your book and run your finger quickly along the lines of type. Stop at and read the words *Baby items* in ad number 2.

• Ask students to finish the exercise on their own. Remind them to scan for the items they are looking for and to skip over everything else.

Teacher Note

Students may be reluctant to try scanning because they may think they will miss something important if they don't read every word. Point out that we use scanning only when we are looking for key pieces of information. Explain that because this skill helps them pick out the information they need and skip over the information they don't need, scanning can save them time.

Reading: Classified Ads

A. Before You Read. What is the name of your local paper? Where is the classified ad section?

Garage Sales

In your local newspaper, you can find ads for garage sales, yard sales, or tag sales in your area. At these sales you can buy furniture, electronic equipment, children's toys and clothing, kitchen items, etc. at very good prices.

1	**Clark** – 16 Poplar Drive – Saturday 9am–3pm. Sofa, child's bedroom set, kitchen table, kitchen items, tools. Rain or shine.	5	**Fanwood** – 33 West End Avenue – Three Family Garage Sale. Saturday 9–4. Dishes, kitchen items, books, clothing, exercise equipment, refrigerator.
2	**Clark** – 32 Standish Way – Friday and Saturday 10am–5pm. Baby items, car seat, playpen, crib, stroller, lots of toys and clothing.	6	**Garwood** – 472 Summit Avenue – Friday and Saturday 9–3. Moving Sale. Twin beds, 2 sofas, washing machine and dryer, bookcase, chairs, coffee table, lamps, and much more!
3	**Cranford** – 55 Holly Street – Moving to Florida! Saturday 8am–6pm. Lots of furniture! Beds, chairs, sofas, end tables, night tables, dining room set, T.V.	7	**Plainfield** – 377 Raritan Road – Saturday Neighborhood Garage Sale – Furniture, kitchen items, small appliances, rugs, lamps, tools, stereo, CDs.
4	**Cranford** – 456 Willow Street – Friday 9 to 5. Something for everyone! Tools, garden equipment, furniture, misc.	8	**Summit** – 44 North Avenue – Friday and Saturday 9–3. Pool table, two bicycles, sports equipment, toys, and games.

B. Scan these ads. Write the number of one or two garage sale ads.

1. This sale has baby items. _____2_____
2. This sale has tools. _1, 4, and 7_
3. This sale has a TV. _____3_____
4. This sale has a sofa. _1, 3, and 6_
5. This sale has kitchen items. _1, 5, and 7_
6. This sale has bicycles. _____8_____
7. This sale has a refrigerator. _____5_____

> What are you looking for? Which garage sale is good for you?

Writing Our Stories: At Home

A. Read.

I rent a room in a house in San Diego. My family is in Poland, and I live alone. I work all day, and I go to school at night. I don't want an apartment. I don't need a kitchen. I only eat breakfast at home. There is a small refrigerator and a micro-wave in the room. My TV is on a small table.

I live in a house in San Diego. It's all on one floor. The house has seven rooms. There are three bedrooms and two bathrooms. There is a family room, too. There is a TV and a computer in the family room. We need a large house. I have three children, and my mother lives with us, too.

B. Check the information that is true about you. (Answers will vary.)

- ☐ I live in a house.
- ☐ I live in an apartment.
- ☐ I live alone.
- ☐ I live with _____.

- ☐ There are _____ rooms.
- ☐ I have a small _____.
- ☐ I have a large _____.
- ☐ There's a TV in my bedroom.

C. Write. (Answers will vary.)

I live at _____ _____ in _____.
        number   street   city

I live in _____. I live with _____.
        a house / an apartment / a room

My home has _____ rooms. _____.

_____

_____

_____

_____

_____

Writing Note
Street names begin with capital letters:
North Avenue

Writing Our Stories: At Home

A. Read.

Read the stories aloud to the students. Ask students to point out any sentences they don't understand. Explain these sentences to students.

B. Check the information that is true about you.

Have students complete this exercise on their own.

Suggestion

Start Exercise C by having several students write on the board one sentence each about their own homes. Correct any spelling or grammar errors. Read the sentences aloud and remind students to watch for these errors in their own writing.

C. Write.

• Instruct students to use the information from Exercise B to help them complete this activity.
• Explain to students that they should use the stories at the top of the page as models for their own writing. Show students how they can adapt sentences to fit their own needs. For example: *There is a TV and a computer in the family room* can become *There is a big red sofa and an old lamp in the living room.*

A. Complete.

- Ask students questions about the picture, such as:

  What room is this?
  What are some of the things you see?
  Does this look like your kitchen at home?

- Check that students know the names of all the items in the picture. Point to and ask students to name these objects: *microwave, clock, table, window, boxes, cups, coffee maker, glasses.*

- Have students complete the activity on their own and check their answers with a partner.

B. Answer.

Students may complete the activity in class or for homework. Suggest that they look at the Grammar Summary on page 59 if they have difficulty with any items.

A. Complete. (Answers may vary. Suggested answers are below.)

1. Where ___is___ the microwave? __It is next to the refrigerator.__
2. Where ___are___ the glasses? __They're next to the sink.__
3. Where ___is___ the clock? __It's over the refrigerator.__
4. Where ___is___ the window? __It's over the sink.__
5. Where ___are___ the cups? __They're on the table.__
6. Where ___is___ the table? __It's next to the stove.__
7. Where ___are___ the boxes? __They're under the table.__
8. Where ___is___ the coffee maker? __It's next to the stove.__

B. Answer.

1. Is the pot on the stove? __Yes, it is.__
2. Are the flowers on the table? __Yes, they are.__
3. Is the window over the stove? __No, it isn't.__
4. Are the cups on the counter? __No, they aren't.__
5. Are the glasses in the sink? __No, they aren't.__
6. Is the clock on the table? __No, it isn't.__
7. Is the stove next to the refrigerator? __No, it isn't.__
8. Are the boxes on the table? __No, they aren't.__

I make flash cards to study vocabulary. On one side, I write the word in English. On the other side, I write the word in my language.

☐ I like this idea.
☐ I don't like this idea.
☐ I'm going to try this idea.

(Answers will vary.)

table

la mesa

Grammar Summary

▶ **1. Prepositions**

The sofa is **in** the living room.

The end table is **next to** the sofa.

The books are **on** the end table.

▶ **2. *Where* questions**

Where is the dresser?	It's next to the bed.
Where are the shoes?	They're under the bed.

▶ **3. *Yes / No* questions**

Is the telephone on the counter?	Yes, it **is.**	No, it **isn't.**
Are the CDs next to the stereo?	Yes, they **are.**	No, they **aren't.**

Learning Tip

Discuss the Learning Tip with students. Take a poll to see how many students have made or used flash cards before. Ask students who have to tell how using flash cards has helped them remember new vocabulary words.

Suggestion

Divide the class into groups by their first language. If all students speak the same first language, create groups of five or six. Give each group a set of ten index cards. Have the students choose ten words from this unit that they need practice with. Show students how to make two-sided flash cards with the English word on one side and the word in their first language on the other side. Encourage students to use the cards to study the words with a partner or on their own.

Grammar Summary

• Review the summary with the class. Invite students to say other statements, questions, and answers that might appear in each of the three sections of the summary.

• See the Grammar Summary Expansion on page 233 for a more complete explanation of these grammar points.

Unit 5
I'm Busy

Discuss the person next to the unit number. Ask:

• *Who is sitting next to the number 5?* (A woman)
• *What is she doing?* (She's sitting on a stool and juggling several items—a telephone, a pencil and paper, and a frying pan.)

Dictionary: Actions

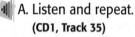

A. Listen and repeat.
(CD1, Track 35)

• Ask students to look at the pictures as you play the audio or read the words. Pause between the sentences and have students repeat each sentence. Repeat this activity again if necessary.
• Say individual sentences and ask students to point to the correct picture. Then have students work in pairs to take turns saying a sentence and pointing to the correct picture.

 **I'm Busy**

Dictionary: Actions

 A. Listen and repeat.

He is eating.　　She is washing the car.　　She is listening to music.　　They are studying.

He is cooking.　　She is sleeping.　　He is reading.　　She is drinking.

They are talking.　　They are watching TV.　　He is doing his homework.　　She is cleaning the house.

She is driving.　　They are walking.　　She is making lunch.　　He is doing the laundry.

B. Complete.

1. He ___is talking___ on the telephone.

2. She ___is reading___ the newspaper.

3. I ___am writing___ in my book.

4. They ___are watching___ a movie.

5. The students ___are studying___ English.

6. He's in bed. He ___is sleeping___.

7. She ___is drinking___ a cup of coffee.

8. They ___are listening___ to the stereo.

9. She ___is cooking___ dinner.

10. He ___is eating___ a hamburger.

is reading
are studying
✓ is talking
am writing
are watching
is drinking
is cooking
is eating
is sleeping
are listening

C. Pronunciation: Contractions. Listen.

Long form	Contraction
She is reading.	She's reading.
He is sleeping.	He's sleeping.
I am studying.	I'm studying.
We are talking.	We're talking.
They are eating.	They're eating.
You are cooking.	You're cooking.

Circle the form you hear.

1. **a.** He is walking.   **(b.)** He's walking.
2. **(a.** She is cleaning.**)**   **b.** She's cleaning.
3. **(a.** I am making lunch.**)**   **b.** I'm making lunch.
4. **a.** You are driving.   **(b.** You're driving.**)**
5. **a.** They are watching TV.   **(b.** They're watching TV.**)**
6. **(a.** We are studying.**)**   **b.** We're studying.

Practice both forms of the sentences above with a partner.

B. Complete.

Have students complete the exercise on their own. Remind them that they can refer to page 60 to check the meaning of the words in the box.

 C. Pronunciation: Contractions. (CD1, Track 36)

• Play the first part of Exercise C on the audio. Repeat several times if you wish.

• Play the second part of Exercise C on the audio. Go over the answers with the class.

• Have students practice the sentences in pairs. As students practice saying the sentences to each other, move around the room offering pronunciation support.

Suggestion

Before asking students to circle their answers, read pairs of similar sentences aloud. Tell students that when you read identical sentences (*She's reading./ She's reading.*), they should call out "*Same!*" When you read different sentences (*She is reading./She's reading.*), they should call out "*Different!*"

Audio Script

C. Circle the form you hear. (CD1, Track 36)

1. He's walking.
2. She is cleaning.
3. I am making lunch.
4. You're driving.
5. They're watching TV.
6. We are studying.

☼ Active Grammar:
Present Continuous Statements

A. Read.

• Read the story with the class. Ask simple comprehension questions to be sure students understand the story. For example:

What day is it?
Where is Jenny?
What is David doing?

• Ask or explain what verbs do. (They describe actions.) Write the first sentence and underline the verbs. Then have students underline the verbs in the paragraph and compare answers with a partner. Review the answers with the class.

Suggestion

• Write on the board: *He is studying. They are studying.* Then ask: *What is the same in the two sentences? What is different in the two sentences?*
• Point out that the sentences with *is/are* plus an *-ing* word talk about actions that are happening right now. Have them find examples in the reading.

B. Match.

Have students match answers on their own and compare their answers in small groups.

Suggestion

After you finish reviewing the answers to Exercise B with the class, have pairs of students use the exercise for conversation practice. One person asks the questions and the other answers. Then students change roles.

Suggestion

Have students cover the text and just look at the picture. Ask them to talk about the picture. Then ask some new questions about the people in the picture.

Active Grammar: Present Continuous Statements

A. Read. Underline the verbs.

It is Saturday morning, and everyone in the Lee family is busy. Jenny is in the bathroom. She is taking a shower. Jenny is getting ready for work. David is in his bedroom. He is studying for a test on Monday. Mrs. Lee is in the living room. She is cleaning. Right now, she is vacuuming the rug. Mr. Lee is in the kitchen. He is cooking lunch for the family. Carla is helping. She is washing the dishes. Grandma Lee is in the kitchen, too. She is doing the laundry.

B. Match.

1. Where is Jenny?   She's in the living room.
2. What is she doing?   He's cooking lunch.
3. Where is Mrs. Lee?   He's studying.
4. What is she doing?   She's in the bathroom.
5. Where is Mr. Lee?   She's cleaning.
6. What is he doing?   She's taking a shower.
7. Where is David?   He's in the kitchen.
8. What is he doing?   He's in his bedroom.

C. Ask and answer.

Short Answers	
Yes, he is.	No, he isn't.
Yes, she is.	No, she isn't.
Yes, they are.	No, they aren't.

1. Is Jenny sleeping?
   No, she isn't. (taking a shower)
2. Is she getting ready for work?
   Yes, she is.
3. Is David in his bedroom?
   Yes, he is.
4. Is he studying?
   Yes, he is.
5. Is Mrs. Lee in the living room?
   Yes, she is.
6. Is she watching TV?
   No, she isn't. (cleaning)

7. Are Mr. Lee and Carla in the kitchen?
   Yes, they are.
8. Are they cooking dinner?
   No, they aren't. (lunch)
9. Is Carla washing the dishes?
   Yes, she is.
10. Are they talking?
    No, they aren't.
11. Is Grandma in the kitchen?
    Yes, she is.
12. Is Grandma doing the laundry?
    Yes, she is.

D. Read.

David: Hello.

Mark: Hi. This is Mark. Can you talk now?

David: I can't. I'm studying for a test. Can I call you later?

Mark: Sure.

Culture Note
On the telephone, say:
This is (name).
Example: This is Maria.

E. Practice this conversation. (Answers will vary.)

A: Hello.

B: Hi, ＿＿＿＿＿＿. This is ＿＿＿＿＿＿. Can you talk now?

A: No, I can't. I'm ＿＿＿＿＿＿. Can I call you later?

B: Sure.

I'm Busy   **63**

Suggestion

Point out the Short Answer box at the top of the page. Students have seen *is/isn't* short answers before, but not short answers with *are/aren't*. Practice the language orally by asking questions about the class. For example, point to the row of students nearest the windows and ask: *Are they sitting near the window?* (Yes, they are.) Then ask: *Are they sitting near the door?* (No, they aren't.)

C. Ask and answer.

Have student work in pairs. One student reads a question and the other gives the correct answer based on the picture on page 62. Encourage students to take turns asking and answering the questions.

D. Read.

Read the conversation as students listen. Then read it again, pausing after each line for students to repeat.

E. Practice this conversation.

• Read the conversation with a student. You read A and let the student read B. Make up a reason you can't talk. For example: *I'm cooking dinner.* or *I'm doing the laundry.*

• Have pairs of students practice the conversation. Invite some pairs to present their conversations to the class.

☀ My, Your, His, Her

A. Act out these classroom directions.

Read aloud the ten classroom directions. Then read the ten directions again and have different students carry out each action. As each student carries out an action, ask these questions: *What are you doing? What's he/she doing?* Repeat correct responses. Rephrase incomplete or incorrect responses using full, correct forms.

B. Complete.

Have students fill in the blanks on their own. Ask them to use the possessive adjective that goes with the subject of the sentence. Point out the Possessive Adjective box at the top of the page.

Suggestion

Have students work in pairs. Prompt them to practice substituting all four possessive adjectives in each sentence. As they say each version of the sentence, ask them to point to a person the possessive adjective might refer to. For example, they can point to themselves (*my*), their partner (*your*), a male in the class (*his*) or a female in the class (*her*) as they say the sentences.

My, Your, His, Her

Possessive Adjectives	
I—my	He—his
You—your	She—her

A. Act out these classroom directions. What are you doing? What is he/she doing?

1. Stand up.
2. Walk to the blackboard.
3. Write your last name on the board.
4. Erase your name.
5. Sit down.
6. Open your book.
7. Close your book.
8. Raise your hand.
9. Point to the clock.
10. Sharpen your pencil.

B. Complete.

1. I'm talking to ___my___ sister.
2. You're doing ___your___ homework.
3. He's opening ___his___ book.
4. She's writing ___her___ address.
5. I'm sharpening ___my___ pencil.
6. He's washing ___his___ car.
7. He's calling ___his___ father.
8. She's talking to ___her___ brother.
9. You're cleaning ___your___ bedroom.
10. She's washing ___her___ hands.

64   UNIT 5

Working Together

A. Sit in a group and write a story about this family. Name each person. Where is each person? What is each person doing? *(Answers will vary.)*

B. Choose two locations. What are people doing? Use your imagination.
(Answers will vary.)

park

cafeteria

student lounge

airplane

computer lab

bus

office

car

Example: car

1. A man is driving.

2. A woman is listening to the radio.

3. A driver is stopping at the red light.

4. A man is talking on his cell phone.

5. A woman is drinking a cup of coffee.

Working Together

A. Sit in a group and write a story about this family.

- Before introducing the activity, invite students to talk about the four pictures. Help them with any new words they want to use.
- Have students form small groups. Suggest that they share the naming of the people in the pictures. They may want to write the names near each picture. Then ask students to write a story about the picture together. One student can be the secretary and write the story on a sheet of paper, or all students can write the story in their own notebooks.

Suggestion

Before doing Exercise B, introduce the words *cafeteria* and *student lounge.* Have students who know these words explain their meanings to the class.

B. Choose two locations.

- Review the sample answers with the class. Ask students to think of other sentences they can say about what people in a cafeteria are doing.
- Have students work in pairs or small groups to choose two of the locations provided (or to make up their own) and tell what people might be doing in these locations. This exercise can also be done as a writing assignment.

☀ The Big Picture:
Where is everybody?

A. Listen to the conversation between Tommy and his mother.

Mom

Katie

Brian

Dad

Tommy

☀ The Big Picture:
Where is everybody?

▪ **A. Listen to the conversation between Tommy and his mother.**

(CD1, Track 37)

• Invite students to talk about what the people in the pictures are doing. Ask:

Where is the family?
Where is the man, the younger boy, the older boy, the girl?
What is _____ doing?
Who is talking on the phone?
Where is the woman?
What do you think she is saying?
What time do you think it is?

• Play the audio.

▪ **D. Listen again and write the names on the picture.**

Play the audio again and ask students to write the name of each person on the picture.

C. Complete.

Have students fill in the answers on their own. Ask a student to write the correct answers on the board.

▪ **B. Listen again and write the names on the picture.**

| Mom | Tommy | Brian | Katie | Dad |

C. Complete.

1. Tommy is in the _kitchen_____.
2. Brian is in the _living room_____.
3. Katie __is___ in her _bedroom_____.
4. Dad __is___ in the _living room_____.
5. Mom __is___ at _work_____.

66   UNIT 5

Audio Script

☀ The Big Picture:
Where is everybody?

A. Listen to the conversation between Tommy and his mother.
(CD1, Track 37)

Tommy: Hello.
  Mom: Hi, Tommy. This is Mommy.
Tommy: Hi, Mommy. Are you at work?
  Mom: Yes, I'm a little late. What are you doing? Are you doing your homework?
Tommy: No, I'm not. I'm watching TV.

  Mom: Where's Brian? Is he doing his homework?
Tommy: Brian's in the living room. He's playing video games.
  Mom: And Katie? Where's Katie?
Tommy: She's in her bedroom.
  Mom: Good! Is she doing her homework?
Tommy: No, Mom. She's talking on the telephone to her boyfriend.
  Mom: Where's Daddy? Is he cooking dinner?
Tommy: Daddy's in the living room. He's sleeping.
  Mom: I'm coming home right now.

D. Listen and answer.

1. _____No, she isn't._____
2. _____Yes, she is._____
3. _____No, he isn't._____
4. _____No, he isn't._____
5. _____Yes, he is._____
6. _____No, she isn't._____
7. _____No, he isn't._____

Yes, he is.
No, he isn't.

Yes, she is.
No, she isn't.

E. Match.

1. Where is Tommy? —————— No, he isn't.
2. What is he doing? He's in the kitchen.
3. Is Tommy playing video games? He's playing video games.
4. Is Tommy talking to his mother? He's watching TV.
5. Where is Brian? No, he isn't.
6. What is he doing? Yes, he is.
7. Is Brian sleeping? He's in the living room.

F. Answer.

1. Where is Dad? _____He's in the living room._____
2. Is he cooking dinner? _No, he isn't._____
3. What's he doing? _He's sleeping._____
4. Where is Katie? _She's in her bedroom._____
5. What's she doing? _She's talking on the telephone to her boyfriend._____
6. Is she doing her homework? _No, she isn't._____

G. Write a story about this family in your notebook. (Answers will vary.)

I'm Busy   **67**

Audio Script

D. Listen and answer.
(CD1, Track 38)

1. Is Mom at home?
2. Is she talking to Tommy?
3. Is Tommy doing his homework?
4. Is Brian doing his homework?
5. Is Brian playing video games?
6. Is Katie doing her homework?
7. Is Dad cooking dinner?

D. Listen and answer.
(CD1, Track 38)

Play the audio three times. The first time through, have students look at the picture on page 66 and just listen. The second time, pause after each sentence while students fill in the answers. The third time, have students check their answers.

E. Match.

Have students match the questions and answers on their own. Check their work by having different students read pairs of questions and answers.

Suggestion

Have students use the questions and answers for conversation practice with a partner.

F. Answer.

Have students look at the picture, complete the sentences, then compare answers with a partner.

G. Write a story about this family in your notebook.

Invite students to write a story about the picture on page 66 on their own.

Suggestion

You may wish to pair a more fluent student with a less fluent student and have them write a story together. The less able students benefit from the guidance they receive. The more able students get a valuable review as well as extra practice with spoken and written English.

Reading: The Phone Book

Suggestion

• Write on the board in random order the last names of several students in the class. Explain that when the first letters are the same, we have to look at the second letter to put the words in alphabetical order. Circle the second letter of each name. Then ask students to tell you the correct order. Rewrite the list on the board. Ask what to do when the first two letters are the same, as in the names *Martin* and *Maddox*. (Use the third letter in each name to put the words in alphabetical order.)

• Ask students to stand up and arrange themselves in alphabetical order. This will involve a lot of talking, laughing, and fun.

A. Before You Read.

Display a local phone book and have students point out the cities it includes.

B. Write the phone number.

• Point out the head words on the telephone book page: *Palmer—Park*. Explain that only names with third letters from *l* to *r* will appear on this page. Ask what three letters the names on this page will start with and write them on the board. (*Pal, Pan, Pao, Pap*, and *Par*)

• Ask students to find and write the correct phone number next to each name.

C. Write the address.

Point out the abbreviations *St*, *Rd*, and *Ave* or *Av* in the phone book. Explain that abbreviations such as these often have a period at the end. Also, point out that the abbreviation used for *Avenue* is *Ave* in places other than the phone book. Write the abbreviations with periods next to the full forms on the board.

Avenue—Ave. or *Av.*
Street—St.   *Road—Rd.*

Reading: The Phone Book

A. Before You Read. Where is your phone book? What cities does it include?

179 Palmer – Park	

	Palmer David 177 Central Av Cranford..............555-1483	Pannullo T 46 Sussex St Plainfield..............555-4316
	Palmer Emily 43 Grand St Cranford..............555-1234	Panosh John 336 Forest Ave Westfield..............555-8274
	Palmer R 34 Broad St Essex..............555-5477	Pantagis Stephen 3 Chester Ave Essex..............555-8682
	Palmer William 6 Linden L Fanwood..............555-6134	Pantagis Susan 200 Broad St Essex..............555-8833
	Palmieri Ann 45 Grove St Fanwood..............555-5579	Pantano N 59 Maple St Plainfield..............555-7604
	Palmieri Fred 114 Maple T Essex..............555-9966	Paoli P 621 Sunny Drive Plainfield..............555-8652
	Palumbo Ed 110 South Ave Warrenville..............555-1024	Paolo Stephen 56 Davis Rd Plainfield..............555-0294
	Palumbo George 110 South Av Essex..............555-6403	Paone Joan 44 Harding St Essex..............555-5657
	Palumbo Henry 184 Second St Essex..............555-4403	Papa's Pizza 77 Main St Plainfield..............555-2534
	Palumbo L 23 Coles Way Fanwood..............555-7761	Papen Chris 204 Euclid Av Plainfield..............555-8541
	Palumbo P 650 Brant Crt Cranford..............555-7463	Papen George 399 Glen Road Fanwood..............555-2538
	Palusci Ellen 67 Main St Warrenville..............555-9832	Papen Theresa 75 Glen Road Fanwood..............555-7520
	Palusci Martin 173 First St Essex..............555-4411	Papik B 34 Hazel Court Warrenville..............555-6852
	Panagos Cleaners 43 South Ave Essex..............555-7764	Pappas John and Marge 12 Lake Ave Essex..............555-6427
	Panagos H 65 Rahway Rd Fanwood..............555-0102	Pappas S 216 State St Plainfield..............555-0208
	Panagos Joseph 76 Third Av Fanwood..............555-2310	Parada Juan 169 Sunset St Plainfield..............555-7314
	Panarese B 876 Park Av Warrenville..............555-8525	Parada Ricardo 14 Forest Ave Essex..............555-6291
P	Panarese Brad 9 Willow Ave Cranford..............555-0113	Parada Teresa 90 South Av Cranford..............555-7326
	Panarese C 453 Rogers Way Essex..............555-7509	Paradise Ed 501 Martin St Fanwood..............555-6491
	Panasik Craig 65 Davis Road Fanwood..............555-8029	Paradise H 36 Grant Av Essex..............555-2509
	Panek Darren 431 Coles Way Essex..............555-7435	Pardo Charles 153 Glen Road Fanwood..............555-8574
	Panek Katherine 107 Charles St Fanwood..............555-1128	Pardon R 54 Paulis St Warrenville..............555-2530
	Panek Bakery 54 Center St Cranford..............555-7039	Parente A 591 Hort St Warrenville..............555-0203
	Panera Richard 87 Route 22 Cranford..............555-2085	Parente E 88 Broad St Westfield..............555-8637
	Pang Hang 43 Grove Av Fanwood..............555-6965	Parisi L 71 Francis Av Plainfield..............555-8630
	Pang J 44 Thomas St Plainfield..............555-7413	Parisi M 490 Kent Place Plainfield..............555-3250
	Pang Y 87 Woods Way Plainfield..............555-8530	Park In-Chui 937 North Av Fanwood..............555-7831
	Pango L 866 Baker St Plainfield..............555-2527	Park Jeong 503 Lake Av Cranford..............555-1509
	Pannone 60 Davis Rd Fanwood..............555-4682	

B. Write the phone number.

Emily Palmer	555-1234	John and Marge Pappas	555-6427
Y Pang	555-8530	Henry Palumbo	555-4403
Juan Parada	555-7314	Charles Pardo	555-8574

C. Write the address.

Papa's Pizza	77 Main St. Plainfield
Panagos Cleaners	43 South Ave. Essex
Jeong Park	503 Lake Ave. Cranford

Writing Our Stories: What's Happening?

A. Read.

My name is Renata. I am studying English at Davis Community College. There are many students in this school. Right now, many students are studying in their classrooms. Some students are studying or reading in the library. Some students are using computers. Some students are eating in the cafeteria. Other students are talking, walking in the halls, or looking at books in the bookstore. This school is busy all the time.

B. Name four places in your school. (Answers will vary.)

_____ _____

_____ _____

C. Write about your school. What is happening now? (Answers will vary.)

My name is _____. I am a student at _____

_____. There are many students in this school. Right now,

many students _____ in their classrooms. Some

students _____ in the

_____. Some students

_____ in the

_____. Other students

_____. My school

is busy all the time.

> **Writing Note**
> The name of your school begins with a capital letter.

Writing Our Stories: What's Happening?

A. Read.

Read the story aloud to students or have them read it silently. Answer any questions they may have.

B. Name four places in your school.

Talk about different places in your school and write the name of each place on the board. Then ask students to write four of these places in their books.

C. Write about your school.

• Students can use the information from Exercise B to complete this activity.

• Explain to students that they should use the story at the top of the page as a model for their writing. Show students how they can adapt sentences from the story to fit their own needs. For example: *Some students are studying or reading in the library* can become *Some students are eating or drinking in the cafeteria.*

Looking at Forms: Bubble Forms

A. Complete this form.

- Point out the name at the top of the form. Then for each letter of the name, say the letter, point to it, and use your finger to trace down to the filled-in bubble below the letter. Repeat for the numbers at the right.
- Have students complete the activity individually, then check each other's work.

Looking at Forms: Bubble Forms

A. Complete this form.

Name:	Orlando J. Gutierrez
Telephone Number:	666-555-4218
Student ID Number:	888-910-6160

Instructions

Use a number 2 pencil

Darken circles completely

Examples:

Wrong ✓

Wrong ✗

Wrong ◔

Right ●

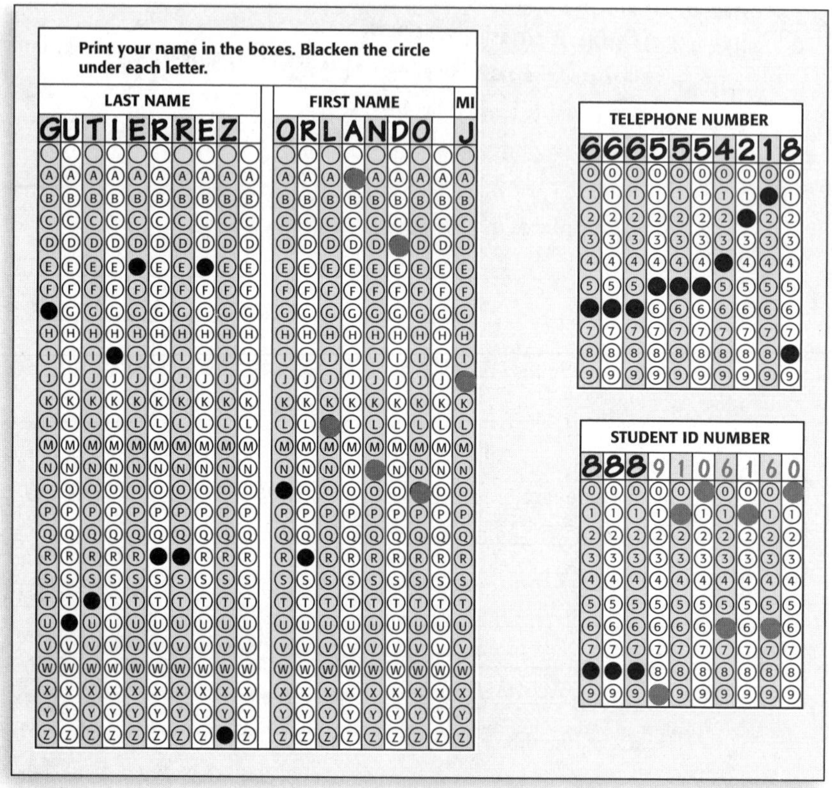

Print your name in the boxes. Blacken the circle under each letter.

LAST NAME: GUTIERREZ

FIRST NAME: ORLANDO MI: J

TELEPHONE NUMBER: 6665554218

STUDENT ID NUMBER: 888 910 6160

B. Complete this form about yourself.

(Answers will vary.)

Name: _____

Telephone Number: _____

Student ID Number: _____

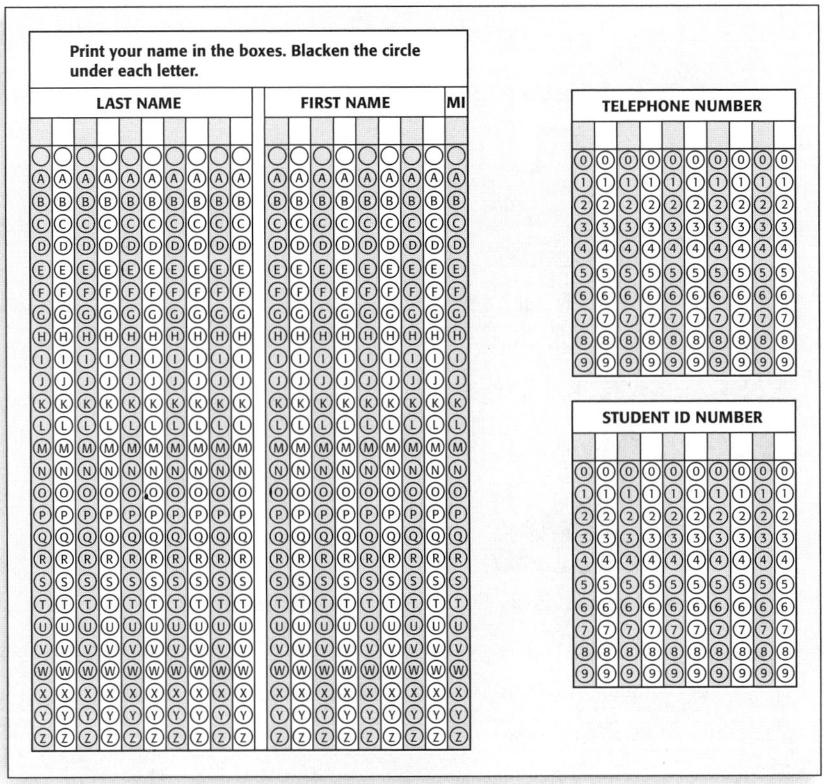

Print your name in the boxes. Blacken the circle under each letter.

| LAST NAME | FIRST NAME | MI |

| TELEPHONE NUMBER |

| STUDENT ID NUMBER |

B. Complete this form about yourself.

Ask students to print their own last name and first name on the form, using all capital letters. Then have students fill in the corresponding bubbles for each letter. Students should then write their own telephone number and student ID number, and fill in the corresponding bubbles. Have pairs of students check each other's work.

Teacher's Note

Move around the room as students fill in the form to make sure that students are using a pencil and filling in the circles completely.

Suggestion

For additional practice, give students real bubble forms from the personal information section of a standardized test to fill out.

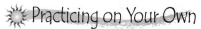 Practicing on Your Own

A. Complete.

Point out that there are several possible correct answers to most of the items in this exercise. Encourage students to include activities that haven't been mentioned in class.

Suggestion

Review students' answers orally in class. Write any sentences containing new words on the board. Suggest that students copy the new words in their notebooks.

B. Answer these questions.

Have students answer these questions on their own.

Suggestion

Students can use the questions and answers for conversation practice with a partner.

Practicing on Your Own

A. Complete. (Answers will vary. Sample answers below.)

1. He _____is cooking_____ in the kitchen.
2. She _____is sleeping_____ in her bedroom.
3. She _____is taking a shower_____ in the bathroom.
4. I _____am eating_____ in the dining room.
5. They _____are watching TV_____ in the living room.
6. We _____are talking_____ in the classroom.
7. I _____am reading_____ in the library.

B. Answer these questions.

1. Where is Bob? _____He's in the kitchen._____
2. Is he eating dinner? _____No, he isn't._____
3. What is he doing? _____He's cooking._____

4. Where is Susan? _____She's in the kitchen._____
5. Is she doing her homework? _____No, she isn't._____
6. What is she doing? _____She's making lunch._____
7. Where are you? _____(Answers will vary.)_____
8. What are you doing? _____(Answers will vary.)_____
9. Are you doing your homework? _____(Answers will vary.)_____

Learning Tip

> **I watch TV in English. I watch easy programs.
> Sometimes I watch TV with my children.**

(Answers may vary.)

☐ I like this idea.
☐ I don't like this idea.
☐ I'm going to try this idea.

Grammar Summary

1. Present continuous statements	
I **am studying.**	**I'm studying.**
He **is sleeping.**	He**'s sleeping.**
She **is eating.**	She**'s eating.**
They **are watching** TV.	They**'re watching** TV.
2. *Yes / No* questions	
Are you watching TV?	Yes, I **am.** No, **I'm not.**
Is she watching TV?	Yes, she **is.** No, she **isn't.**
Is he watching TV?	Yes, he **is.** No, he **isn't.**
Are they watching TV?	Yes, they **are.** No, they **aren't.**
3. *Wh-* questions	
Where is he?	He's in the kitchen.
What is he doing?	He's cooking.

I'm Busy **73**

Learning Tip

Discuss the Learning Tip with students. Take a poll to see which TV programs most students watch. Ask which ones they think help them learn more English and why.

Suggestion

On the board, make a list of the children's shows that students say they have watched. Ask what kind of English they have learned while watching these shows.

Grammar Summary

• Review the summary with the class. Invite students to say other statements, questions, and answers that might appear in each of the three sections of the summary.
• See the Grammar Summary Expansion on page 234 for a more complete explanation of these grammar points.

Unit 6
My City

Discuss the person next to the unit number. Ask:

- *Who is next to the number 6?* (A woman)
- *What is she doing?* (She's holding a city skyline and dancing.)

☀Dictionary:
Adjectives, Locations, Climate

A. Listen and repeat.
(CD1, Track 39)

- For now, focus only on the *Adjectives* section on pages 74 and 75. Ask students to look at the words and pictures. Answer any questions students may have with simple English sentences. For example:
  - **S:** *What does "dirty" mean?*
  - **T:** *There is garbage in the street. It isn't clean. It's dirty.*

- Invite students to comment on the pictures. Restate student comments in simple English. For example: *That's right. She's covering her ears. It's noisy.*

- Play the *Adjectives* section of the audio. Have students listen and repeat each adjective.

6 My City

Dictionary: Adjectives, Locations, Climate

A. Listen and repeat.

Adjectives

large	small	quiet	noisy

busy	clean	dirty	fun

safe	dangerous	beautiful	ugly

cheap	expensive	interesting	boring

heavy/light

hardworking

friendly

unfriendly

Location

in the north

in the mountains

in the east

in the west

in the center

in the middle

capital ★

near the ocean

in the south

Climate

wet

dry

humid

hot

cold

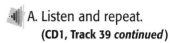

A. Listen and repeat.
(CD1, Track 39 *continued*)

• Now focus on the words on the *Location* and *Climate* sections on page 75. Answer student questions and invite comments.

• Play the *Location* and *Climate* sections of the audio and have students listen and repeat the words and phrases.

Suggestion

To review the adjectives, write the following headings on the board: *People, Places, Things.* Explain each heading. Then have students decide which adjectives are used to describe people, which are used to describe places, and which are used to describe things. Invite students to take turns choosing one of the adjectives from pages 74 and 75 and writing it under an appropriate heading. Then, ask a volunteer to make up a sentence using that adjective. For example, one student might write the adjective *hardworking* under the *People* heading. Another might then make up the following sentence: *Olivia is hardworking.*

☀ Active Grammar:
Adjective Review

A. Match the opposites

Have students complete the activity individually and check their answers with a partner.

Suggestion

To provide an oral review, ask students to take turns using each pair of opposite adjectives in a pair of sentences. For example:

It's a busy street.
It's a quiet street.

 B. Listen and complete with an adjective. (CD1, Track 40)

Play the audio once as students just listen. Then have them fill in the adjectives as they listen to the audio a second time. Play the audio a third time so students can check their answers.

Suggestion

Ask students to describe places, such as:
• their state
• their city
• a place in their city, such as a museum
• the street their school is on

Active Grammar: Adjective Review

A. Match the opposites.

1. busy (h.)	a. ugly
2. wet (g.)	b. expensive
3. clean (i.)	c. unfriendly
4. quiet (f.)	d. boring
5. cheap (b.)	e. light
6. beautiful (a.)	f. noisy
7. interesting (d.)	g. dry
8. small (j.)	h. quiet
9. friendly (c.)	i. dirty
10. heavy (e.)	j. large

B. Listen and complete with an adjective.

1. Miles City, Montana, is a _____small_____ city.
2. The movies in New York City are _____expensive_____.
3. Downtown Chicago is _____busy_____.
4. The weather in Phoenix, Arizona, is _____hot_____ and _____dry_____.
5. The people in Atlanta, Georgia, are _____friendly_____.
6. The streets in San Francisco, California, are _____clean_____.
7. The traffic in Boston, Massachusetts, is _____heavy_____.
8. New Orleans, Louisiana, is an _____interesting_____ city.

76 UNIT 6

Audio Script

B. Listen and complete with an adjective.
(CD1, Track 40)

1. Miles City, Montana, is a small city.
2. The movies in New York City are expensive.
3. Downtown Chicago is busy.
4. The weather in Phoenix, Arizona, is hot and dry.
5. The people in Atlanta, Georgia, are friendly.
6. The streets in San Francisco, California, are clean.
7. The traffic in Boston, Massachusetts, is heavy.
8. New Orleans, Louisiana, is an interesting city.

C. Can you label the U.S. map?

Boston,
Massachusetts

New York City,
New York

Seattle,
Washington

Detroit,
Michigan

Chicago,
Illinois

Philadelphia,
Pennsylvania

Los Angeles,
California

Phoenix,
Arizona

Houston,
Texas

Miami,
Florida

Boston, Massachusetts	Los Angeles, California	New York City, New York
Chicago, Illinois	Miami, Florida	Phoenix, Arizona
Detroit, Michigan	Philadelphia, Pennsylvania	Seattle, Washington
Houston, Texas		

 D. *Or* questions. Ask and answer with a partner.

1. Is Boston small or large? (Answers may vary.)

2. Is Los Angeles hot or cold? It's hot.

3. Is Miami near the mountains or near the ocean? It's near the ocean.

4. Is Seattle in the north or in the south? It's in the north.

5. Is New York City clean or dirty? (Answers may vary.)

6. Are the people in Houston friendly or unfriendly? (Answers may vary.)

7. Are the stores in Chicago cheap or expensive? They're expensive.

8. Are the streets in Seattle busy or quiet? They're busy.

C. Can you label the U.S. map?

• Before starting the exercise, make sure students can locate where they are on the map. Say:

What state do we live in? Where is it on the map? Make an X in the location.

• Invite students to work in pairs, labeling as many of the cities as they can. Then display a map of the United States and help students locate the other cities. Write each new city and state on the board. Have students complete their maps individually.

D. *Or* questions.

Role-play one or two questions and answers with a student. Then have pairs complete the activity.

E. Pair practice.

Say the short answers in the box and ask students to repeat. Read the sample dialogue with a student. Then ask pairs of students to practice asking and answering questions about their city using the adjectives provided. Move around the room checking students' use of the adjectives and monitoring their pronunciation.

F. As a class, write the names of six international cities.

Copy the chart on the board and complete it with the whole class.

Suggestion

Create a larger chart with the cities, nationalities, and languages of all of the students in the class.

G. Complete from the chart.

Have students complete the sentences on their own. Then call on volunteers to read their answers to the class.

E. Pair practice. Ask and answer questions about your city.

F. As a class, write the names of six international cities. Complete the chart. (Answers will vary.)

City	Nationality	Language
Paris	French	French
1.		
2.		
3.		
4.		
5.		
6.		

G. Complete from the chart. (Answers will vary.)

1. _____ is from _____ .
       male classmate   city

2. He is _____ , and he speaks _____ .
       nationality   language

3. _____ is from _____ .
       female classmate   city

4. She is _____ , and she speaks _____ .
       nationality   language

What city do you want to visit?

 A. Listen and complete.

Janet

Steven

Caroline and Susan

1. Janet wants to visit ___San Diego___ because it is ___a beautiful city___.
2. Steven wants to visit ___New York City___ because it is ___very exciting___.
3. Caroline and Susan want to visit ___Orlando___ because it is ___fun___.

B. Pair practice. Talk about a city you want to visit.

What city do you want to visit?

Why?

I want to visit New York.

I want to go to New York because it is exciting.

Chicago	Houston	Miami
Los Angeles	New York	San Francisco
Phoenix	Boston	_____

quiet
safe
clean
interesting
beautiful
cheap
hot
friendly
exciting
fun

☀ What city do you want to visit?

 A. Listen and complete.
(CD1, Track 41)

- Point out the pictures of the people and the incomplete sentence related to each one.
- The first time you play the audio, have students only listen. The second time through, ask them to complete the sentences. The third time through, have students check their work.

B. Pair practice.

Have students complete this activity with a partner. When they finish, call on different pairs to present a dialogue to the class. Question any factual errors (for example: *I want to go to Chicago because it's always warm.*) and ask students to revise their conversations accordingly.

Audio Script

A. Listen and complete.
(CD1, Track 41)

Conversation 1
A: What city do you want to visit?
Janet: I want to visit San Diego.
A: Why do you want to visit San Diego?
Janet: I want to visit San Diego because it is a beautiful city.

Conversation 2
A: What city do you want to visit?
Steven: I want to visit New York City.
A: Why do you want to visit New York City?
Steven: I want to visit New York because it's very exciting.

Conversation 3
A: What city do you want to visit?
Caroline: We want to visit Orlando.
A: Why do you want to visit Orlando?
Caroline: We want to visit Orlando because it's fun.

City Populations

Suggestion

Before starting the listening exercises on this page, write numbers in the hundreds (such as *375, 291,* and *465*) on the board. Say the numbers and have students repeat them. Then build up to larger numbers containing the word *thousand*, such as *2,461, 7,523,* and *27,691.*

 ### A. Listen. (CD1, Track 42)

After students listen to the audio several times, ask them to take turns reading the numbers aloud.

 ### B. Listen and write the populations. (CD1, Track 43)

The first time you play the audio, tell students to only listen. The second time, have students write their answers. Then have some volunteers write their answers on the board. Play the audio a third time and ask the class to check the answers on the board.

 ### C. Pronunciation.

Say the first two or three numbers aloud and ask students to repeat. Next, call on different students to say them aloud. Then have students practice the numbers in pairs. Prompt students to make sentences with the numbers and cities, like the sentence in the speech bubble to the right of the exercise.

Suggestion

Invite several students to come to the board. Dictate several numbers, starting with small ones and moving on to larger ones. Note which numbers cause problems. Show students the correct way to write these numbers.

City Populations

 A. Listen.

1.	Miami, Florida	369,253
2.	Atlanta, Georgia	401,766
3.	Las Vegas, Nevada	418,658
4.	Washington, D.C.	519,000
5.	Detroit, Michigan	965,084
6.	San Antonio, Texas	1,147,213
7.	Philadelphia, Pennsylvania	1,417,601
8.	Houston, Texas	1,845,967
9.	Los Angeles, California	3,633,591
10.	New York, New York	7,428,162

 B. Listen and write the populations.

1. Seattle, Washington — 563,374
2. Phoenix, Arizona — 1,211,466
3. San Francisco, California — 745,774
4. Boston, Massachusetts — 555,249
5. Chicago, Illinois — 2,799,050
6. Fresno, California — 404,141
7. Honolulu, Hawaii — 395,327
8. Dallas, Texas — 1,075,894

 C. Pronunciation. Practice these numbers with a partner.

1. 2,890,000 (Ankara, Turkey)
2. 34,800,000 (Tokyo, Japan)
3. 17,900,000 (São Paolo, Brazil)
4. 14,350,000 (Cairo, Egypt)
5. 10,150,000 (Paris, France)
6. 1,719,000 (Cali, Colombia)
7. 13,200,000 (Moscow, Russia)
8. 11,800,000 (Shanghai, China)

> The population of Ankara, Turkey, is 2,890,000.

Audio Script

A. Listen.
(CD1, Track 42)

1. The population of Miami, Florida, is 369,253.
2. The population of Atlanta, Georgia, is 401,766.
3. The population of Las Vegas, Nevada, is 418,658.
4. The population of Washington, D.C., is 519,000.
5. The population of Detroit, Michigan, is 965,084.80
6. The population of San Antonio, Texas, is 1,147,213.
7. The population of Philadelphia, Pennsylvania, is 1,417,601.
8. The population of Houston, Texas, is 1,845,967.
9. The population of Los Angeles, California, is 3,633,591.
10. The population of New York, New York, is 7,428,162.

B. Listen and write the populations.
(CD1, Track 43)

1. The population of Seattle, Washington, is 563,374.

(Continued on next page.)

Which city is this?

A. Look at the photographs. Guess the city.

1. San Francisco

2. New York

3. Chicago

4. San Antonio

San Antonio, Texas
Fairbanks, Alaska
San Francisco, California
Chicago, Illinois
New York, New York
Miami, Florida
Honolulu, Hawaii

B. Answer.

1. It's in **California.** 2. It's in **New York.** 3. It's in **Illinois.** 4. It's in **Texas.**

1. What state is the city in?
2. Is the city beautiful? **(Answers may vary.)**
3. Is the city near the mountains or near the ocean? 1. It's near the ocean.
   2. It's near the ocean. 3. It's not near to either. 4. It's not near to either.
4. Is the city safe? **(Answers may vary.)**
5. Is the city exciting? **(Answers may vary.)**
6. What do you know about the city? **(Answers will vary.)**

☀ Which city is this?

Suggestion

Have students identify as many of the cities pictured on this page as they can. Help them identify the others: *San Francisco, New York, Chicago,* and *San Antonio.*

A. Look at the photographs.

• Invite students to talk about the pictures and tell what they see. Rephrase any incomplete or incorrect responses in standard English and expand on them. For example:

S: *Is San Francisco. Is a big bridge.*
T: *That's right. That's a picture of San Francisco and there is a big bridge. Do you know the name of the bridge?*
S: *Golden Gate.*
T: *Right. It's the Golden Gate Bridge.*

• Have students label the pictures.

B. Answer.

• Point to each picture in Exercise A and discuss each city's qualities using the list of six questions as a guide. Write new words on the board and provide pronunciation practice.
• Select the cities one by one and call on different students to answer each of the questions.

(Continued from page 80.)

2. The population of Phoenix, Arizona, is 1,211,466.
3. The population of San Francisco, California, is 745,774.
4. The population of Boston, Massachusetts, is 555,249.
5. The population of Chicago, Illinois, is 2,799,050.
6. The population of Fresno, California, is 404,141.
7. The population of Honolulu, Hawaii, is 395,327.
8. The population of Dallas, Texas, is 1,075,894.

☀Working Together

A. Interview.

Review the questions and possible answers with the class. Then have students ask and answer the questions in groups of three.

Suggestion

Display a world map and invite students to point out their home country and the city they are from. Invite them to say one or two things about their country and city.

B. Complete.

Point out that the first five questions relate to one city and the second five relate to another city. Have students complete the sentences on their own based on the information they wrote in Exercise A. Then ask students to check their sentences with the people they wrote about.

Suggestion

Ask students to use the questions in Exercise A to interview someone outside of class. Have students write out the answers in the Exercise B format. They can share their reports at the next class meeting.

Working Together

A. Interview. In a group of three students, ask the questions. (Answers will vary.)

Yes, it is.	Yes, they are,
No, it isn't.	No, they aren't.

Question	Student 1	Student 2
1. What city are you from?		
2. Is your city in the East, West, North, or South?		
3. Is your city the capital city of your country?		
4. Is your city beautiful?		
5. Is your city busy?		
6. Are the people hardworking?		

B. Complete. (Answers will vary.)

1. _____ is from _____.
   Student 1   city

2. _____ is _____.
   city   location

3. _____ **is / isn't** the capital city.

4. _____ **is / isn't** _____.
                                        adjective

5. The people **are / aren't** _____.

6. _____ is from _____.
   Student 2   city

7. _____ is _____.
   city   location

8. _____ **is / isn't** the capital city.

9. _____ **is / isn't** _____.
                                        adjective

10. The people **are / aren't** _____.

C. Complete the sentences about the city where you are studying.
(Answers will vary.)

Our City

1. Our school is in _____, _____.
   city   state

2. The population of _____ is about _____.
   city   population

3. The largest city in our state is _____.

4. _____ _____ the capital city.
   city   is / isn't

5. _____ is _____.
   city   adjective

6. _____ is _____.
                     adjective

7. _____ isn't _____

8. _____ isn't _____.

9. The people _____ friendly.
              are / aren't

10. The people _____ hardworking.
               are / aren't

D. Look at the map on the inside back cover of the book. Draw a simple map of your state. Show your city and the capital of your state. (Answers will vary.)

Suggestion

Before class, look up the population of the city you are living in as well as the largest city in the state and the capital city of the state.

C. Complete the sentences about the city where you are studying.

Complete the first four items in this exercise with the whole class. Ask students to complete the exercise on their own. Then have students compare their answers with a partner. Invite some students to read their sentences aloud. Discuss any differences of opinion with the class.

D. Look at the map on the inside back cover of the book.

Help students find their state on the map. Have them draw the outline of the state and mark both the city they are in and the state's capital. If you are using this book outside of the United States, have students draw a map of the local state or territory where they live.

☀ The Big Picture:
Chicago, Illinois

A. Can you identify these places and people?

Have students work alone to identify as many of the people and places as they can. Then review the answers with the whole class.

B. Listen. (CD1, Track 44)

Play the audio and ask students to just listen. Play the audio again. This time, have students point to the pictures of things they hear about on the audio. Play the audio once again. This time, pause the audio after each paragraph and ask simple comprehension questions. For example: *Is Chicago a big city?* (Yes, it is.) *Is it near the mountains?* (No, it isn't. It's near a lake.)

C. Match

Have students work in pairs to match the two lists.

The Big Picture: Chicago, Illinois

A. Can you identify these places and people?

The Brookfield Zoo	The Sears Tower	Blues club
The Art Institute of Chicago	Oprah Winfrey	Wrigley Field
Lake Michigan		

Oprah Winfrey  Lake Michigan Brookfield Zoo

The Sears Tower   Blues club   The Art Institute of Chicago   Wrigley Field

B. Listen.

C. Match.

1. __c__ paintings   a. blues clubs
2. __a__ musicians   b. Wrigley Field
3. __f__ Oprah Winfrey   c. Art Institute of Chicago
4. __b__ baseball   d. Brookfield Zoo
5. __d__ animals   e. Sears Tower
6. __e__ office building   f. TV talk show host

Audio Script

☀ The Big Picture:
Chicago, Illinois

B. Listen. (CD1, Track 44)

Chicago, Illinois, is one of the largest cities in the U.S. It's in the Midwest of the country next to beautiful Lake Michigan. The summers are hot, and the winters are cold, so visit Chicago in the spring or in the fall.

There are many interesting places to visit. Many places are in busy downtown Chicago. If you like art, go to the Art Institute of Chicago. There are many famous paintings there. But, if you like something different, go to one of Chicago's blues clubs. You'll see Chicago's great blues musicians. Maybe you'll want to dance.

If you like sports, Chicago is for you. It's a great sports town. There are seven professional teams in Chicago. Wrigley Field, a baseball park, is the oldest baseball park in the United States. It's home to the Chicago Cubs baseball team.

For children, there are also many places to visit. The Brookfield Zoo is a fun place for children. Children will also like the Sears Tower office building. It is one of the tallest buildings in the world. It has 110 floors. You can take an elevator to the top and see all of Chicago.

Do you watch TV talk shows? Then you know Oprah Winfrey. Her talk show is very popular. Millions of people watch her TV show every afternoon. If you go to Chicago, maybe you can watch the Oprah show live!

So, when do you want to visit Chicago? Chicago is waiting for you.

D. Listen again and circle.

Yes | (No) | **1.** Chicago is in the south of the United States.
(Yes) | No | **2.** Chicago is near water.
(Yes) | No | **3.** Spring is a good time to visit Chicago.
(Yes) | No | **4.** Chicago's summers are hot.
(Yes) | No | **5.** You can enjoy art and music in Chicago.
Yes | (No) | **6.** Oprah Winfrey is a popular blues musician.
Yes | (No) | **7.** Chicago has one professional sports team.

E. *Or* Questions. Ask and answer with a partner.

> Is Chicago a city or a state?
> It's a city.

1. Is Chicago in the midwest or in the south?
It's in the midwest.
2. Are the winters in Chicago warm or cold?
They're cold.
3. Is Chicago near a lake or an ocean?
It's near a lake.
4. Is Chicago famous for rock music or blues music?
It's famous for blues music.
5. Is Wrigley Field for baseball or for football?
It's for baseball.
6. Is the Brookfield Zoo interesting or boring for children?
It's interesting.
7. Is the Sears Tower a large or a small building?
It's a large building.
8. Is downtown Chicago quiet or busy?
It's busy.

F. Complete with *is, isn't, are,* or *aren't.*

1. It ___is___ fun for people to see professional sports in Chicago.

2. Lake Michigan ___is___ a beautiful lake.

3. Winters in Chicago ___aren't___ hot and humid.

4. Downtown Chicago ___is___ busy.

5. The Sears Tower ___isn't___ a small building.

6. The Art Institute of Chicago ___isn't___ a boring museum.

7. The Brookfield Zoo ___is___ fun for children.

8. Chicago blues clubs ___are___ exciting and interesting.

D. Listen again and circle.
(CD1, Track 44)

Play the Exercise B audio once more and ask students to answer the questions on their own. Then review the correct answers with the class.

E. *Or* questions.

Have pairs of students take turns asking and answering the questions.

F. Complete with *is, isn't, are,* or *aren't.*

Have students fill in the answers on their own, then check their answers with a partner.

☀Reading:
Seattle, Washington

Suggestion

Ask students to locate Washington on a large map. Then ask them to find Seattle. Discuss the difference between Seattle, Washington, and Washington, D.C.

A. Before You Read.

• As you discuss the three questions with the class, ask students to use the map on page 246 to verify their answers.

• Invite students to comment on the pictures that accompany the reading. Rephrase any incomplete or incorrect responses in standard English and expand on them. For example:

S: *There's boats.*
T: *That's right. There are a lot of boats in the harbor. What else do you see in that picture?*

• Ask students to read through the story without stopping to look up new words.

B. Circle the answer.

• Have students answer the questions on their own.

• Review the answers by asking students to go back to the story and point out the sentence or sentences that lead to each answer.

C. Which adjectives describe Seattle?

Make a list on the board of the adjectives students suggest. As you go over the completed list, have students go back to the story and point out the sentence or sentences that led them to choose each adjective.

Reading: Seattle, Washington

A. Before You Read.

1. Where is Washington state? It is in the northwest of the United States.
2. Is Seattle in the north or the south of the state? It is in the north of the state.
3. Is Seattle near the mountains? Is it near the ocean? It is near both.

Seattle is the largest city in Washington state. The population of Seattle is 563,374. It is in the northwest of the United States. It is in a beautiful location near the Pacific Ocean and Canada. Seattle is one of the major seaports in the United States. You can find many boats and houseboats in the water near Seattle. When the weather is clear, you can see the famous sleeping volcano, Mount Rainier.

Seattle is a beautiful city, but it is a rainy city. It gets 36.2 inches, or 92 cm, of rain every year.

Many people know Seattle because of the Space Needle. You can take an elevator to the top of the Space Needle. On the top floor, there is a restaurant that revolves 360°. You can see all of Seattle.

There are many large companies in Seattle. One develops computer software. Another makes coffee. A third sells books on-line.

The University of Washington is in Seattle, and there are many professional sports teams in Seattle. You can see that Seattle is a good place for a vacation, for work, and for relaxation.

B. Circle the answer.

Yes	No	1.	Seattle is a large city.
Yes	No	2.	Seattle is in the Southwest of the United States.
Yes	No	3.	Seattle has warm, sunny weather all year.
Yes	No	4.	Many large companies are in Seattle.
Yes	No	5.	Seattle is a good place for a vacation.

C. Which adjectives describe Seattle? (beautiful, rainy)

Writing Our Stories: My City

A. Read.

My name is Steven Lee. I am from Taipei, Taiwan. Taipei is the largest city in Taiwan. The population of my city is about 7,700,000. Taipei is in the north of the island. It has mountains and rivers. My city is big, and it is interesting. The Taipei City Zoo is a famous zoo. The National Palace Museum has a wonderful collection of Chinese art. The weather in Taipei is good all year, but it is often humid. The Taiwanese people are hardworking and friendly.

B. Write. (Answers will vary.)

I am from _____, _____. The
           city   country

population of my city is about _____. It is _____.
                     population   location

My city is _____. _____ is _____.
    large / small   city   adjective

_____ is _____ and _____.

The people in my city are _____ and

_____

_____

_____

_____

Writing Note

Use a comma between the name of a city and the name of a country: Taipei, Taiwan.

☀Writing Our Stories: My City

A. Read.

Ask students to read the story all the way through without stopping. Then read the story to the students. Ask: *Do you have any questions about the story?*

B. Write.

• Explain to students that they can use Exercise A as a model for their writing.
• Review students' writing and copy on the board some of the original sentences they wrote at the end of their stories. Ask other students to read these sentences aloud.

Suggestion

Have students copy some of the sentences from the board into their notebooks. For homework, students can rewrite these sentences to fit their own stories.

Practicing on Your Own

A. Answer.

Point out the short answers in the box and have students complete the activity on their own.

B. Complete the sentences with an adjective.

Have students complete the activity orally with partners before writing the answers in their books.

C. Complete about the city where you live now.

Have students complete the activity on their own.

Suggestion

Play a guessing game using sentences from Exercise C. Have students take turns describing a city in another part of the world. The student who is speaking completes one or two sentences from Exercise C about the city, and the rest of the class tries to guess the city. If the class guesses wrong, the speaker keeps adding sentences until the class guesses the right city.

Practicing on Your Own

| Yes, it is. | No, it isn't. |
| Yes, they are. | No, they aren't. |

A. Answer. (Answers will vary.)

1. Is your city near the mountains? _____
2. Is your city safe at night? _____
3. Are the people in your city friendly? _____
4. Are the streets in your city clean? _____
5. Is your city expensive to live in? _____
6. Is your city fun? _____
7. Is your city exciting? _____
8. Are the buildings in your city large? _____

B. Complete the sentences with an adjective. (Answers will vary.)

1. I want to visit Chicago because it's _____
2. I want to visit Seattle because it's _____
3. I want to visit Miami because it's _____
4. I want to visit Phoenix because it's _____
5. I want to visit _____ because _____
6. I want to visit _____ because _____

C. Complete about the city where you live now. | is   isn't   are   aren't |
(Answers will vary.)

1. My city _____ big.
2. The streets _____ clean.
3. The summers _____ hot.
4. The people _____ hardworking.
5. The people _____ friendly.
6. The stores _____ expensive.
7. My city _____ near an ocean.
8. My city _____ interesting.

We come to class a few minutes early.
We give each other spelling tests.

(Answers will vary.)

☐ I like this idea.
☐ I don't like this idea.
☐ I'm going to try this idea.

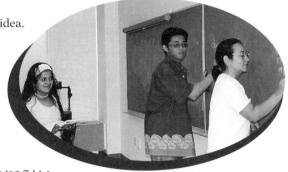

Grammar Summary

1. Want / Wants

I **want** to go to New York City because it's exciting.

We **want** to go to Chicago because it's a good sports town.

He **wants** to go to Miami because it's hot and sunny.

She **wants** to go to Denver because it's a good place for winter sports.

2. Yes / No questions

Is Chicago in the Midwest?	Yes, it **is.**
Is Seattle in the Midwest?	No, it **isn't.**
Are winters cold in Chicago?	Yes, they **are.**
Are summers hot in Seattle?	No, they **aren't.**

3. Or questions

Is Chicago in the north **or** in the south?	It's in the north.
Are the streets in Chicago quiet **or** busy?	They're busy.

My City   **89**

• Discuss the Learning Tip with students. Point out that the picture shows a woman reading spelling words while her classmates write the words on the board.

• Ask:

How many students arrive early for class?
Do you study together?
Do you talk?
Do you give each other spelling tests?

Grammar Summary

• Review the summary with the class. Invite students to say other statements, questions, and answers that might appear in each of the three sections of the summary.

• See the Grammar Summary Expansion on page 235 for a more complete explanation of these grammar points.

Unit 7
Downtown

Discuss the person next to the unit number. Ask:

• *Who is standing next to the number 7?* (A man)
• *What is he doing?* (He's looking at a sign. He's pointing in different directions with his hands.)

☀ Dictionary: Stores, Places Downtown, Prepositions

A. Listen and repeat.
(CD1, Track 45)

• For now, focus only on the *Stores* and *Places Downtown* sections on page 90. Invite students to comment on the pictures. Rephrase any incomplete or incorrect statements and expand on them. For example:

S: *Bread in bakery.*
T: *That's right. You can buy bread in a bakery. What else can you buy in a bakery?*

• Play the *Stores* and *Places Downtown* portion of the audio and have students listen and repeat.

7 Downtown

Dictionary: Stores, Places Downtown, Prepositions

 A. Listen and repeat.

Stores

bank

bakery

bookstore

coffee shop

laundromat

shoe store

supermarket

drugstore

Places Downtown

City Hall

library

police station

park

post office

hospital

parking lot

Prepositions

The bank is **on the corner of** First Street and Main Street.

Mr. Garcia is standing **in front of** the bank.

Mr. Garcia is standing **behind** the bank.

Mr. Garcia is standing **next to** the bank.

Mr. Garcia is standing **across from** the bank.

Mr. Garcia is standing **between** the bank and the coffee shop.

B. Complete.

1. I can mail a letter at the _____post office_____.

2. I can borrow books at the _____library_____.

3. I can buy food at the _____supermarket_____.

4. I can buy a book at the _____bookstore_____.

5. I can wash my clothes at the _____laundromat_____.

6. I can deposit money at the _____bank_____.

7. I can get a prescription filled at the _____pharmacy_____.

8. I can walk in the _____park_____.

9. I can buy sneakers at the _____shoe store_____.

(CD1, Track 45 *continued*)

• Ask students to look at the *Prepositions* section at the top of page 91. Point to the pictures and say the sentences.

• Use a desk and chair to demonstrate the prepositional phrases *in front of, behind, next to,* and *between*. For example, stand between your desk and your chair and say: *I'm standing between the desk and the chair.*

• Use the pictures to clarify *on the corner of* and *across from*.

• Play the *Prepositions* portion of the audio. Have students listen and repeat.

B. Complete.

Have students complete the sentences and check their answers with a partner.

Active Grammar:
Prepositions

A. Listen and complete the map. (CD1, Track 46)

Review the pronunciation of the places in the box. Play the audio once and have students just listen. Play the audio a second time and have them fill in the places on the map. Play the audio a third time as pairs of students check each other's work.

B. Pair practice.

Have students ask and answer questions about the places in pairs.

C. Complete.

Have students fill in the answers. When they finish, have some students put the answers on the board. Go over the answers with the class.

Active Grammar: Prepositions

A. Listen and complete the map.

bakery	bookstore	library	shoe store
bank	coffee shop	laundromat	supermarket

B. Pair practice. Talk about the locations on the map above.

Where's the _____ ?   It's on _____

C. Complete. Look at the map above.

across from	between	on
behind	next to	on the corner of

1. The supermarket is ___across from___ the bank.
2. The parking lot is ___behind___ the supermarket.
3. The bank is ___on the corner of___ First Street and Main Street.
4. The post office is ___between___ the bank and the coffee shop.
5. The bakery is ___next to___ the park.
6. The laundromat is ___on___ Second Street.
7. The bus station is ___across from___ the parking lot.
8. The bookstore is ___on the corner of___ Main Street and Second Street.

Audio Script

A. Listen and complete the map.
(CD1, Track 46)

1. A: Where's the bakery?
   B: It's on Main Street, next to the park.
2. A: Where's the supermarket?
   B: It's across from the post office.
3. A: Where's the shoe store?
   B: It's on Main Street, across from the drugstore.
4. A: Where's the bookstore?
   B: It's next to the shoe store.

5. A: Where's the library?
   B: It's on Maple Avenue. It's behind the post office.
6. A: Where's the bank?
   B: It's on the corner of Main Street and First Street.
7. A: Where's the coffee shop?
   B: It's next to the post office.
8. A: Where's the laundromat?
   B: It's on the corner of Second Street and Maple Avenue.

Reading a Map

A. Talk about the map.

The bookstore is next to the bakery.
The parking lot is behind the school.

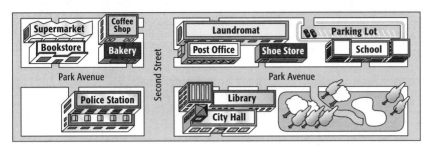

B. Write the locations of five buildings. (Answers may vary.)

1. _____

2. _____

3. _____

4. _____

5. _____

 C. Pronunciation. Listen and repeat the conversations.

1. **A:** Where's the shoe store?
   B: It's on Park Avenue.
   A: On Park Avenue?
   B: Yes.

2. **A:** Where's the parking lot?
   B: It's behind the school.
   A: Behind the school?
   B: Yes.

3. **A:** Where's the park?
   B: It's next to the library.
   A: Next to the library?
   B: Yes.

4. **A:** Where's the bakery?
   B: It's across from the police station.
   A: Across from the police station?
   B: Yes.

Practice these conversations with a partner.

Downtown **93**

Reading a Map

A. Talk about the map.

Ask different students to read the sample sentences in the box in the top right hand corner of the page. Then call on students to tell the locations of other stores and places on the map.

B. Write the locations of five buildings.

Have students write down some of their sentences from Exercise A.

 C. Pronunciation.
(CD1, Track 47)

Have students just listen as you play the audio the first time. Play the audio a second time. This time, pause after each line and ask students to repeat.

 Practice these conversations with a partner.

Have students work with a partner to practice the conversations in Exercise C.

Suggestion

After students have practiced for a few minutes, ask one student in each pair to cover Exercise C, and the other to ask the first student questions from the exercise. Have them change roles so that both students have a chance to answer questions. Alternatively, ask students to write and practice other conversations using the map. For example:

S1: *Where's the library?*
S2: *It's next to the park.*
S1: *Next to the park?*
S2: *Yes.*

☀ Where's the park?

A. Read and write these locations on the map.

• Say the new words and phrases (*traffic light, stop sign, turn left,* and *turn right*) and point out the part of the picture that demonstrates the meaning of each. Ask students to repeat each word and phrase.

• Ask students to use a finger to trace the route on the map as you read each dialogue. Then ask students to read the dialogues to themselves and complete the activity. If students have difficulty with this activity, have them work in pairs.

Where's the park? **(Words in parentheses are answers for page 95, Ex. B.)**

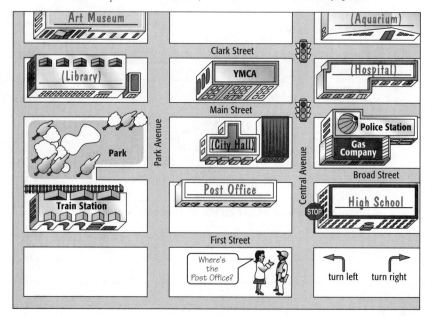

A. Read and write these locations on the map.

1. **A:** Where's the post office?
   B: Walk two blocks to Broad Street.
   Turn left.
   The post office is on your left.

2. **A:** Where's the art museum?
   B: Walk four blocks to the second traffic light. That's Clark Street.
   Turn left.
   The art museum is about two blocks up on your right.

3. **A:** Where's the high school?
   B: Walk one block to the first stop sign. That's First Street.
   Turn right.
   The high school is on your left.

traffic light

stop sign

B. Listen and write the locations on the map.

1. City Hall   2. library   3. hospital   4. aquarium

C. Read and complete.

traffic light	stop sign	right	left
Clark	Main	Broad	First

1. **A:** Where's the gas company?
   B: Walk two blocks to _____**Broad**_____ Street.
   Turn _____**right**_____.
   The gas company is on your _____**left**_____.

2. **A:** Where's the train station?
   B: Walk one block to the first _____**stop sign**_____.
   That's _____**First**_____ Street.
   Turn _____**left**_____.
   The train station is two blocks up on your _____**right**_____.

3. **A:** Where's the park?
   B: Walk two blocks to _____**Broad**_____ Street.
   Turn _____**left**_____.
   The park is about two blocks up, in front of you.

D. Write the directions to each of these locations. (Answers will vary.)

1. City Hall   2. the police station   3. the aquarium

Walk _____ blocks.
Walk _____ blocks to the first _____.
That's _____ Street.
Turn right.
Turn left.
The _____ is on your right/left.

B. Listen and write the locations on the map.
(CD1, Track 48)

As students listen to the audio, have them write the locations on the map on page 94. Play the audio several times as students complete the activity. Have students check each other's work.

C. Read and complete.

Have students use the map on page 94 to complete this activity. Then ask one student to read the directions as the other students check their answers.

D. Write the directions to each of these locations.

Ask students to use one or more of the phrases in the box to give directions to each of the locations. Have students complete this activity on a sheet of paper or in their notebooks. Students can work individually or in pairs.

Audio Script

B. Listen and write the locations on the map.
(CD1, Track 48)

1. **A:** Where's City Hall?
   B: Walk two blocks to Broad Street. Turn left. City Hall is on your right.
2. **A:** Where's the library?
   B: Walk three blocks to the first traffic light. Turn left. The library is two blocks up on your right.
3. **A:** Where's the hospital?
   B: Walk three blocks to the first traffic light. Turn right. The hospital is on your left.
4. **A:** Where's the aquarium?
   B: Walk four blocks to the second traffic light. That's Clark Street. Turn right. The aquarium is on your left.

☀ The Public Library

👥 A. Ask and answer questions about the library.

• Discuss the picture with the class. Ask:

What is this person doing?
Who is this?
What signs do you see?
What does this sign mean?

Encourage students to name familiar items in the picture. Then introduce any new words to students and have them repeat.

• Write these words and phrases on the board: *upstairs, on the main floor, downstairs, in front of, behind, next to, between.* Tell students they can use these words to answer the questions in this activity. As students talk in pairs, move around the room offering language support as needed.

B. Complete these sentences about your local library.

• Ask students to tell about any experiences they have had in a library. Prompt students with questions. For example: *Where is the library in this town? Is there a library in this school?*

• Have students complete the sentences in Exercise B with information about their own local library. Have students research any information they do not know for homework.

Suggestion

Ask students the following question: *How can the library help you learn English?* List students' ideas on the board. Prompt suggestions with questions, such as:

Are libraries quiet or noisy?
Are libraries a good place to study?
What books and other reading materials can you find in the library? (dictionaries, newspapers, easy reading books)
What other things do libraries have? (audiotapes, videotapes, computers)

The Public Library

👥 A. Ask and answer questions about the library.

Where are the children's books?

They're downstairs.

1. the reference books	4. the periodicals
2. the new books	5. the computers
3. the maps	6. the newspapers

B. Complete these sentences about your local library. (Answers will vary.)

1. The library is on ———————————.

2. The telephone number of the library is ———————————

3. I **have / don't have** a library card.

Working Together

A. Write the name of a store or location in your community.
(Answers will vary.)

1. park: _____Central Park_____
2. hospital: _____
3. supermarket: _____
4. drugstore: _____
5. bakery: _____
6. bank: _____
7. bookstore: _____
8. music store: _____
9. movie theater: _____
10. shoe store: _____

B. Give directions. (Answers will vary.)

The hospital in this area is _____.

It is on _____.
                        street

For an emergency, I need to call _____.
                                 telephone number

Write directions from your school to the hospital.

_____

_____

_____

_____

_____

☀ Working Together

A. Write the name of a store or location in your community.

Do this activity together as a class. Invite students to come up with the names of several different places for each category. Students will enjoy telling each other their favorite places to shop.

B. Give directions.

• Display a local map or draw one on the board. (Some phone books contain a map showing important places in the community.) Locate your school and the local hospital on the map. If you draw the map on the board, include the names of the streets that connect the two as well.
• As students give directions, trace the route on the map with your finger.
• Have pairs of student practice giving the directions to each other several times before they write the directions in their books.

The Big Picture: Downtown

A. Listen.

The Big Picture: Downtown

A. Listen. (CD1, Track 49)

• Ask questions about the people in the picture, such as:

Who are these two people?
What are they doing?
What happened to the truck?
What is the policeman doing?

Accept all reasonable responses and rephrase one-word answers or incomplete sentences into full-sentence form.

• Play the audio or read the story once or twice. Then ask students more questions about the picture. Model some of the new language and ask students to repeat. For example: *Joseph is sitting at a table. He's reading the newspaper.*

B. Listen and circle.
(CD1, Track 50)

Read aloud the choices after each number. Then play the audio and ask students to choose answers on their own. Play the audio once or twice more so students can check to see if their answers agree with the picture.

B. Listen and circle.

1. **a.** Elena is. — **b.** Jane is. — **c.** Mrs. Lee is.
2. **a.** Michael is. — **b.** Luisa is. — **c.** Michael and Luisa are.
3. **a.** Officer Ortiz is. — **b.** Mr. Thomas is. — **c.** Mark is.
4. **a.** Officer Ortiz is. — **b.** Jane is. — **c.** Mrs. Lee is.
5. **a.** Mark is. — **b.** Joseph is. — **c.** Jane is.
6. **a.** Joseph is. — **b.** Jane is. — **c.** Luisa is.
7. **a.** Joseph is. — **b.** Officer Ortiz is. — **c.** Michael and Luisa are.
8. **a.** Mr. Thomas is. — **b.** Mrs. Lee is. — **c.** Officer Ortiz is.

Audio Script

The Big Picture: Downtown

A. Listen. (CD1, Track 49)

It's a busy afternoon downtown. People are busy, and the stores are busy, too. Oh, look! There's an accident at the intersection of Smith Street and North Main Street. Mr. Thomas works at the bakery, and he drives the delivery truck. He's talking to the other driver. Over in the park, Elena is watching the children. The chil-dren are playing on swings. They're having a good time. There's a coffee shop on North Main Street. There are two tables in front of the coffee shop. Joseph is sitting at a table. He's reading the newspaper and drinking a cup of coffee. Jane is sitting at the other table. She's reading a good book. Mark is the waiter. He's bringing Jane some ice cream. Uh, oh. Mrs. Lee is running to her car. Officer Ortiz is standing next to her car. He's writing her a ticket. Oh, how wonderful! Michael and Luisa are in front of City Hall. I think they're getting married today.

B. Listen and circle. (CD1, Track 50)

1. Who is watching the children?
2. Who is getting married?
3. Who is standing at the corner of Smith Street and North Main Street?
4. Who is running?
5. Who is working at the coffee shop?
6. Who is reading a book?
7. Who is drinking a cup of coffee?
8. Who is writing a ticket?

C. (Circle) and complete.

1. The playground is _____ on _____ Smith Street.
   a. across from   **b.** on   **c.** between

2. City Hall is _____ next to _____ the playground.
   a. across from   **b.** next to   **c.** on the corner of

3. The coffee shop is _____ next to _____ the bakery.
   a. next to   **b.** between   **c.** behind

4. The parking lot is _____ across from _____ the laundromat.
   a. across from   **b.** behind   **c.** between

5. Jane and Joseph are sitting _____ in front of _____ the coffee shop.
   a. behind   **b.** in front of   **c.** next to

6. The police station is _____ across from _____ City Hall.
   a. across from   **b.** behind   **c.** on

7. Officer Ortiz is standing _____ next to _____ Mrs. Lee's car.
   a. next to   **b.** on   **c.** in front of

D. Complete with the name of a person(s) in the picture.

1. _____ Officer Ortiz _____ is behind the bookstore.

2. _____ Mrs. Lee _____ is between the bookstore and the bank.

3. _____ Mark, Joseph, and Jane _____ are in front of the coffee shop.

4. _____ Michael and Luisa _____ are in front of City Hall.

5. _____ Mr. Thomas _____ is on the corner of North Main Street and Smith Street.

E. Complete.

1. Mr. Thomas _____ is talking _____ to the other driver.
2. Elena _____ is watching _____ the children.
3. The children _____ are playing _____.
4. Joseph and Jane _____ are sitting _____ at tables.
5. Joseph _____ is reading _____ a newspaper.
6. Mark _____ is working _____ at the coffee shop.
7. Michael and Luisa _____ are getting _____ married.

watch
read
sit
✓talk
work
play
get

C. Circle and complete.

Have students look at the picture on page 98 as they complete this exercise.

D. Complete with the name of a person(s) in the picture.

Invite students to complete this activity individually or in pairs.

E. Complete.

Have students complete the sentences individually. Review the answers orally with the class.

Suggestion

Ask groups to write and act out two-line exchanges between people in the picture. For example:

Michael: *I love you, Luisa.*
  Luisa: *I love you, too.*

Suggestion

Ask small groups or pairs to write short stories about the picture.

Reading: The Library

A. What can you do at the library?

- Discuss what the woman and boy are doing. Ask: *What else can they do at the library?*
- Have students read the story without stopping to look up individual words. Then have them check what they can and can't do at the library.

Teacher Note

Show students how they can use context to figure out the meaning of unfamiliar words in the story. For example, if a student doesn't know what *borrow* means, point out that the words that come after *borrow* in this story are: *books for one month* and *a video for three days*. Have students ask themselves, *What do people do with books for one month? What do they do with videos for three days?* (Take them home.) So *borrow* means *take for some time* (two days or two weeks or a month) *and then bring back.*

Reading: The Library

Every Saturday morning, my son and I go to the public library. The library is only four blocks from our apartment. We can walk there.

My son and I have library cards. We go to the children's section, and he takes out books and videos about animals. He can borrow books for one month, but he can only borrow a video for three days.

Story Time is at 10:00. He stays downstairs and listens to the librarian read stories. I go upstairs and take a computer class. I don't have a computer at home. I am learning how to use the Internet and how to send e-mail to my family. At the library, I can use the computer for free. After my class, I stop in the reference section and read a newspaper from my country for a few minutes.

The library is a wonderful place for both me and my son. And best of all, it's free!

A. What can you do at the library?

- ☑ 1. I can borrow books.
- ☑ 2. I can borrow videos.
- ☑ 3. I can do my homework in the library.
- ☐ 4. I can buy magazines.
- ☑ 5. I can use the Internet.
- ☑ 6. I can read books to my children.
- ☑ 7. I can read the newspaper.
- ☐ 8. I can leave my child for the day.
- ☑ 9. I can get a library card.

Writing Our Stories:
Our School

A. Read.

I am a student at Union County College in Elizabeth, New Jersey. Our school is on West Jersey Street. West Jersey Street is a busy street. The traffic is heavy and noisy all day. There are many stores and buildings on West Jersey Street. Our school is between a small parking lot and the gas company. There is a large clothing store across the street. Our school is convenient to transportation. The train station is across the street, and the bus stop is on the corner. We have one problem. Because our school is in a city, it is difficult to find a parking space.

B. Write about the location of your school. (Answers will vary.)

I am a student at _____ in _____,
                        school   town

_____. Our school in on _____.
       state   street

The traffic is _____ and _____.

Our school is _____

_____

_____

_____

_____

_____

Writing Note

Read your story two or three times. Check the spelling.

Writing Our Stories:
Our School

A. Read.

Ask students to read through the story without stopping to look up new words.

Suggestion

Have students underline all the prepositions in the story.

B. Write about the location of your school.

• Before students begin writing, talk about the location of their own school. Write the name of the school and the name of the street on the board. Point out that the name of the school and the street begin with capital letters. Ask questions, such as:

What street is the school on?
Is the street quiet or noisy?
Is it busy?
What is next to the school?
What is across from the school?
Where is the parking lot?

After the discussion, ask students to write about the location of their school in their books.

• Explain to students that they can use the story at the top of the page as a model for their writing. Show how students can adapt sentences to fit their own stories. For example: *Our school is between a small parking lot and the gas company* can become *My school is between a factory and a park.*

A. Look at the map.

Have students complete the activity individually. Then ask them to check their questions and answers with a partner.

Suggestion

Have students use their questions and answers for paired oral practice.

Practicing on Your Own

A. Look at the map. Complete the sentences.

1. Where _____is_____ the bank?

   It's _____across from_____ the bakery.

2. Where _____is_____ the school?

   It's _____next to_____ the park.

3. Where _____are_____ the children?

   They _____are_____ in the _____park_____.

4. What _____are they_____ doing?

   They _____are playing_____.

5. Where _____(Answers will vary.)_____?

   _____.

6. Where _____(Answers will vary.)_____?

   _____.

7. Where _____(Answers will vary.)_____?

   _____.

8. Where _____(Answers will vary.)_____?

   _____.

Looking at Forms: Library Card Application

A. Complete. (Answers will vary.)

```
┌─────────────────────────────────────────────────────────────────┐
│                 Public Library Card Application                   │
│                                                                   │
│  _____   _____  _____   __/__/__          │
│       Last name           First name      MI    Today's date      │
│  ☐ Adult  ☐ Child   ___-___-_____   _____       │
│                     Social Security Number  (If child, signature of parent/guardian) │
│                                                                   │
│  _____  │
│                            Address                                │
│  _____   _____   _____   │
│             City                       State      Zip Code        │
│  Telephone:  (_____) _____-_____                        │
└─────────────────────────────────────────────────────────────────┘
```

Grammar Summary

▶ **1. Prepositions**
Where is the library?   It's **on** Maple Avenue.
Where are the foreign newspapers?   They are **next to** the computers.
▶ **2. *Who* questions**
Who is watching the children?   Elena is.
Who is drinking coffee?   Joseph and Jane are.
▶ **3. *Can* statements**
I **can** mail a letter at the post office.

Looking at Forms: Library Card Application

A. Complete.

Ask students to complete the Public Library Card Application form with their own information. Walk around the classroom and check students' applications. Provide assistance as needed.

Suggestion

Bring in actual library card application forms. Have students who do not yet have a library card complete a form in class. Students can then bring their application to the local library to receive their own library card.

Grammar Summary

• Review the summary with the class. Invite students to name the other prepositions they have studied, and to say other statements, questions, and answers that might appear in each of the three sections of the summary.

• See the Grammar Summary Expansion on page 236 for a more complete explanation of these grammar points.

Unit 8
Money

Discuss the person standing next to the unit number. Ask:

- *Who is standing next to the number 8?* (A woman)
- *What is she doing?* (She's holding up a giant dollar bill.)

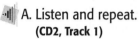

☀Dictionary:
Coins and Bills

 A. Listen and repeat.
   (CD2, Track 1)

> Play the audio or read the monetary amounts aloud and have students repeat. Point out that the words in the second line and the numbers in the third line under each coin are said the same way.

Teacher Note

Explain that English speakers rarely use the word *one* with the word *dollar*. They usually say *a dollar* or *a dollar and twenty-five cents*.

Suggestion

Expand on the culture note. Ask students to take out any quarters they may have in their pocket or purse and to look for quarters with states on the back. Ask students to tell the class what state(s) are on their quarter(s).

 # 8 Money

Dictionary: Coins and Bills

 A. Listen and repeat.

Coins

a penny	a nickel	a dime	a quarter
one cent	five cents	ten cents	twenty-five cents
$.01	$.05	$.10	$.25

Culture Note
From 1999 to 2009, the United States is issuing a new series of quarters. These quarters will honor the different states. Do you have any of these quarters? What state is on the back?

Bills

a dollar
$1.00

five dollars
$5.00

ten dollars
$10.00

twenty dollars
$20.00

Active Grammar: *How much* Questions

A. Listen and repeat.

a.	4¢	$.04	f.	50¢	$.50
b.	10¢	$.10	g.	62¢	$.62
c.	25¢	$.25	h.	75¢	$.75
d.	30¢	$.30	i.	85¢	$.85
e.	35¢	$.35	j.	99¢	$.99

> **Money**
> There are three ways to write cents.
> ten cents
> 10¢
> $.10

B. Write the amount.

a.

35¢ / $.35

b.

11¢ / $.11

c.

41¢ / $.41

d.

31¢ / $.31

e.

35¢ / $.35

> Sit in a group.
> Take out your change
> Count it together.
> Write the amount.
> Who has the most change?

C. Listen and write the amount.

a.	$.02 / 2¢	d. $.25 / 25¢	g. $.50 / 50¢
b.	$.10 / 10¢	e. $.38 / 38¢	h. $.69 / 69¢
c.	$.17 / 17¢	f. $.49 / 49¢	i. $.98 / 98¢

Money **105**

Active Grammar: *How much* Questions

A. Listen and repeat.
(CD2, Track 2)

Play the audio or say the amounts as many times as necessary for students to master the pronunciation.

B. Write the amount.

• Have students count the money in each picture and write the amounts on their own. Then have students work with a partner to check their answers.
• Ask students to take out the change in their own pockets and purses and count it together. Have students write the amounts. Find out who has the most change.

Teacher Note

Before doing Exercise C, have students practice making dollar signs if necessary. You also may wish to introduce the term *decimal point* and explain that a decimal point goes between the number of dollars and the number of cents.

C. Listen and write the amount.
(CD2, Track 3)

Play the audio and have students write the amounts they hear.

Audio Script

C. Listen and write the amount.
(CD2, Track 3)

a. two cents
b. ten cents
c. seventeen cents
d. twenty-five cents
e. thirty-eight cents
f. forty-nine cents
g. fifty cents
h. sixty-nine cents
i. ninety-eight cents

Bills

 A. Listen and repeat.
(CD2, Track 4)

Play the audio or say the monetary amounts and have students repeat each one. Repeat the exercise several times if necessary.

 B. Listen and write the amount.
(CD2, Track 5)

Play the audio three times so that students can listen, write, and check their answers.

Suggestion

Have students go to the board five or six at a time. Dictate amounts of money and have students write the amounts on the board.

 C. Listen and repeat.
(CD2, Track 6)

• Have students listen and repeat each of the numbers in the boxes.
• Say pairs of similar numbers (such as *13 and 30*) and ask students to say *same* if the numbers are the same or *different* if they are different.

Circle. (CD2, Track 7)

Play the audio and have students circle the numbers they hear.

Bills

> **Dollars and Cents**
> $ 2.50: two <u>dollars</u> and fifty <u>cents</u>   *or*   two fifty
> $ 10.99: ten <u>dollars</u> and ninety-nine <u>cents</u>   *or*   ten ninety-nine
> $498.79: four hundred and ninety-eight dollars and seventy-nine cents
>   *or*   four ninety-eight seventy-nine.

 A. Listen and repeat.

a. $1.00	d. $4.99	g. $127.98
b. $1.50	e. $17.49	h. $249.99
c. $2.75	f. $59.50	i. $629.77

 B. Listen and write the amount.

a. $1.00	f. $79.25
b. $1.25	g. $157.62
c. $2.50	h. $230.99
d. $3.75	i. $457.24
e. $15.08	

Culture Note

The dollar is the monetary unit of the United States. What is the monetary unit in your country?

C. Listen and repeat.

13	14	15	16	17	18	19	20
30	40	50	60	70	80	90	100

Circle.

a. (13) 30	h. ($13.50) $13.15
b. 14 (40)	i. ($15.99) $50.99
c. (15) 50	j. ($19.99) $90.99
d. 16 (60)	k. $14.40 ($14.14)
e. 17 (70)	l. ($17.20) $70.20
f. (18) 80	m. ($16.16) $60.16
g. (19) 90	n. ($18.75) $80.75

106   UNIT 8

Audio Script

B. Listen and write the amount.
(CD2, Track 5)

a. a dollar
b. a dollar twenty-five
c. two dollars and fifty cents
d. three seventy-five
e. fifteen dollars and eight cents
f. seventy-nine twenty-five
g. one hundred fifty-seven dollars and sixty-two cents
h. two hundred thirty dollars and ninety-nine cents
i. four hundred fifty-seven dollars and twenty-four cents

C. Listen and repeat.
(CD2, Track 6)

13, 14, 15, 16, 17, 18, 19, 20
30, 40, 50, 60, 70, 80, 90, 100

Circle. (CD2, Track 7)

a. 13		h. $13.50
b. 40		i. $15.99
c. 15		j. $19.99
d. 60		k. $14.14
e. 70		l. $17.20
f. 18		m. $16.16
g. 19		n. $18.75

Looking at Forms: Checks

A. Read.

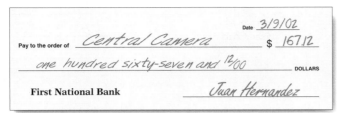

Date 3/9/02

Pay to the order of _Central Camera_ $ _167.12_

one hundred sixty-seven and ¹²/00 ————— DOLLARS

First National Bank _Juan Hernandez_

B. Write these check amounts.

$21.40   twenty-one and $^{40}/_{00}$

$137.95   one hundred thirty-seven and $^{95}/_{00}$

$359.80   three hundred fifty-nine and $^{80}/_{00}$

a. $7.50   seven and $^{50}/_{00}$

b. $34.25   thirty-four and $^{25}/_{00}$

c. $59.49   fifty-nine and $^{49}/_{00}$

d. $137.12   one hundred thirty-seven and $^{12}/_{00}$

e. $429.67   four hundred twenty-nine and $^{67}/_{00}$

Writing Note
Put the cents amount over /00.

C. Complete these checks. (Name and date will vary.)

To: The Electronics Center #84.95

Date _____

Pay to the order of _The Electronics Center_ $ 84.95

eighty-four and 95/00 ————— DOLLARS

First National Bank _____

To: United Credit #237.52

Date _____

Pay to the order of _United Credit_ $ 237.52

two hundred thirty-seven and 52/00 ————— DOLLARS

First National Bank _____

☀ Looking at Forms: Checks

Suggestion

Help students understand checking accounts. Ask:

What bank do you use?
Do you have a checking account?
Do you pay for your checking account?
Do you get a statement every month?

A. Read.

Review the check with students. Point out the slash between the number of cents and the *00*. Answer any questions students have about how to write words and numbers on checks.

B. Write these check amounts.

Explain that the word amounts on checks are said the same way as the number amounts. Ask different students to read aloud the three amounts written out in words. Read the rest of the amounts to the class. Then have students write the amounts in words.

C. Complete these checks.

Have students complete the checks on their own, then check their work with a partner. Have one student write each check on the board. Review the checks with the class.

I need a fax machine.

A. Write seven other items you can buy in an electronics store.

Have students try to complete their lists on their own. If students have difficulty coming up with seven items, have them work in small groups.

Teacher Note

You may wish to bring in catalogs from electronics stores and have students use the catalog to find names of electronic items.

 ## B. Pronunciation.
(CD2, Track 8)

• Play the audio or read the words at least twice as students write their answers.
• Correct the exercise as a class, writing on the board any words students disagree about. Use slashes to divide each of the words into syllables. Invite students to practice saying the words aloud.

I need a fax machine.

A. Write seven other items you can buy in an electronics store. (Answers will vary.)

fax machine	_____
answering machine	_____
TV	_____
speakers	_____
computer	_____
	_____
	_____

B. Pronunciation. Listen. How many syllables do you hear?

store	1	notebook	2
sale	1	stereo	3
printer	2	camcorder	3
computer	3	tapes	1
telephone	3	headphones	2
CDs	2	VCR	3
batteries	3	speakers	2
scanner	2	camera	2
movies	2	stereo	3
disk	1	games	1

C. Look at the list in Exercise B. Write five singular words. Write five plural words. (Answers will vary.)

Singular	Plural
_____	_____
_____	_____
_____	_____
_____	_____
_____	_____

D. Label the computer with a partner.

CD-ROM	keyboard	mouse
floppy disk	keys	mouse pad
monitor	speakers	screen

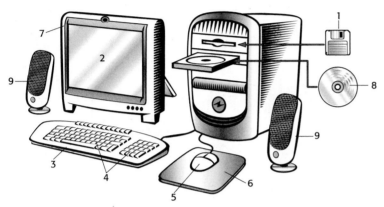

1. _____floppy disk_____   5. _____mouse_____

2. _____screen_____   6. _____mousepad_____

3. _____keyboard_____   7. _____monitor_____

4. _____keys_____   8. _____CD-ROM_____

     9. _____speakers_____

C. Look at the list in Exercise B.

Have students complete the activity on their own and compare lists with a partner.

Suggestion

Show students the picture of the computer on this page. Ask students questions about their experience with computers, such as:

Can you use a computer?
Do you have a computer at home?
What kind of computer do you have?
How much does a computer cost?
Do you use a computer at work?
Do you use the Internet?

D. Label the computer with a partner.

After the pairs finish labeling the computer, review the answers with the class. Say the name of each part and have students repeat.

☀ How much is it?

Suggestion

Invite students to talk about the items in the picture. Supply vocabulary and model pronunciation as necessary. Encourage students to talk about what electronic equipment they have and what they want.

A. Pair practice.

Read the sample dialogue with a student. Ask students what they think *I'll take it* means. (I will buy it.) Then have students work in pairs to create dialogues for the other items.

A. Pair practice.

A: How much is this camera?

B: It's on sale. It's $179.

A: I'll take it.

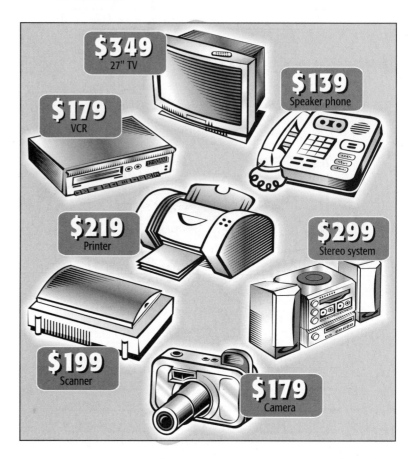

$349
27" TV

$179
VCR

$139
Speaker phone

$219
Printer

$299
Stereo system

$199
Scanner

$179
Camera

How much are they?

A. Pair practice.

A: How much are these headphones?

B: They're on sale. They're $29.95.

A: I'll take them.

$29.⁹⁵ Headphones

$4.⁹⁹ each Games

$159 each Speakers

$8.⁵⁰ (Pack of 3) Tapes

$7.²⁵ (Pack of 4) Batteries

$16.⁹⁹ each DVDs

$14.⁴⁹ each CDs

☀How much are they?

Suggestion

Invite students to talk about the items in the picture. Supply vocabulary and model pronunciation as needed. Encourage students to talk about which items they have bought recently.

Teacher Note

Point out to students that we use *they* and *them* to talk about plural objects.

A. Pair practice.

Read the sample dialogue with a student. Then have students work in pairs to create dialogues for the other items.

Working Together

Suggestion

Before doing Exercise A, brainstorm with students a list of local stores. Write the list on the board. Have students take turns coming to the board and writing the names of things they can buy at each store.

A. Sit in a group of four students.

Have students take turns telling where they shop for each of the items.

B. Sit in a group.

• Have each group discuss the answer to each question before writing it. Explain that there are several correct answers to some questions, depending on where you buy the item.

• Go over the answers with the whole class. Call on one person from each group to tell the prices their group came up with.

C. Bring in sales circulars from different stores.

As the groups discuss the circulars, move around the room offering support. Model new language as necessary. For example: *The sale is next week.* or *The sale price is $15.*

Working Together

A. Sit in a group of four students. Talk about the places you like to shop. (Answers will vary.)

1. I shop at _____ for clothes.

2. I shop at _____ for shoes.

3. I shop at _____ for food.

4. I shop at _____ for sports equipment.

5. I shop at _____ for CDs.

6. I shop at _____ for toys.

7. I shop at _____ for _____.

B. Sit in a group. Complete with a price. (Answers will vary.)

1. A first-class stamp is _____.

2. A local telephone call is _____.

3. The local newspaper is _____.

4. A gallon of regular gas is _____.

5. A cup of coffee is _____.

6. A CD is _____.

7. A video rental is _____.

8. A movie at the movie theater is _____.

9. A round-trip airline ticket to my country is _____.

10. A computer is _____.

C. Bring in sales circulars from different stores. Sit in a group and discuss. (Answers will vary.)

Where is the sale? Do you shop there?

What kind of store is it? When is the sale?

List four items on sale. What is the regular price? What is the sale price?

D. Complete about a bank in your area. (Answers will vary.)

Bank: _____

Street: _____

The bank is open from _____ to _____ on weekdays.

The bank is open late on _____ night.

The bank is open on Saturday from _____ to _____.

E. Interview a partner. Check your partner's answers. (Answers will vary.)

ATM: Automated Teller Machine

How do you pay for . . .	I pay cash.	I use a credit card.	I write a check.	I get a money order.	I use my ATM card.
gas					
rent					
food					
your telephone bill					
your electric bill					
clothes					

F. Put these ATM steps in order.

___3___ Select *Withdraw cash.*

___5___ Take your cash.

___1___ Insert your ATM card.

___6___ Take your receipt.

___2___ Put in your PIN number.

___7___ Remember your ATM card!

___4___ Choose the amount you want.

D. Complete about a bank in your area.

Have students write about a bank they use. If students do not know the information, have them find out the information for homework.

E. Interview a partner.

Review the five payment methods at the top of the chart. Then have students interview each other in pairs.

F. Put these ATM steps in order.

• Explain or demonstrate the meaning of any new words in this exercise. For example:

T: *What does "withdraw" mean? It doesn't mean to put money in the bank.*
S: *Take out?*
T: *Right. When you withdraw money you take money out of the bank.*

• Have students number the steps on their own. To check the answers, have a student read out the correct steps in order. Call on a different student to read each step.

Suggestion

Invite a volunteer to come to the front of the class and pantomime the ATM steps while the class reads the steps aloud in the correct order.

☀ The Big Picture:
The Electronics Store

A. Circle the equipment you see in the store.

• Talk about the pictures with the class. Invite students to comment on the people and the items they see. Ask questions to get them started. For example:

Picture 1
What is this boy looking at?
What does the woman want to buy?
What kind of TV is that?
What are the young man and woman looking at?
The woman is pregnant. What does "pregnant" mean?

Picture 2
What is this woman buying?
What is this boy doing?
Who is standing behind him?

• Have students work alone to circle the items they see in the picture.

B. Listen. (CD2, Track 9)

Play the audio once and ask students to tell the class everything they can remember about the sale.

The Big Picture: The Electronics Store

A. Circle the equipment you see in the store.

(Names in white boxes are responses to page 115, Ex. C.)

TVs   camcorders   speakers
headphones   electronic dictionaries   scanners
game systems   computers   fax machines
DVDs   printers   telephones

 B. Listen.

Audio Script

☀ The Big Picture:
The Electronics Store

B. Listen. (CD2, Track 9)

Electronics City is having a July 4th sale, and all their electronic equipment is on sale. A lot of customers are in the store and the salespeople are busy.

Marta is standing in front of the big-screen TVs. She watches TV a lot. On Saturday and Sunday she watches sports, like soccer, baseball, and tennis. She wants a big-screen to enjoy the games. Tammy and Sean are expecting their first baby soon. They are looking at video cameras. They want to take lots of pictures of the baby for their parents. George is looking at the DVDs. He likes movies, and the DVDs are on sale for $12.99 each or three for $30.00. He's going to buy three. Tamara is Russian, and she's studying English. She's buying an English-Russian electronic dictionary to help her with vocabulary.

Mr. and Mrs. Jackson want to buy their first computer. They want to e-mail their children and their grandchildren. They don't know anything about computers. Their grandson is helping them buy the right computer. Then he is going to show them how to use it.

C. Listen again and write the correct name under each person.

| Marta | George | Mr. and Mrs. Jackson |
| Tammy and Sean | Tamara | |

D. Complete.

1. Marta _____is standing_____ in front of the TVs.

2. Tammy and Sean _____are expecting_____ a baby.

   They _____are looking_____ at camcorders.

3. George _____is looking_____ at DVDs.

4. Tamara _____is studying_____ English.

   She _____is buying_____ an electronic dictionary.

5. Mr. and Mrs. Jackson _____are_____ at the store with their grandson.

   He _____is helping_____ them buy a computer.

> is studying
> is looking
> is buying
> are
> ✓ is standing
> are looking
> is helping
> are expecting

E. Listen to each conversation. Write the item and the price.

Conversation 1: ___Russian-English dictionary___ $___39.99___

Conversation 2: ___50" TV___ $___1,549___

Conversation 3: ___computer___ $___599___

Conversation 4: ___video camera___ $___799___

F. Match.

1. This is a nice camcorder. Is it easy to use? — It's on sale for $799. And there's a $100 rebate.

2. Can I connect it to my TV? — Yes, it's very easy to use.

3. How long is the warranty? — Yes, you can connect it to your TV or your computer.

4. How much is it? — Send this card and a copy of your receipt to the manufacturer. They will send you $100.

5. What's a rebate? — It's one year.

C. Listen again and write the correct name under each person. (CD2, Track 9)

Play the audio for Exercise B once or twice more as students write the names of the people on the picture on page 114. Have students check their answers with a partner.

D. Complete.

Point out that the answers are in the box next to the exercise. Have students use the picture on page 114 to complete the exercise.

E. Listen to each conversation.

Play the audio for each conversation as many times as students need to fill in the answers. After students have written the item and price for each conversation, review the answers together.

F. Match.

Have students match the questions and answers on their own. Answer any questions students have about warranties and rebates. When students have completed the exercise, ask them to read the conversation with a partner.

Audio Script

E. Listen to each conversation. Write the item and the price. (CD2, Track 10)

Conversation 1
A: Is this a Russian-English dictionary?
B: Yes, it is.
A: How much is it?
B: It's $39.99.
A: I'll take it.

Conversation 2
A: What size is this TV?
B: It's a 50".
A: Is it on sale?
B: Yes. It's usually $1,699. But it's on sale today for $1,549.

Conversation 3
A: How much is this computer?
B: It's $1,999.
A: We need an easy-to-use computer. We just need it for e-mail. What else do you have?
B: This is our basic model. It's very easy to use. It's only $599.

Conversation 4
A: This is a nice video camera. Is it easy to use?
B: Yes, it's very easy to use. And the pictures are great.
A: Can I connect it to my TV?
B: You can connect it to your TV or your computer.

A: How long is the warranty?
B: It's one year.
A: How much is it?
B: It's on sale for $799. And there's a $100 rebate.
A: What's a rebate?
B: Send this card and a copy of your receipt to the manufacturer. They will send you $100.

 Reading

A. Before You Read.

Discuss the questions with the whole class.

B. Answer.

• Invite students to talk about the advertisement. Ask: *Which items do you think are expensive? Which are cheap?*

• Have students look at the ad and ask questions about any words they don't understand.

• Discuss the answers to the questions with the whole class.

Reading

A. Before You Read. (Answers will vary.)

1. Do you shop at sales?
2. Where can you find information about sales?

B. Answer.

1. What's the name of this store? Electronics City.
2. When is the sale? July 4th and 5th from 9 A.M. to 10 P.M.
3. How much will you save on the notebook computer? $400.
4. What features does the cordless phone include? Caller ID and answering system.
5. What size is the TV? 36" (inches).
6. What does the stereo system include? A receiver and five speakers.
7. How much is the digital camera? $499.
8. Is this a good sale? Yes, it is.

Writing Our Stories: Spending Money

A. Read.

I have a home entertainment center. In my living room, I have a large-screen TV with four speakers. I have a DVD player, too. I'm saving my money now for a video camera. I want to take pictures of my vacation. The camera I want is $795. I want to buy it on sale.

B. Write. What electronic equipment do you have? What are you planning to buy? (Answers will vary.)

I have a(n) _____. I also have a(n) _____.

I want a(n) _____.

I'm saving my money for a _____. _____

_____

_____

_____

Writing Note
Use capital letters for these words: TV, VCR, DVD, PC.

☀Writing Our Stories: Spending Money

A. Read.

- Ask students: *How do you think the man in the picture feels?* (happy, proud, excited) Encourage students to tell about something they bought that made them very happy.
- Read the story aloud to the students or have them read it silently. Answer any questions they may have.

B. Write.

- Have students write their stories individually. Remind them that they can use sentences from the story at the top of the page as models. For example: *I have a large-screen TV with four speakers* can become *I have a new computer with a 17-inch screen.*

Suggestion

Before students begin writing, have them help you write your own story on the board. Some students can ask you questions about what equipment you own. Others can write one sentence each on the board as you dictate.

Practicing on Your Own

A. Write the amount.

After students write the answers, ask them to check their work with a partner.

B. Complete each question with *is* or *are*.

Point out the two forms (singular and plural) students can use for their answers.

Suggestion

Do the exercise orally in class before having students write the answers. Call on different students to ask and answer the questions.

Practicing on Your Own

Dollars and Cents
$ 2.50: two <u>dollars</u> and fifty <u>cents</u>
$10.99: ten <u>dollars</u> and ninety-nine <u>cents</u>

A. Write the amount.

a. $1.00   one dollar

b. $4.50   four dollars and fifty cents

c. $7.98   seven dollars and ninety-eight cents

d. $18.75   eighteen dollars and seventy-five cents

e. $79.63   seventy-nine dollars and sixty-three cents

f. $135.72   one hundred thirty-five dollars and seventy-two cents

g. $199.00   one hundred ninety-nine dollars

B. Complete each question with *is* or *are*. Write the answer.

It's $_____.   They're $_____.

1. How much __are__ the speakers?   They're $89 each.
2. How much __is__ the DVD player?   It's $329.
3. How much __are__ batteries?   They're $5.99.
4. How much __are__ the CDs?   They're $11.49 each.
5. How much __is__ the electronic dictionary?   It's $29.50.
6. How much __is__ the scanner?   It's $149.
7. How much __are__ the headphones?   They're $19.49.

Looking at Forms: Mail-In Rebate

A. Complete this rebate form. (Answers will vary.)

Many electronics stores offer mail-in rebates. You must send an application form and your receipt to the manufacturer.

$399
$449 – $50
Manufacturer's
Mail-in Rebate

Name: _____	
Last First	

Name: _____
               Last   First

Address: _____

City: _____ State: _____ Zip code: _____

Phone number: (_____) _____

E-mail address: _____

Product (circle): printer fax scanner copier monitor computer

Model number: _____

Store: _____

Date of purchase: _____

Signature: _____

Send this form and your receipt to the manufacturer.

Grammar Summary

1. **How much questions**	
How much is the printer?	It's $129.00.
How much is it?	It's $129.00.
How much are the speakers?	They're $249.00.
How much are they?	They're $249.00.

2. **Dollars and cents**
$4.95: four dollars and ninety-five cents
four ninety-five

3. **Writing check amounts**
$4.95: *four and 95/00*

Looking at Forms: Mail-In Rebate

A. Complete this rebate form.

- Discuss what a *rebate* is. (Money a company gives back to you after you buy their product.) Ask students to tell about specific rebates they know about or have actually received. For example, automobile companies often give rebates on certain models. Electronics manufacturers also frequently give rebates.
- Ask students to complete the form individually.

Suggestion

If students prepare the rebate form at home, ask them to use an actual model number and date of purchase.

Grammar Summary

- Review the summary with the class. Invite students to make up other *How much* questions and answers.
- See the Grammar Summary Expansion on page 236 for a more complete explanation of this grammar point.

Unit 9
Working at the Mall

Discuss the person next to the unit number. Ask:

• *Who is standing next to the number 9?* (A man)
• *What is he doing?* (He's holding up items of clothing.)

☀ Dictionary: Jobs

📶 A. Listen and repeat.
(CD2, Track 11)

• Ask students to tell you some adjectives that describe the jobs shown (such as *easy, difficult, boring, interesting, safe,* and *dangerous*). Write these adjectives on the board.
• Prompt students to talk about these jobs. Ask questions such as:

> *Are you a _____?*
> *Where do you work?*
> *Do you know a _____?*
> *Where does he/she work?*

• Play the audio or read the words on the page. Have students point to each job as they hear about the job. Do the activity again, this time pausing to give students a chance to repeat the words and sentences.

 # 9 Working at the Mall

Dictionary: Jobs

📶 A. Listen and repeat.

Jobs

hairstylist
A hairstylist cuts hair.

manicurist
A manicurist colors nails.

cashier
A cashier takes money.

security guard
A security guard watches customers.

cook
A cook prepares food.

waiter
A waiter serves food.

salesperson
A salesperson helps customers.

pharmacist
A pharmacist fills prescriptions.

photographer
A photographer takes pictures.

120 UNIT 9

florist
A florist sells flowers.

painter
A painter paints walls and ceilings.

custodian
A custodian cleans floors.

B. Complete.

1. A hairstylist _____cuts_____ hair.
2. A custodian _____cleans_____ the floor.
3. A security guard _____watches_____ customers.
4. A florist _____sells_____ flowers.
5. A cook _____prepares_____ food.
6. A manicurist _____colors_____ nails.
7. A pharmacist _____fills_____ prescriptions.
8. A photographer _____takes_____ pictures.

cleans
sells
takes
colors
✓cuts
watches
fills
prepares

C. Complete. (Answers may vary. Sample answers below.)

1. A _____hairstylist/waiter_____ stands all day.
2. A _____manicurist/secretary_____ sits at work.
3. A _____pharmacist/florist_____ has to write orders.
4. A _____security guard_____ wears a uniform.
5. A _____photographer_____ talks to customers.

D. Discuss other jobs. (Answers may vary. Sample answers below.)

1. Who works at your school? teacher/counselor/custodian/secretary
2. Who works in an office? secretary/manager/receptionist/accountant
3. Who works in a hospital? doctor/nurse/lab technician/custodian
4. Who works at a mall? salesperson/manager/fast-food cook/security guard

Working at the Mall **121**

B. Complete.

Ask students to fill in the blanks using the words in the box. Check answers by calling on different students to read each of the sentences.

C. Complete.

Have students complete the sentences and discuss the answers with a partner. Many sentences have several correct answers. If a student uses the name of a new job, write that occupation on the board and ask students to repeat.

D. Discuss other jobs.

Discuss the questions with the whole class. Write any new words that come up on the board. Add a defining sentence and have the class practice pronouncing the words and sentences. For example: *Receptionist.*
A receptionist greets people.

A. Complete.

• Invite students to talk about the pictures. Have them identify the jobs of the people in the pictures and tell what the people are doing.

• Ask students to complete the sentences on their own. Check answers by calling on different students to read their answers to the class.

Active Grammar: Present Tense

A. Complete.

1. Luis works at _____ Cosimo's _____. He's a _____ waiter _____.
2. Richard works at _____ Hair Plus _____. He's a _____ hairstylist _____.
3. Marie works at _____ Family Pharmacy _____. She's a _____ pharmacist _____.
4. Sam works at _____ Cosimo's _____. He's a _____ cook _____.
5. Carlos works at _____ The Clothes Closet _____. He's a _____ cashier _____.
6. Sheri works at _____ Hair Plus _____. She's a _____ manicurist _____.
7. Kenji works at _____ The Clothes Closet _____. He's a _____ salesperson _____.

B. Read.

A: Where does Ahmed work?

B: He works at the Parkside Mall.

A: What does he do?

B: He's a security guard.

> **Present Tense**
> I work at the mall.
> She work<u>s</u> at the mall.
> He work<u>s</u> at the mall.

C. Pair practice. Talk about the jobs in the mall.

Where does Sam work?

What does he do?

He works at Cosimo's.

He's a cook.

D. Read the schedule. Complete the information below.

	Sunday	Monday	Tuesday	Wednesday	Thursday	Friday	Saturday
Sam			3–11	3–11	3–11	3–11	3–11
Luis		12–5	12–5			12–5	12–5

1. Sam works __8__ hours a day.

2. Sam works __5__ days a week.

3. Sam works (full time) / part time.

4. Luis works __5__ hours a day.

5. Luis works __4__ days a week.

6. Luis works full time /(part time.)

7. I work _____ hours a day. (Answers will vary.)

8. I work _____ days a week. (Answers will vary.)

9. I work full time / part time. (Answers will vary.)

> Full time: 35–40 hours a week
> Part time: less than that a week

B. Read.

Ask different pairs of students to read the dialogue to the class.

Suggestion

• Point out the Present Tense note in the box to the right of the dialogue. Ask students to tell you what is different about the word *work* in the sentences. (There's no *s* at the end of *work* in the sentence that begins with *I*. There's an *s* at the end of *work* in the sentences that begin with *he* and *she*.)

• Ask students to look at pages 120 and 121 to find other examples of verbs with *s* at the end. (A hairstylist cut<u>s</u> hair, etc.)

C. Pair practice.

• Read the dialogue with a student. If necessary, explain the meaning of *Where does _____ work?* and *What does _____ do?*

• Have students work in pairs to talk about the jobs in the pictures on pages 120 and 121. When they finish, ask them to look at the word *work* in the sample dialogue. Ask:

Does it have an s *in the question?* (No)
Why does it have an s *in the statement?* (You add an *s* at the end of a verb after statements with *he* and *she*.)

D. Read the schedule.

• Ask students about their own schedules. Write on the board:

I'm a _____.
I work _____ hours a day.
I work _____ days a week.
I work _____. (full time or part time)

Ask volunteers to fill in the information about their own schedules.

• Have students complete the activity on their own and check their answers with a partner.

☀ What time is it?

 A. Listen and repeat.
(CD2, Track 12)

Ask students to look at the clock faces as you play the audio or read the times. Then present the times again and have students repeat each one. You may do this step several times.

B. Show the time on the clocks.

Ask students to draw the hands on the clocks. Then call on different students to read the times.

Suggestion

Have students work in pairs. Show them how to cover the row of numbers below the clocks with a pencil. Then have them take turns saying the times using only the pictures of the clocks.

C. Listen and show the time on the clocks.
(CD2, Track 13)

Have students draw hands on the clocks as they listen to the audio. Review the answers by having different students draw their clocks on the board.

What time is it?

 A. Listen and repeat.

| two o'clock | two oh-five | two ten | two fifteen | two thirty |
| 2:00 | 2:05 | 2:10 | 2:15 | 2:30 |

| two forty | two forty-five | two fifty | two fifty-five | three o'clock |
| 2:40 | 2:45 | 2:50 | 2:55 | 3:00 |

B. Show the time on the clocks. Say the time.

| 1:00 | 6:30 | 7:15 | 11:45 |

| 2:10 | 3:40 | 5:25 | 4:55 |

 C. Listen and show the time on the clocks.

| 4:00 | 6:30 | 8:15 | 10:55 |

124 UNIT 9

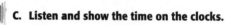

Audio Script

C. Listen and show the times on the clocks.
(CD2, Track 13)

a. four o'clock
b. six thirty
c. eight fifteen
d. ten fifty-five

What time do you get up?

A. Complete about your schedule. (Answers will vary.)

I get up at
__:__.

I eat breakfast at
__:__.

I leave the house at
__:__.

I work from
__:__ to __:__.

I eat dinner at
__:__.

I study from
__:__ to __:__.

I get home at
__:__.

I watch TV from
__:__ to __:__.

I go to bed at
__:__.

B. Complete.

1. I get up ___at___ 6:00.

2. I eat breakfast ___at___ 7:00.

3. I go to school ___from___ 9:00 ___to___ 12:00.

4. I eat lunch ___at___ 1:00.

5. I work ___from___ 3:00 ___to___ 11:00.

6. I go to bed ___at___ 12:00.

> **Prepositions**
> I go to school <u>at</u> 7:20.
> I study <u>from</u> 7:30 <u>to</u> 9:00.

☀ What time do you get up?

Teacher Note

Tell students that English speakers often leave off *o'clock* when saying the time. Explain that we usually say *I get up at seven,* not *I get up at seven o'clock.* Also explain that *o'clock* is never used with half or quarter hours: *I start work at two-thirty,* not *I start work at two-thirty o'clock.*

A. Complete about your schedule.

Ask students to fill in the times that they do each activity.

Suggestion

Have students share their work with a partner.

B. Complete.

- Point out the Prepositions box on the right and briefly discuss the use of *from* and *to* to show how long an activity takes.
- Have students fill in the prepositions on their own.

C. Sit with a partner.

Have students complete the chart with a partner.

D. Complete about the chart.

Have students fill in the missing prepositions and times using the information about their partner from Exercise C.

Suggestion

Have two or three pairs form a group. Have students take turns reporting to the group on their partner's schedule.

☀ My job

A. Read.

Read the dialogue to the students or have them read it on their own. Answer any questions students may have.

Suggestion

Have pairs of students read the dialogue together. Suggest that they switch roles so that each student has the chance to practice both parts. Move around the room to help with pronunciation.

C. Sit with a partner. Ask the questions and complete the times. (Answers will vary.)

		Me	My Partner
1.	What time do you get up?		
2.	What time do you eat breakfast?		
3.	What time do you leave the house?		
4.	What time do you work?		
5.	What time do you study?		
6.	What time do you go to bed?		

D. Complete about the chart. (Answers will vary.)

> **Present Tense**
> I get up at 7:00.
> He ge<u>ts</u> up at 7:00.

1. My partner gets up <u>at</u> __:__.

2. My partner eats breakfast _____ __:__.

3. My partner leaves the house _____ __:__.

4. My partner works <u>from</u> __:__ <u>to</u> __:__.

5. My partner studies _____ __:__ _____ __:__.

6. My partner goes to bed _____ __:__.

My Job

A. Read.

A: Where do you work?

B: I work at Photo-Mart.

A: What do you do?

B: I'm a photographer. I take pictures of children and families. I take passport photos, too.

A: Do you work full time or part time?

B: I work full time.

A: What's your schedule?

B: I work from Wednesday to Sunday, from 11:00 to 7:00. I have Monday and Tuesday off.

A: Do you like your job?

B: Yes, I do.

B. Listen and complete.

1. Marie works at ___Family Pharmacy___.
2. She's a ___pharmacist___.
3. She works **(full time)** / part time.
4. She works from ___Monday___ to ___Friday___.
5. She works from ___12___ : ___00___ to ___8___ : ___00___.
6. She **(likes)** / doesn't like her job.

7. Juan works at ___The Flower Basket___.
8. He's a ___florist___.
9. He works full time / **(part time)**.
10. He works from ___Wednesday___ to ___Saturday___.
11. He works from ___9___ : ___00___ to ___2___ : ___00___.
12. He **(likes)** / doesn't like his job.

C. Practice this conversation with a partner. (Answers will vary.)

A: Where do you work?

B: I work at _____.

A: What do you do?

B: I'm a _____.

A: Do you work full time or part time?

B: I work _____.

A: What's your schedule?

B: I work from _____ to _____, from ___:___ to ___:___.
I have _____ and _____ off.

A: Do you like your job?

B: _____

B. Listen and complete.
(CD2, Track 14)

Play the audio several times as students fill in the answers. Present the dialogue again so that students can check their answers.

C. Practice this conversation with a partner.

Have students fill in their own information. Then have them take turns interviewing several different partners.

Audio Script

B. Listen and complete.
(CD2, Track 14)
Picture 1
A: Where do you work?
B: I work at Family Pharmacy.
A: What do you do?
B: I'm a pharmacist. I fill prescriptions and talk to customers.
A: Do you work full time or part time?
B: Full time.
A: What's your schedule?
B: I work from Monday to Friday, from 12:00 to 8:00.
A: Do you like your job?
B: Yes, I do.

Picture 2
A: Where do you work?
B: I work at the Flower Basket.
A: What do you do?
B: I'm a florist. I sell flowers and plants.
A: Do you work full time or part time?
B: I work part time.
A: What's your schedule?
B: I work from Wednesday to Saturday, from 9:00 to 2:00.
A: Do you like your job?
B: Yes, I do.

☀ Sam's Day

A. Pronunciaton.

(CD2, Track 15)

Have students listen several times and then repeat the sounds and words.

Teacher Note

As you introduce the pronunciation of the -s endings, alternate between the two sounds, *ssss* and *zzzz*, and ask students to copy you. Have students place their fingers on their throats. Point out that the voice box vibrates when they are making the *zzzz* sound, but that it doesn't vibrate when they are making the *ssss* sound.

B. Listen and repeat.

(CD2, Track 16)

For each sentence, demonstrate how to link the /s/ or /z/ sound with the following vowel. Then have students practice it several times with you.

Practice these sentences with a partner.

Have students practice the sentences in Exercise B with a partner.

C. Complete the story.

Have students use the words in the box to complete the sentences. Then ask the students to read the story to a partner, remembering the *s* at the end of each of the verbs.

 Sam's Day

A. Pronunciation. Listen and repeat.

/s/	/z/	/əz/
get—gets	drive—drives	watch—watches
work—works	go—goes	punch—punches
take—takes	study—studies	

Pronounce these words.

1. eats
2. lives
3. prepares
4. sells
5. brushes
6. cuts

B. Listen and repeat. Link the final *s* with the following vowel.

1. Sam lives_alone.
2. He gets_up at 8:00 in the morning.
3. He takes_a shower.
4. He studies_English from 9:00 to 12:00.
5. He punches_in at 4:00.
6. He works_at Cosimo's five or six days a week.

Practice these sentences with a partner.

C. Complete the story. Then read the story to your partner.

Sam ___lives___ alone in a small apartment. He is busy all day. He ___gets___ up at 8:00 in the morning. He ___takes___ a shower; then he gets dressed. Sam doesn't eat breakfast. He drives to school and ___studies___ English from 9:00 to 12:00. He goes home and ___eats___ lunch at 1:00. Sam leaves for work at 3:30, and he punches in at 4:00. Sam is a cook at the Parkside Mall. He ___works___ at Cosimo's five or six days a week. He ___prepares___ pizza and Italian food. He ___works___ from 4:00 to 11:00. He takes two breaks. Sam ___eats___ dinner at the restaurant at 9:00. Sam goes home at 11:30. He ___watches___ TV for an hour; then he ___goes___ to bed at 1:00.

prepares
goes
studies
✓lives
takes
✓gets
works
eats
works
watches
eats

Working Together

A. Laura's Day. Laura has a busy day. She works full time, and she goes to school. Sit with a partner. Put her schedule in order from 1 to 10. (Answers may vary.)

B. Write a story about Laura's day. (Answers will vary.)

Laura gets up at . . .

_____
_____
_____
_____
_____
_____
_____
_____

☀Working Together

A. Laura's Day.

• Discuss the pictures with the whole class. Answer any questions students may have.

• Explain that the pictures are not in the correct order, and that students can put them in any order that makes sense to them. For example, one group might say she goes to school in the morning and another group might say she does this at night.

• Have pairs number the pictures in order and explain their choices to another pair of students.

B. Write a story about Laura's day.

Have students write their stories with a partner or in groups of three.

Suggestion

Ask several pairs or groups to write their stories on the board. Review the stories on the board and ask the rest of the class to correct the errors.

The Big Picture: The CD Den

A. Listen. (CD2, Track 17)

- Invite students to talk about the picture. Ask:

  What kind of store is this?
  What is this person looking at?
  Who is this?
  What is the woman buying?

- Say the words in the box at the top of the page and ask students to repeat. Define words as necessary. For example: *A "supervisor" is a person who checks on the work of employees.*
- Tell students to just listen as you play the audio.

B. Check *Yes* or *No*.

Have students read the ten sentences. Then play the audio for Exercise A again. This time, have students check the *yes* or *no* box after each sentence. Play the audio as many times as students require. If necessary, pause the tape. Play the audio once more so that students can check their answers.

The Big Picture: The CD Den

employer: owner, company
boss: supervisor, manager
employee: worker

A. Listen.

B. Check (✓) *Yes* or *No*.

	Yes	No
1. Eric is the manager of the CD Den.	☑	☐
2. He works part time.	☐	☑
3. This store sells CDs and tapes.	☑	☐
4. The store opens at 12:00.	☐	☑
5. Mei-Lin is the assistant manager.	☑	☐
6. All the other employees are full time.	☐	☑
7. Most employees are students.	☑	☐
8. The store is busy on the weekends.	☑	☐
9. There is a security guard during the week.	☐	☑
10. The security guard wears a uniform.	☐	☑

Audio Script

The Big Picture: The CD Den

A. Listen. (CD2, Track 17)

My name is Eric. I'm the manager of the CD Den in the Summit Mall. We sell CDs and tapes of all kinds of music—rock, pop, jazz, classical. We have the music you want. In our store, there is always music playing.

The CD Den is open seven days a week from 10 A.M. to 9 P.M. I work full time, about 50 hours a week. My assistant manager, Mei-Lin, also works full time. All the other employees are part time. We have 10 part-time workers. Most of them are high school and college students. They work about 15 to 20 hours a week, after school and on the weekends. Those are our busiest times. On the weekends, we have a security guard, too. She is young, and she doesn't wear a uniform. She looks like a customer. She walks around the store and watches people.

C. Circle the correct verb.

Present Tense
I work at the mall.
She works at the mall.
He works at the mall.

1. I **work** / works full time.
2. Mei-Lin **work** / **works** full time.
3. The store **open** / **opens** at 10:00.
4. The store **have** / **has** two managers.
5. The security guard **walk** / **walks** around the store.
6. Many employees **work** / **works** part time.

D. Listen. Write the day and times.

Sunday	Monday	Tuesday	Wednesday	Thursday	Friday	Saturday

1. James can work on _____Monday_____ from _5_:_00_ to _9_:_00_.
2. Gloria can work on _____Tuesday_____ from _3_:_00_ to _7_:_00_.
3. Makiko can work on _____Saturday_____ from _10_:_00_ to _5_:_00_.
4. Andre can work on _____Sunday_____ from _12_:_00_ to _6_:_00_.
5. Lucy can work on _____Friday_____ from _5_:_00_ to _10_:_00_.

Looking at Forms: A Job Application

A. You are applying for a job at the CD Den. Complete this application.
(Answers will vary.)

THE CD DEN

Name: _____
    First   Last   Middle Initial

Address: _____
              Street

_____
    City   State   Zip Code

Telephone Number: (_____)_____

Social Security Number: _____

I can work _____ hours a week.

I can work (circle): Sunday Monday Tuesday Wednesday Thursday Friday Saturday

I can work from ____ : ____ to ____ : ____.

C. Circle the correct verb.

Have students complete the exercise on their own. As you review the answers, ask students to tell why they chose each answer.

Teacher Note

Item 4 introduces *have* and *has* for the first time. Briefly point out that *has* works like the other present tense verbs that end in -*s*. (*Have* and *has* are covered in more detail in Unit 14.)

D. Listen. (CD2, Track 18)

Play the audio as many times as necessary for students to fill in and check their answers.

Looking at Forms: A Job Application

A. Complete this application.

Ask students to use true information about themselves as they fill out the application.

Audio Script

D. Listen. Write the day and times.
(CD2, Track 18)

1. Eric: James, can you work Monday?
James: What time Monday?
Eric: From 5:00 to 9:00.
James: Sure. 5:00 to 9:00. That's OK.

2. Eric: Gloria, I need someone Tuesday, from 3:00 to 7:00. Can you work then?
Gloria: Tuesday. 3:00 to 7:00. No problem. I can work.

3. Eric: Makiko, I need another person Saturday. Can you work this Saturday from 10:00 to 5:00?
Makiko: Yes, I can work Saturday.

4. Eric: Andre, can you work Sunday from 10:00 to 6:00?
Andre: I can't start at 10:00. I can start at 12:00.
Eric: OK. Sunday, from 12:00 to 6:00. That's good.

5. Eric: Lucy, can you work Friday this week? I need you from 5:00 to 10:00.
Lucy: That's good for me. I can work Friday.

Reading: Working at the Mall

A. Before You Read.

• Ask general questions about malls, such as:

What is a mall?
Is there a mall near here?
Do you ever shop there?

• Talk about the people in the pictures. Ask:

Where are they?
What are they doing?

• Ask students to read the stories individually. Answer any questions they may have. Then read the stories to the class.

B. Check.

Read through the seven questions with students. Ask students to scan the two stories to find the answers to the questions.

Teacher Note

Remind students how to scan:
• Choose a word or phrase to look for.
• Read quickly only looking for that word or phrase.
• Read that part of the story carefully to find the answer you are looking for.

Reading: Working at the Mall

A. Before You Read. Do you know anyone who works at a mall? What do they do?

Richard is a hairstylist. He works from Tuesday to Saturday. He works 40 hours a week, from 10:00 to 6:00. He is very busy on Friday and Saturday because everyone wants to look good for the weekend. Most of Richard's customers are his "regulars"; they come in once a week for a wash and a blow-dry. Richard enjoys talking with them. Richard stands all day, and he's tired at the end of the day. He takes a long, hot bath when he gets home.

Andre is a cashier at the CD Den. He's a college student, and he goes to school every day. He works two evenings a week and all day Saturday and Sunday. People buy CDs and tapes, and Andre takes their money. Some people pay with cash; other people use credit cards. Andre gives them change and their receipts. Andre likes his job. He can listen to music all day.

B. Check (✓).

	Richard	Andre
1. He works full time.	☑	☐
2. He works part time.	☐	☑
3. He works in the evening.	☐	☑
4. He works all weekend.	☐	☑
5. He goes to school.	☐	☑
6. He stands all day.	☑	☐
7. He has regular customers.	☑	☐

Writing Our Stories:
My Job

A. Read.

I am a security guard. I work at the Summit Mall in Westbrook. I work full time. I work 40 hours a week, from Tuesday to Saturday. My hours are from 10:00 to 6:00. I walk up and down the mall all day. I answer questions and give directions. I carry a cell phone. In an emergency, I call the police or the ambulance.

B. Write about your job. (Answers will vary.)

I am a _____. I work at _____.
           job   company

It's in _____, on _____.
       city   street

I work _____. I work _____ hours a week.
      full time / part time

_____

_____

_____

_____

Writing Note

The days of the week begin with capital letters: Monday, Tuesday, Wednesday, Thursday, Friday, Saturday, Sunday

The names of companies begin with capital letters: Clothes Closet, Hair Plus, MacDougal's

Writing Our Stories:
My Job

A. Read.

Read the story aloud or ask a student to. Clarify vocabulary as necessary through demonstrations or simple definitions.

B. Write about your job.

Explain to students that they can use the story in Exercise A as a guide for this writing activity. Show how they can adapt sentences to fit their own needs. For example, *I walk up and down the mall all day* can become *I prepare food all day.*

Suggestion

Invite students to share their stories in groups. Encourage them to show their employee ID cards or other work-related objects, such as badges or beepers.

Practicing on Your Own

A. What time is it?

Ask students to write the answers using numbers.

B. Write the answer.

Review the meaning of the sentences in the box before having students complete the activity.

C. Complete with *at* or *from . . . to.*

Have students do the activity individually.

Suggestion

Students who want further practice can choose a friend or family member to write about. Have these students use Exercise C as a model to describe their friend or family member's work and school life.

Practicing on Your Own

A. What time is it?

It's ___3:00___ .   It's ___5:30___ .   It's ___8:20___ .   It's ___3:10___ .

B. Write the answer.

> No, she works part time.   ✓She's a manicurist.
> She works four days a week.   She works from 10:00 to 6:00.
> Yes, she does.   She works at Hair Plus.
> She was a hairstylist.

1. What does Sheri do?   She's a manicurist.
2. Where does she work?   She works at Hair Plus.
3. How many days does she work?   She works four days a week.
4. Does she work full time?   No, she works part time.
5. What hours does she work?   She works from 10:00 to 6:00.
6. Does she like her job?   Yes, she does.
7. What was her job in her country? She was a hairstylist.

C. Complete with *at* or *from . . . to.*

> at 10:00
> from 10:00 to 6:00

Eric gets up ___at___ 8:00. He takes a shower and has a small breakfast, and then he drives to work. Eric arrives at work ___at___ 9:45. He works ___from___ 10:00 ___to___ 6:00 six days a week. Two nights a week, Eric goes to school ___from___ 7:00 ___to___ 10:00. He's studying for a degree in business. He studies or watches TV ___from___ 10:00 ___to___ 12:00. He goes to bed ___at___ 12:30.

Learning Tip

It's important to continue reading in my native language.
I read the newspaper in my language every day.

☐ I like this idea.
☐ I don't like this idea.
☐ I'm going to do this.
(Answers will vary.)

Grammar Summary

1. Present tense		
I work at Hair Plus.		
He work**s** at Hair Plus.		
She work**s** at Hair Plus.		
2. Yes/No questions		
Does he **work** at Hair Plus?	Yes, he **does.**	No, he **doesn't.**
Do you **work** at Hair Plus?	Yes, I **do.**	No, I **don't.**
3. Wh- questions		
Where does he work?	He works at Cosimo's.	
What does he do?	He's a waiter.	
What does he do there?	He takes people's orders.	
What hours does he work?	He works from 5:00 to 10:00.	
4. Prepositions: at, from . . . to		
She gets up **at** 7:00.		
She goes to school **from** 8:00 **to** 3:00.		

☀ Learning Tip

Discuss the Learning Tip with students. Ask:

Who reads the newspaper in their native language every day?
Who reads a native language newspaper every week?
What newspaper do you read?

Suggestion

Invite students to bring in a copy of a newspaper written in their native language to show their classmates. Students are usually very interested in seeing the letters and writing symbols of other languages.

Grammar Summary

• Review the summary with the class. Invite students to say other statements, questions, answers, and sentences with prepositions that might appear in each of the four sections of the summary.
• See the Grammar Summary Expansion on page 237 for a more complete explanation of these grammar points.

Unit 10
Clothing and Weather

Discuss the person next to the unit number. Ask:

• *Who is standing next to the number 10?* (A man)
• *What is he doing?* (He's running through the rain carrying an umbrella.)

Dictionary: Clothing and Colors

A. Listen and repeat.
(CD2, Track 19)

• For now, focus only on the *Clothing* section on pages 136 and 137. Invite students to comment on the pictures.
• Play the audio or read the words on the page. Have students point to each word as they hear it. Do the activity again, this time pausing for students to repeat each word.

10 Clothing and Weather

Dictionary: Clothing and Colors

A. Listen and repeat.

Clothing

shirt   pants   jeans   shorts

jacket   belt   suit   sweater

dress   skirt   blouse   underpants   bra

tie   briefs   T-shirt   socks   bathing suit

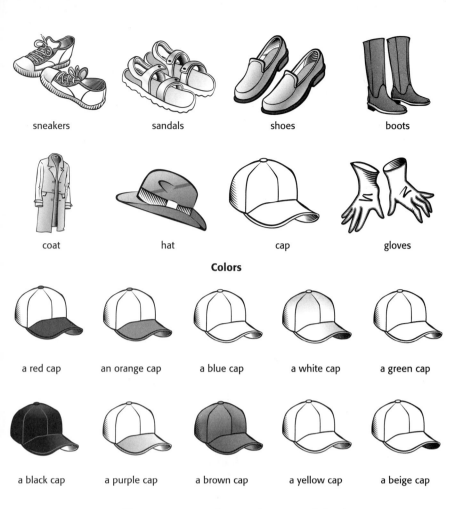

sneakers   sandals   shoes   boots

coat   hat   cap   gloves

Colors

a red cap   an orange cap   a blue cap   a white cap   a green cap

a black cap   a purple cap   a brown cap   a yellow cap   a beige cap

B. Complete. (Answers may vary. Suggested responses below.)

Clothes for hot weather		**Clothes for cold weather**	
shorts	T-shirt	jacket	hat
bathing suit	sandals	coat	sweater
skirt	cap	gloves	boots

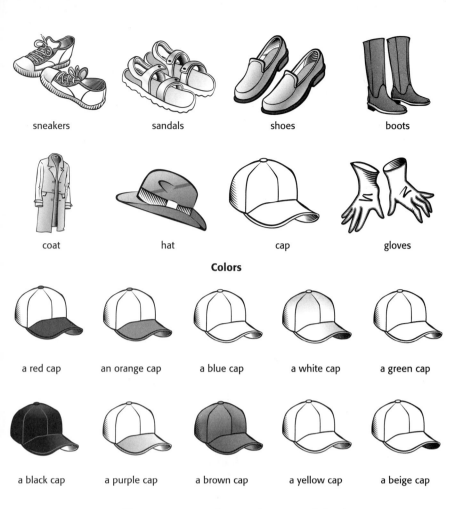

Teacher's Guide right column:

🔊 **A. Listen and repeat.**
(CD2, Track 19 *continued*)

• Ask students to look at the *Colors* section in the middle of page 137.
• Play the audio or read the words as you point to the pictures. Have students listen and repeat. Play the audio again if necessary.

Suggestion

Point to different articles of clothing on pages 136 and 137 and have students say the color and the name of the item. For example: *brown shoes.*

B. Complete.

Have students complete the sentences and check their answers with a partner.

Suggestion

Ask students to categorize the words on pages 136 and 137 in other ways. For example, students might categorize the words under the groupings *Clothes for men* and *Clothes for women.*

☀Active Grammar:
Present Continuous

A. Cross out the word that doesn't belong.

• Read the instructions aloud and review the first example with students. Point out that the first three items are similar; they are all different types of pants. The fourth item is different; it's a type of shirt.

• Have students finish the exercise with a partner.

B. Look around your classroom.

Do this activity with the whole class. Call on different students to ask and answer the questions. You can elicit more than one answer to each question. For example:

T: *Who is wearing sneakers?*
S1: *Tina is.*
S2: *Gino is.*

👥 C. Discuss with a partner.

Have a pair of students read the sample dialogue. Model one or two exchanges with a student. Then have pairs continue on their own.

Suggestion

Prompt students to talk about what their classmates are wearing.

Active Grammar: Present Continuous

A. Cross out the word that doesn't belong.

1. pants, jeans, shorts, ~~T-shirt~~   5. blouse, ~~tie~~, skirt, dress
2. shirt, blouse, T-shirt, ~~sandals~~   6. ~~sweater~~, briefs, underpants, bra
3. sneakers, sandals, ~~hat~~, shoes   7. jacket, sweater, coat, ~~shorts~~
4. coat, hat, gloves, ~~bathing suit~~

B. Look around your classroom. Who is wearing _____?
(Answers will vary.)

> Marek is.
> No one is.

1. Who is wearing sneakers?
2. Who is wearing a sweater?   5. Who is wearing a tie?
3. Who is wearing a dress?   6. Who is wearing sandals?
4. Who is wearing a white shirt?   7. Who is wearing black pants?

👥 C. Discuss with a partner.

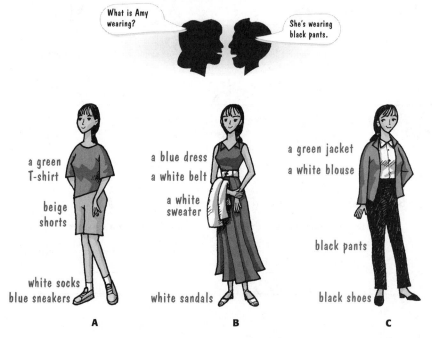

What is Amy wearing?

She's wearing black pants.

a green T-shirt

beige shorts

white socks
blue sneakers

A

a blue dress
a white belt

a white sweater

white sandals

B

a green jacket
a white blouse

black pants

black shoes

C

D. Listen. What is Amy wearing? Write the letter of the correct picture.

1. __B__   5. __A__
2. __A__   6. __C__
3. __C__   7. __A__
4. __B__   8. __C__

 E. Pronunciation. Listen for the stress.

1. Is Amy wearing white pants?   No, she's wearing black pants.
2. Is Amy wearing a blue jacket?   No, she's wearing a green jacket.
3. Is Amy wearing a red dress?   No, she's wearing a blue dress.

Mark the stress.

4. Is Amy wearing a blue belt?   No, she's wearing a white belt.
5. Is Amy wearing brown sandals?   No, she's wearing white sandals.
6. Is Amy wearing black shorts?   No, she's wearing beige shorts.
7. Is Amy wearing a purple shirt?   No, she's wearing a green shirt.
8. Is Amy wearing beige socks?   No, she's wearing white socks.

Practice these sentences with a partner.

F. Look at the pictures of Amy on page 138. Complete with a, an, or X.

1. Amy is going to work. She is wearing __X__ black pants and __a__ white blouse. She's wearing __a__ green jacket, too. Amy is wearing __X__ black shoes.

2. Amy is going to a party. She's wearing __a__ blue dress with __a__ white belt. Amy is wearing __X__ white sandals. She is taking __a__ white sweater to wear if she is cold.

3. Amy is at home. She's wearing comfortable clothing. Amy is wearing
   a green T-shirt. She's wearing beige shorts, too. Amy is wearing white socks and blue sneakers. (Suggested response. Answers may vary.)

D. Listen. (CD2, Track 20)

Explain that each sentence describes one of the three pictures of Amy on page 138. Then play the audio and have students mark their answers. Present the sentences again so that students can check their work.

E. Pronunciation. (CD2, Track 21)

• Explain that in English each sentence usually has one word that is stressed, and that this word is usually said louder than the others. Have students listen as you play the audio.
• Instruct students to mark the stressed word in sentences 4 through 8 as you play the audio again.

Practice these sentences with a partner.

Have students monitor their partners' use of stress.

F. Look at the pictures of Amy on page 138.

Explain that the X means there is no need for the word *a* or *an*.

Audio Script

D. Listen. What is Amy wearing? Write the letter of the correct picture.

(CD2, Track 20)

1. She's wearing a blue dress.
2. She's wearing beige shorts.
3. She's wearing black pants.
4. She's wearing a big white belt.
5. She's wearing a green shirt.
6. She's wearing a white blouse.
7. She's wearing sneakers.
8. She's wearing a green jacket.
9. She's wearing white sandals.
10. She's carrying a white sweater.

☀ The Clothing Store

A. Complete.

- Model the use of *this* with singular items and *these* with plurals by naming items on pages 136–137. For example: *This is a dress. These are pants.*
- Review the sample questions and answers in this exercise. Complete the exercise orally with the whole class. Then have students write in the correct words individually.

B. Pair practice.

- Ask two students to read the dialogue. Point out the empty tags where students should write their answers.
- Tell students they can choose any price they wish for each item. Then have different students ask and answer the questions as the rest of the class listens.
- Have pairs of students take turns asking the prices of items and marking the answers their partner gives them on the appropriate tags. Students can then check each other's answers.

The Clothing Store

A. Complete.

1. How much __is__ __this__ hat? __It's__ $15.
2. How much __are__ __these__ sandals? __They're__ $20.
3. How much __is__ __this__ skirt? __It's__ $28.
4. How much __are__ __these__ gloves? __They're__ $17.
5. How much __are__ __these__ briefs? __They're__ $7.
6. How much __is__ __this__ sweater? __It's__ $30.
7. How much __is__ __this__ tie? __It's__ $17.
8. How much __are__ __these__ shorts? __They're__ $22.

B. Pair practice. Ask and answer questions about the price of each item. Put a price on the empty tags. (Answers will vary.)

C. Read and practice.

Clerk: Hello. Can I help you?

Customer: Yes, I'm looking for a shirt.

Clerk: What size?

Customer: Medium.

Clerk: Our shirts are here.

Customer: I like this shirt.

Clerk: Try it on. The mirror is over there.

Customer: I like it. How much is it?

Clerk: It's $50. But today it's on sale for $35.

Customer: Great. I'll take it.

👥 **D. Write a conversation between a clerk and a customer.** (Answers will vary.)

> **Be careful!** Look at the changes for singular and plural in the conversation.

Clerk: Hello. _____.

Customer: Yes, I'm looking for _____.

Clerk: What size?

Customer: _____.

Clerk: Our _____ are here.

Customer: I like **this / these** _____.

Clerk: Try **it / them** on. The mirror is over there.

Customer: I like **it / them**. How much _____?

Clerk: _____ $_____, but today _____ on sale for $_____.

Customer: Great. I'll take **it / them**.

C. Read and practice.

- Read the dialogue to the class. Answer any questions students may have.
- Have students practice the dialogue in pairs.

👥 D. Write a conversation between a clerk and a customer.

- Ask students to think of an item of clothing they want to buy. They can look at the items on pages 136–137 for ideas. Then have students write complete conversations. Remind them to use *they* and *them* if they are talking about a plural noun such as *pants* or *socks*.
- Have students practice their conversations with partners. Invite some pairs to perform their conversations for the class.

The Weather:
Dictionary

 A. Listen and repeat.
(CD2, Track 22)

Have students point at the
pictures as you play the
audio or read the words.
Then play the audio again,
this time pausing after each
word or phrase and having
students repeat.

Suggestion

Ask students what season it is. Then
have them look out the window and
make as many true statements about
the weather as they can.

 **A. Listen and repeat.**

Weather

It's sunny.   It's cloudy.   It's windy.

It's raining.   It's snowing.   It's foggy.

It's hot.   It's warm.   It's cool.   It's cold.

Seasons

spring   summer   fall   winter

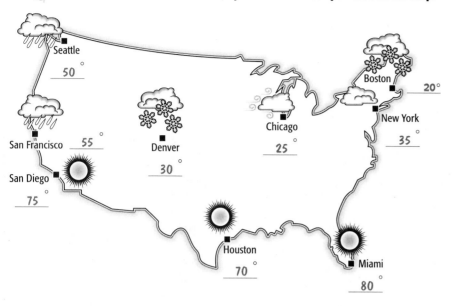

B. Listen to the weather. Find the city and write the temperature on the map.

Seattle 50°

San Francisco 55°

San Diego 75°

Denver 30°

Chicago 25°

Houston 70°

Boston 20°

New York 35°

Miami 80°

C. **Write the weather conditions from the map above.**

1. It's ___snowing and cold___ in Boston.
2. It's ___cloudy and cold___ in New York.
3. It's ___hot___ in Miami.
4. It's ___warm___ in Houston.
5. It's ___warm___ in San Diego.
6. It's ___raining and cool___ in San Francisco.
7. It's ___raining___ in Seattle.
8. It's ___snowing___ in Denver.
9. It's ___cloudy, cold, and windy___ in Chicago.

cold
cloudy
raining
windy
snowing
hot
warm
cool
cold

B. Listen to the weather.
(CD2, Track 23)

• Point to various weather symbols on the map and ask students to say what each symbol means.
• Play the audio. Then play it again, pausing after each sentence. Have students point to places and symbols mentioned in each sentence.
• Present the weather report a third time. This time have students fill in the temperatures on the map.

C. Write the weather conditions from the map above.

Point out the words in the box and tell students they can use the same word more than once. Have students finish the exercise individually and check their answers with a partner.

Audio Script

B. Listen to the weather. Find the city and write the temperature on the map.
(CD2, Track 23)

Look at the map of the United States. Find Boston. It's cold in Boston today. It's snowing. The temperature is 20 degrees.
Find New York. It's cloudy and cold in New York today. The temperature is 35 degrees.
Find Miami. It's sunny and hot in Miami. The temperature is 80 degrees.
Find Houston. It's sunny and warm in Houston today. The temperature is 70 degrees.
Find San Diego. The weather is beautiful in San Diego all year. It's sunny and 75 degrees.

Find San Francisco. It's raining today in San Francisco. It's cool. The temperature is 55 degrees.
Find Seattle. It's raining in Seattle, too. It's 50 degrees in Seattle. You will need your umbrella and raincoat.
Find Denver. It's snowing in Denver today. It's 30 degrees in Denver.
Find Chicago. It's cloudy and cold in Chicago today. It's very windy. The temperature is 25 degrees.

☀ Working Together

A. Sit in a group.

Have students discuss the pictures in groups of four or five. Suggest that they look at the vocabulary on pages 136, 137, and 142 for help with clothing and weather vocabulary.

Suggestion

• Have each group choose a leader. The leader reads the questions to the group. He or she also summarizes the answers as they finish discussing each question.
• Set a time limit of ten minutes for the discussion. At the end of that time, ask different group leaders to report their group's answers to one of the questions.

Suggestion

Have students work in small groups to choose one of the four pictures and write a short paragraph about it. Walk around the room providing any new vocabulary words as needed.

Working Together

A. Sit in a group. Discuss these pictures. (Answers may vary.)

1. Where are these people?
2. What are they doing?
3. What season is it? What's the weather?
4. What is each person wearing?

B. What are they wearing? Describe two classmates. Describe your teacher. What are they wearing? *(Answers will vary.)*

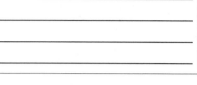

Juan is wearing blue jeans and a black T-shirt.
He's wearing sneakers and socks. On his desk,
Juan has a white Yankee baseball cap.

_____

_____
_____
_____
_____

_____
_____
_____
_____

 C. Get dressed! Dress Roberto. Don't show your picture to your partner. Describe Roberto's clothing. Can your partner draw him? *(Answers will vary.)*

Put some clothes on Roberto!
Describe your picture to your partner.

Listen to your partner.
Draw Roberto's clothes.

B. What are they wearing?

Discuss the directions and read the sample description aloud. Then have students complete the activity on their own.

Suggestion

You can pair more fluent students with less fluent students to work on this activity together. The less fluent students benefit from the guidance they receive. The more fluent students get a valuable review as well as extra practice with spoken and written English.

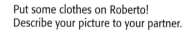 **C. Get dressed!**

- Read the instructions aloud. Make sure students understand that they should draw clothes on the left-hand picture of Roberto. Walk around the room encouraging students as they draw the clothing.
- Ask students to sit with a partner. Tell them not to look at their partner's drawing. Student 1 slowly describes the clothes he drew on the left-hand picture. Student 2 listens carefully and draws these articles of clothing on the man in the right-hand picture. Then they switch roles. When both students finish, have each student compare their right-hand drawing to their partner's original left-hand drawing.

The Big Picture: The Clothing Store

The Clothing Store

A. Listen. (CD2, Track 24)

• Encourage students to comment on the picture. Ask:

Who are these people?
Where are they?
What are they doing?
What season is it?
What is she trying on?
What are they saying to each other?

• Play the audio and have students circle the items Monica is going to buy. Present the story at least once more so that students can check their answers.

B. Circle *Yes* or *No.*

• Review the eight statements with students. If there are any statements the students don't understand, explain or rephrase them in simple English.

• Point out sentence 5 and ask students what they think *spend* means. (It means *pay money* in this case.)

• Ask students to answer the questions without listening to the audio again.

A. Listen. Circle the clothes Monica is going to buy.

coat	dress	gloves	skirt
sneakers	sweater	hat	socks

(circled: coat, gloves, sweater, hat)

B. Circle Yes or No.

1. Monica is in the clothing store.   **Yes**   No
2. Monica is shopping alone.   Yes   **No**
3. It's cold now.   **Yes**   No
4. Monica likes the coat she is trying on.   Yes   **No**
5. Monica is going to spend a lot of money today.   **Yes**   No
6. Monica needs winter clothes.   **Yes**   No
7. Monica was in the United States last winter.   Yes   **No**
8. It's hot all year in Boston.   Yes   **No**

146   UNIT 10

Audio Script

The Big Picture: The Clothing Store

A. Listen. Circle the clothes Monica is going to buy. (CD2, Track 24)

Monica is from Cuba. Cuba is an island in the Caribbean, and it's hot there all year. Monica is living in Boston. Monica came to the United States in May. She liked the weather in Boston in May, June, July, and August. It was sunny and hot. September was warm, and Monica was comfortable.

But now it is December. Monica can't believe the weather! It's very cold. It's 30 degrees. Her friends tell her, "This isn't cold yet! In January, it's going to be colder. And it's going to snow soon." Monica is at the clothing store with her sister. She needs warm clothes. She needs a coat. She needs a hat and gloves. She is also going to buy a sweater. Monica is standing in front of the mirror. She's trying on coats. She isn't comfortable. She's saying, "This coat feels so heavy."

C. Complete.

1. Monica is from ___Cuba___.
2. She came to the United States in ___May___.
3. She lives in ___Boston___.
4. In Boston, it is hot in the ___summer___.
5. In Boston, it is cold in the ___winter___.
6. In January, it is going to ___snow___.
7. In Cuba, the weather is ___hot___.
8. Right now, Monica is in a ___clothing store___.
9. The ___temperature___ is 30°.
10. It's very ___cold___ outside now.

Boston
winter
cold
snow
clothing store
temperature
May
summer
✓Cuba
hot

D. Check the tense.

	Past	Present	Future
1. Monica is trying on coats.	☐	☑	☐
2. Monica lives in Boston.	☐	☑	☐
3. Monica lived in Cuba last year.	☑	☐	☐
4. It's going to snow in January.	☐	☐	☑
5. Monica is going to buy a sweater.	☐	☐	☑
6. Monica came to the United States last May.	☑	☐	☐
7. It's 30 degrees outside.	☐	☑	☐
8. It was sunny and hot in the summer.	☑	☐	☐
9. Monica is going to buy a hat.	☐	☐	☑
10. Monica needs warm clothes.	☐	☑	☐

E. In your notebook, write about Monica at the clothing store. (Answers will vary.)

C. Complete.

Have students fill in the answers individually and check them with a partner.

D. Check the tense.

- Ask students to look at Exercises B and C. Ask: *What sentences show past events? What sentences show future events?* Explain: *The phrase "going to" sometimes describes future events.*
- Have students complete the activity in pairs.

Suggestion

Review the answers by calling on different students to read aloud a sentence and give the correct answer.

E. In your notebook, write about Monica in the clothing store.

Students can use the sentences in Exercises B, C, and D for ideas.

Suggestion

To help students organize their ideas in a logical sequence, suggest that they write several sentences on scrap paper, and then place the ideas in an order that makes sense to them. The simplest order may be time order: *What happened first? What happened next? What happened at the end?*

☀Reading: Climate Zones

A. Before You Read.

Ask students to locate where they live on the map. Say the words in bold type in the article and ask students to repeat. Then have them read the article straight through without stopping.

Suggestion

Have students use the U.S. map on page 246 to help pinpoint the place where they live.

B. Complete.

Have students answer the questions individually. Review the answers with the whole class.

Suggestion

Invite students to point out any sentences in the reading they don't understand. Paraphrase these sentences in simple English.

Reading: Climate Zones

A. Before You Read. Look at the map. What zone do you live in?

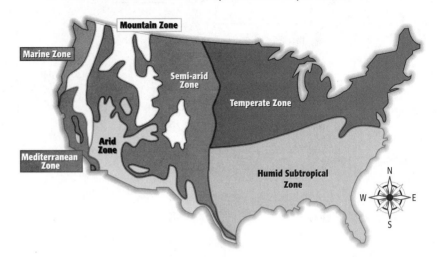

The United States is very large, so it has many kinds of weather. There are seven climate zones in the United States. The **temperate** zone is in the north. There are four seasons. The summers are warm and humid, and the winters are cold, with four or five snowstorms. The **humid subtropical** zone has long, hot summers. The winters are short and can have a lot of rain. These areas can receive 60" of rain a year. The **mountain** zone has a long, cold winter with heavy snow. Some areas receive over 200" of snow a year. A large part of the Southwest is **arid** or **semi-arid**. These areas are very dry. There are many large deserts. The West Coast is in two climate zones. In the **marine** zone, there are long, cool summers and mild winters. There is often fog and light rain. In the **Mediterranean** area in the south, the summers are long and dry. The winters are rainy and mild.

B. Complete.

1. The ___Mediterranean___ zone has mild winters with a lot of rain.
2. The ___mountain___ zone has long, cold winters with heavy snow.
3. The ___marine___ zone has fog and light rain all year.
4. The ___arid___ zone has very dry weather all year.
5. The ___humid subtropical___ zone has long, hot summers.
6. I live in the (Answers will vary.) zone. The weather is _____.

Writing Our Stories:
Weather

A. Read.

San Juan
PUERTO RICO

I live in Virginia. We have four seasons. The summer is long and hot, and the winter is mild. It doesn't snow very often. Right now, it's spring, my favorite season. The days are warm, and the nights are cool. I usually wear jeans and a shirt.

I am from Puerto Rico. The climate is hot and tropical. It is sunny and hot almost every day. The fall is hurricane season, and we sometimes have bad storms with heavy wind and rain. But most of the time, the weather is beautiful.

B. Complete these sentences. (Answers will vary.)

I live in _____. We have _____ seasons.

The weather is _____

_____.

Right now, it's _____.

I am from _____. We have _____ seasons.

The weather is _____

_____.

Writing Note
Names of states and countries begin with a capital letter.

C. In your notebook, write about the weather in your area. What is the weather in your country?
(Answers will vary.)

Writing Our Stories:
Weather

A. Read.

Have students read the story all the way through without stopping. Ask them to discuss any questions they have with a partner.

B. Complete these sentences.

Have students complete this exercise on their own and check their answers with a partner.

C. In your notebook, write about the weather in your area.

• Students can use the information from Exercise B to complete this activity.

• Explain to students that they should use the story in Exercise A as a model for their writing. Show students how they can adapt sentences to fit their own needs. For example, *The summer is long and hot, and the winter is mild* can become *The winter is long and cold, and the summer is short.*

Suggestion

Invite students to share their stories in groups.

☼Practicing on Your Own

A. Answer.

Have students write the answers on their own.

Suggestion

Check for correct answers by having pairs of students ask and answer the questions in class.

B. Answer.

Point out that questions 1–3 refer to Boston, 4–6 refer to Houston, and 7–9 refer to Seattle. Have students write short answers on their own.

Suggestion

Have students practice the questions and answers in pairs.

C. What is the weather in your area today?

Have students answer the question individually. Invite different students to read their answer to the class.

Practicing on Your Own

A. Answer. (Answers may vary. Suggested responses below.)

What is So Jung wearing?
1. She is wearing a gray cap.
2. She is wearing a black jacket and a white T-shirt.
3. She is wearing blue jeans.
4. She is wearing black sneakers.

What is Victor wearing?
1. He is wearing sunglasses.
2. He is wearing a black coat.
3. He is wearing black leather pants with a black belt.
4. He is wearing a gray shirt.

B. Answer.

		Yes, it is. No, it isn't.
1.	Is it raining in Boston?	No, it isn't.
2.	Is it snowing in Boston?	Yes, it is.
3.	Is it cold there?	Yes, it is.
4.	Is it hot in Houston?	Yes, it is.
5.	Is it sunny in Houston?	Yes, it is.
6.	Is it going to rain there?	No, it isn't.
7.	Is it cool in Seattle?	Yes, it is.
8.	Is it cloudy in Seattle?	Yes, it is.
9.	Is it going to rain there?	Yes, it is.

C. What is the weather in your area today?
(Answers will vary.)

Looking at Numbers

A. Figure it out!

1. Monica is buying a red coat for $75. Her hat is $15, and her gloves are $20. How much is she going to spend? **$110**

2. Monica is buying a hat for her sister. It's $17. Monica is giving the clerk $50. How much is her change? **$33**

3. Monica likes a blue sweater. It is $60, but it's on sale for 50% off. How much is the sweater? **$30**

4. Monica is trying on a red dress. It's $40. All the dresses in the store are 10% off today. How much is the dress? **$36**

5. Monica bought a lot of clothes. She has only $50 in her wallet. She likes some black boots. They are $90, but they're on sale today for half price. Can she buy the boots? **Yes**

Grammar Summary

1. Present continuous	
I **am wearing** a cap.	
He **is wearing** a sweater.	
She **is wearing** sneakers.	
2. *How much* questions	
How much is this shirt?	It's $34.
How much are these briefs?	They're $8.
3. Short questions and answers	
Is it cold in Alaska?	Yes, it **is.**
Is it cold in Arizona?	No, it **isn't.**

Looking at Numbers

A. Figure it out!

Read through the five questions with the class and answer any questions students may have.

Suggestion

Have students form groups and answer the questions together. Call on different groups to present and explain their answers to the class.

Grammar Summary

• Review the summary with the class. Invite students to say other statements, questions, and answers that might appear in each of the three sections of the summary.

• See the Grammar Summary Expansion on page 238 for a more complete explanation of these grammar points.

Unit 11
Food

Discuss the person next to the unit number. Ask:

• *Who is next to the number 11?* (A woman)
• *What is she doing?* (She's sitting on a stool and holding a plate and a mug.)

☀ Dictionary:

Breakfast, Lunch, Dinner, Beverages, Dessert, Fruit

A. Listen and repeat.
(CD1, Track 25)

• Ask students to look at the pictures as you play the audio or read the words for the *Breakfast* and *Lunch* sections on page 152.
• Say individual words and ask students to point to the corresponding picture.
• Have students sit in pairs and take turns saying words and pointing to the corresponding pictures.

11 Food

Dictionary: Breakfast, Lunch, Dinner, Beverages, Dessert, Fruit

A. Listen and repeat.

Breakfast

eggs   cereal   pancakes   bacon

toast   donut   bagel

Lunch

hamburger   french fries   salad   soup

turkey sandwich   tuna salad sandwich   lettuce   tomato   cucumber

Dinner

pasta   chicken   fish   steak

rice   pizza   potatoes

green beans   corn   beans

Beverages

a cup of coffee   a cup of tea   a soda   iced tea   juice   milk

Dessert

ice cream   cake   cookies   pie

Fruit

bananas   an apple   oranges   grapes   mangoes

Food   **153**

A. Listen and repeat.
(CD2, Track 25 *continued*)

• Ask students to look at the pictures as you play the audio or read the words for the *Dinner, Beverages, Dessert,* and *Fruit* sections on page 153.
• Say individual words and ask students to point to the corresponding picture.
• Have students sit in pairs and take turns saying words and pointing to the corresponding pictures.

Suggestion

Write the six categories on the board. Ask students to name other foods that could go in each column. Prompt suggestions with questions, such as: *What do you eat for breakfast? What other beverages do you like?* Write students' suggestions under the appropriate category.

Suggestion

Students can hold spelling quizzes on the words on pages 152 and 153. Have students form small groups. Assign one student in the group the role of "teacher." This student says ten words from pages 152 and 153, repeating them as often as necessary. The other students try to spell the words correctly.

Active Grammar: Present Tense

A. Complete.

Have students write their lists individually. Call on several students to read their lists to the class using the sentence starters *I like . . .* and *I don't like . . . .*

B. Listen. (CD2, Track 26)

• Discuss the photo. Ask:

Where is this man?
What is he doing?
What meal is he eating?
Do you eat breakfast?

• Explain that the audio will contain more words than are printed on the page. Make sure students understand that they don't have to understand all the words; they just need to understand enough to fill in the blanks.
• Point out the sample answers.
• Play the audio and have students just listen. Play the audio a second time and have students fill in their answers. Play it a third time so that students can check their work.

Active Grammar: Present Tense

A. Complete. What do you like to eat? Look at the dictionary. Write five foods that you like. Write five foods that you don't like. (Answers will vary.)

I like . . .

1. _____
2. _____
3. _____
4. _____
5. _____

I don't like . . .

6. _____
7. _____
8. _____
9. _____
10. _____

B. Listen. What does he eat?

Breakfast

Time: __7__ : __15__

He eats __a bagel__ and __fruit__.

He drinks __a cup of coffee__.

Lunch

Time: __1__ : __00__ to __2__ : __00__

He eats __a sandwich__ and __french fries__.

He drinks __a soda__.

For dessert, he has __some cookies__.

Dinner

Time: __7__ : __00__

He eats __chicken__ and __green beans and potato.__

He drinks __water__.

Audio Script

B. Listen. What does he eat? (CD2, Track 26)

Hi, my name is Mike. I eat three meals a day. In the morning, I am always in a hurry, so I eat a small breakfast at 7:15. I eat a bagel and a piece of fruit. I always have a cup of coffee. Then I go to work. I eat lunch at 1:00. I have an hour for lunch. I like to have a sandwich, french fries, and a soda. Sometimes I buy some cookies for dessert. I eat dinner at home at 7:00. I like to cook, so I have a nice dinner. I have chicken, green beans, and a potato. I drink water. I don't have any dessert.

C. Complete. What do you eat for breakfast? (Answers will vary.)

1. What time do you eat breakfast?

    I eat breakfast at _____ : _____ .

2. What do you eat for breakfast?

    I eat _____

    _____ .

3. What time do you eat lunch?

    I eat lunch at _____ : _____ .

4. What do you eat for lunch?

    I eat _____ .

5. What time do you eat dinner?

    I eat dinner at _____ : _____ .

6. What do you eat for dinner?

    I eat _____ .

Culture Note
Americans usually eat three meals a day. The biggest meal is dinner.

D. The typical food of my country. Make a list of the typical foods in your country. Compare with a partner. (Answers will vary.)

Breakfast	Lunch	Dinner
_____	_____	_____
_____	_____	_____
_____	_____	_____

Dessert	Fruit	Beverages
_____	_____	_____
_____	_____	_____
_____	_____	_____

C. Complete.

Have students complete the activity independently. Invite volunteers to write their answers on the board.

D. The typical food of my country.

Have students complete the activity individually and then discuss their lists with a partner.

Suggestion

As a follow-up, you can have students from the same country or geographical area sit together and share their lists. Then they can tell the rest of the class about typical foods from their part of the world. Encourage students to draw pictures on the board to show what the foods look like.

E. Complete with *always, sometimes,* or *never*.

Review the meaning of the words *always, sometimes,* and *never.* Then have students complete the sentences on their own. Have several different students read their answers to the class.

Suggestion

Make signs that say:

- *I always . . .*
- *I sometimes . . .*
- *I never . . .*

Place the signs in different parts of the room. Then provide a sentence ending from Exercise E, such as *eat breakfast.* Ask students to stand in front of the sign that is true for them. Ask a student in each group to say what is true for their group in a complete sentence. For example, *We always eat breakfast.* Repeat the activity with other items from Exercise E.

F. Answer.

Ask several different students to answer each question. Write any new words on the board. Say the words and have students repeat.

G. Complete and compare your answers with a partner.

Have students complete the activity on their own, then discuss their answers with a partner.

E. Complete with *always, sometimes,* or *never*. (Answers will vary.)

1. I _____ eat breakfast.
2. I _____ drink juice at breakfast.
3. I _____ drink coffee in the morning.
4. I _____ eat lunch.
5. I _____ eat dinner with my family.
6. I _____ drink coffee at night.
7. I _____ prepare my own meals.
8. I _____ eat at restaurants.
9. I _____ eat fast food.

> Always = 100%
> Sometimes = 50%
> Never = 0%

F. Answer. (Answers will vary.)

1. Do you eat fast food?
2. Do you like fast food?
3. Give an example of a fast-food restaurant.
4. Is fast food good for your health?
5. What kind of food do children like?
6. Which do you like more, fast food or food cooked at home?

> **Culture Note**
> Fast food is food that is prepared quickly. Hamburgers and hot dogs are two fast foods.

G. Complete and compare your answers with a partner. (Answers will vary.)

1. My favorite food is _____
2. My favorite drink is _____
3. My favorite restaurant is _____
4. My favorite fast-food restaurant is _____
5. My favorite dessert is _____

Ordering Lunch

A. Read the menu.

LUNCH MENU

SANDWICHES		SOUPS	
Tuna salad sandwich	$5.25	Vegetable Soup	$2.00
Turkey sandwich	$5.25	Soup of the day	$2.50
Roast beef sandwich	$5.75		
Hamburger	$4.00	**BEVERAGES**	
Cheeseburger	$4.50	Coffee, tea	$ .75
Hot dog	$2.25	Iced tea	$1.00
French fries	$1.25	Soda	$ .75
		Milkshake	$2.50
SALADS			
Small green salad	$2.75	**DESSERTS**	
Large green salad	$4.00	Ice cream	$1.50
Chef's salad	$6.50	Pie	$2.50

B. What'll you have? Listen and write the order.

Woman: I'll have _a large green salad, the soup of the day, and water._

Man: I'll have _a cheeseburger and iced tea._

C. Read and practice.

Waiter: What'll you have today?

Customer: I'll have a turkey sandwich on whole wheat toast.

Waiter: Lettuce and tomato?

Customer: Lettuce, but no tomato.

Waiter: Anything to drink?

Customer: I'll have iced tea, please.

> Bread
> white
> whole wheat
> rye
> a roll

Food **157**

☀ Ordering Lunch

A. Read the menu.

Have different students read parts of the menu aloud. Correct pronunciation of the food items and any incorrect reading of dollars and cents prices. Discuss new words and phrases such as *milkshake* and *soup of the day*.

Suggestion

You might ask students to take turns telling about each food item on the food menu in a complete sentence. For example:

• *The tuna salad sandwich is five dollars and twenty-five cents.*
• *The french fries are a dollar twenty-five.*

B. What'll you have?
(CD2, Track 27)

Have students listen and write in the food orders. Explain that they don't need to write every word they hear. To check the answers, have different students write the orders on the board.

C. Read and practice.

Have students repeat each line. Then have them practice the conversation in pairs. Call on some pairs to present the conversation to the class.

Audio Script

B. What'll you have? Listen and write the order. (CD2, Track 27)

Waiter: May I take your order?

Woman: Yes, I'll have a large green salad. What's the soup of the day?

Waiter: Black bean.

Woman: I'll have the soup, too.

Waiter: Anything to drink?

Woman: Just water, please.

Waiter: And you, sir, what'll you have?

Man: I'll have a cheeseburger.

Waiter: How do you want your cheeseburger cooked?

Man: Medium, please.

Waiter: Anything to drink?

Man: I'll have iced tea.

☀ Pronunciation: 'll

🔊 A. Pronunciation.
(CD2, Track 28)

Play the audio several times. The first time have students just listen. The second time have them fill in the words. Pause and review the answers by having different students write them on the board.

👥 Practice the sentences with a partner.

Have students practice the sentences in pairs.

☀ Containers

📢 A. Listen and repeat.
(CD2, Track 29)

Ask students to just listen to the four phrases the first time you play the audio. Present the audio again, pausing to have students repeat each phrase.

Teacher Note

On the audio, the word *of* is shortened and sounds like "uh." This is how Americans usually pronounce *of* in short phrases like these in Exercise A.

B. Put the drinks in the correct columns on page 159.

Have students fill in the chart on their own. Discuss the answers with the class. You may wish to put a large chart on the board where students can write in their answers.

Pronunciation: 'll

🔊 A. Pronunciation. Listen and complete. Then, listen and repeat.

1. ___I'll have___ a salad.
2. ___She'll have___ a cup of tea.
3. ___He'll have___ a hamburger.
4. ___He'll have___ a small soda.
5. ___I'll have___ a glass of juice.
6. ___She'll have___ pancakes.
7. ___We'll have___ a cheese pizza.
8. ___They'll have___ pasta.

👥 Practice the sentences with a partner.

Containers

📢 A. Listen and repeat.

a can of soda   a glass of milk   a cup of coffee   a bottle of juice

B. Put the drinks in the correct columns on page 159. You may put a drink in more than one column. (Answers may vary.)

soda   chocolate milk   iced coffee   espresso

hot chocolate   orange juice   milk   ✓coffee

water   lemonade   iced tea   tea

Audio Script

A. Pronunciation. Listen and complete. Then, listen and repeat. **(CD2, Track 28)**

1. **I'll have** a salad.
2. **She'll have** a cup of tea.
3. **He'll have** a hamburger.
4. **He'll have** a small soda.
5. **I'll have** a glass of juice.
6. **She'll have** pancakes.
7. **We'll have** a cheese pizza.
8. **They'll have** pasta.

a can of	a bottle of	a cup of	a glass of
soda	orange juice	coffee	chocolate milk
iced tea	water	tea	lemonade
lemonade	iced tea	espresso	milk
iced coffee	milk	hot chocolate	orange juice

Working Together

A. Pair practice. Sit with a partner. Ask questions and check (✓) the answers.
(Answers will vary.)

	Yes	No
Do you like hamburgers?		
Do you like hot dogs?		
Do you like chicken?		
Do you like rice?		
Do you like fish?		
Do you like vegetables?		

B. Complete the sentences about you and your partner. (Answers will vary.)

1. I _____ hamburgers.

2. I _____ chicken.

3. I _____ rice.

4. My partner _____ hot dogs.

5. My partner _____ fish.

6. My partner _____ vegetables.

7. I _____ .

> **Present Tense**
> I like pizza.
> I don't like chicken.
>
> He likes pizza.
> He doesn't like beans.
>
> She likes chicken.
> She doesn't like rice.

Working Together

A. Pair practice.

Have students complete the check-off activity with a partner.

B. Complete the sentences about you and your partner.

• Point out the present tense sentences in the box and read them aloud. Ask students what is different about the verb *like* in the three statements. (*Like* has an -s ending after the words *he* and *she*. There is no -s ending on *like* after the word *I*.)

• Have students complete the sentences on their own. Ask students to look at the answers their partner gave in Exercise A to complete items 4, 5, and 6. Then have students check each other's work.

C. In a group of three students, decide the prices on the menu.

Discuss new words and phrases such as *cheesecake* and *cheeseburger special*. Students can then decide on the prices in small groups. Move around the classroom as students work, checking on their oral and written expressions of dollars and cents prices.

D. Read and practice the conversation.

Have students remain in the same groups they formed for Exercise C to practice this conversation. Invite different groups to read the conversation to the class.

C. In a group of three students, decide the prices on the menu. (Answers will vary.)

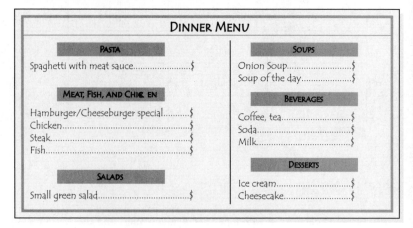

DINNER MENU

PASTA		SOUPS	
Spaghetti with meat sauce.....................$		Onion Soup..........................$	
		Soup of the day...................$	

MEAT, FISH, AND CHICKEN		BEVERAGES	
Hamburger/Cheeseburger special...........$		Coffee, tea...........................$	
Chicken...$		Soda....................................$	
Steak..$		Milk.....................................$	
Fish..$			

SALADS		DESSERTS	
Small green salad...................................$		Ice cream.............................$	
		Cheesecake..........................$	

D. Read and practice the conversation.

Waiter:	Are you ready to order?
Customer 1:	Yes, we are.
Waiter:	What'll you have?
Customer 1:	I'll have onion soup and spaghetti with meat sauce.
Waiter:	Anything to drink?
Customer 1:	I'll have coffee.
Waiter:	And you? What'll you have?
Customer 2:	I'll have the cheeseburger special.
Waiter:	Would you like a salad?
Customer 2:	No, thank you.
Waiter:	Anything to drink?
Customer 2:	I'll have a diet soda.

E. Sit in a group of three students. Complete the conversation. (Answers will vary.)

Waiter:	Are you ready to order?
Customer 1:	Yes, we are.
Waiter:	What'll you have?
Customer 1:	I'll have _____.
Waiter:	Anything to drink?
Customer 1:	I'll have _____.
Waiter:	And you? What'll you have?
Customer 2:	I'll have _____.
Waiter:	Anything to drink?
Customer 2:	_____
Waiter:	_____

Culture Note

In the United States, Americans leave a tip for the waiter or waitress. Waiters and waitresses do not receive large salaries, so tips are important. People usually leave 15% of the check total.

F. Sit in a group. Talk and complete. (Answers will vary.)

My Community

1. A good Chinese restaurant in my area is _____.
2. A good Mexican restaurant in my area is _____.
3. A good Italian restaurant in my area is _____.
4. A good pizzeria in my area is _____.
5. A good _____ restaurant in my area is _____.

E. Sit in a group of three students.

Ask students to form new groups. Have students look at the menu on page 160, then decide together how to fill in the blanks in this conversation. Encourage students to discuss different ways to complete each line. Ask them to practice the completed conversation. Then invite groups to read their conversations to the class.

Suggestion

Bring copies of a very simple take-out menu to class. Ask students to study it and ask questions about anything they don't understand. Then have groups of three use the items on the menu to role-play the conversation in Exercise E again. Invite groups to present their new conversations to the class.

Suggestion

Discuss the cultural note. Ask students: *Do you tip in your country?*

F. Sit in a group.

Ask students who live in the same neighborhood to sit together for this activity. After they complete the sentences, invite each group to tell the rest of the class about the restaurants in their neighborhood.

☀The Big Picture:
At Mario's Italian Restaurant

🎵 **A. Listen. (CD2, Track 30)**

- Ask students to describe the picture. You might use questions like these to get started:

  Where are these people?
  What is he/she doing?
  Where are they sitting?
  What are they eating?
  How many _____ are there in the restaurant?

- Ask students to talk about the picture using *There is* and *There are*. For example: *There are flowers on the table. There is one slice of pizza on the table.*

- Instruct students to just listen as you play the audio.

🎵 **B. Listen again and write the names on the correct person. (CD2, Track 30)**

Point to and say each of the seven names. Have students repeat each name. Then play the audio again and ask students to write the correct names in the boxes in the picture.

Teacher Note

Remind students that it is not necessary to understand everything on the audio. Explain that the best way to understand rapid spoken English is to focus only on the key information needed (in this case the people's names).

The Big Picture: At Mario's Italian Restaurant

🎵 **A. Listen.**

🎵 **B. Listen again and write the names on the correct person.**

Troy	Emma	Faye	Bob	Ann	Lori	Matthew

162 UNIT 11

Audio Script

☀The Big Picture:
At Mario's Italian Restaurant

A. Listen. (CD2, Track 30)

It's Friday night at Mario's Italian Restaurant. Troy and Emma always eat at Mario's on Friday nights. They're sitting at their favorite table, near the window. Faye is the waitress. She always works on Friday nights, so Troy and Emma always sit at her table. Faye is friendly, so Troy and Emma give her a good tip. Right now, she is taking Troy's and Emma's orders. Troy is ordering a salad and chicken. Emma is ordering a salad and pasta. Bob and Ann are at the restaurant with their children, Lori and Matthew. Bob and Ann like to go out to eat on Fridays because they're always tired on Friday nights after a busy week. They're eating a large cheese-and-pepperoni pizza. They're all drinking soda.

162 ENGLISH IN ACTION 1

C. Read and circle.

1. It's Saturday night.   Yes   (No)
2. Troy and Emma eat at Mario's on Friday nights.   (Yes)   No
3. Troy and Emma like to sit by the door.   Yes   (No)
4. Faye always works on Fridays.   (Yes)   No
5. Faye is a good waitress.   (Yes)   No
6. Troy and Emma are good customers.   (Yes)   No
7. Troy and Emma are ordering pasta.   Yes   (No)

D. Read and circle.

1. Who is sitting next to the window?

   (a.) Troy and   b. Bob and   c. Faye is.   d. Lori is.
       Emma are.   Ann are.

2. When do Troy and Emma eat at Mario's?

   a. Every day.   b. Every night.   (c.) On Fridays.   d. Italian.

3. Why do Troy and Emma sit at Faye's table?

   a. Because they like the food.   c. Because they're hungry.

   (b.) Because they like her.

4. When do Bob and Ann like to eat out?

   (a.) On Fridays.   b. Every   c. Every   d. Every
                          weekend.   night.   morning.

5. Why are Bob and Ann eating out tonight?

   a. Because they're hungry.   (c.) Because they're tired.

   b. Because they like to cook.

E. Complete.

1. Troy and Emma _____are eating_____ at Mario's.
2. They _____are sitting_____ at Faye's table.
3. Emma _____is looking_____ at the menu.
4. Troy _____is ordering_____ a salad and chicken.
5. Faye _____is taking_____ Troy's and Emma's orders.
6. Bob's family _____is eating_____ pizza.
7. They _____are drinking_____ soda.

> is ordering
> are sitting
> is eating
> ✓ are eating
> are drinking
> is taking
> is looking

C. Read and circle.

Ask students to answer the questions individually. Go over the answers with the whole class. You can replay portions of the audio to confirm any answers students have difficulty with.

D. Read and circle.

Have students complete the answers individually. Check the answers by having one student read the questions aloud and calling on different students to answer the questions.

E. Complete.

Ask students to complete the sentences individually and check their answers with a partner.

Suggestion

Ask groups of students to work together to write a conversation in which Troy and Emma are ordering dinner and Faye is taking their order. Tell students they can include any Italian food items they wish.

Reading:
Pizza Delivery

A. Before You Read.

- Invite several different students to answer the three questions.
- Point out the pizza toppings in the illustration. Explain that different pizza toppings are popular in different parts of the country. For example, pineapple is a popular topping in Hawaii.
- Ask students to read the stories to themselves. When they finish, invite them to ask about anything they don't understand. You can use the illustrations at the top right to clarify the meanings of the pizza toppings. Invite students to add their comments about the reading.

B. Complete.

Have students answer the questions individually. Then have four students write one answer each on the board. Review the answers with the class.

Reading: Pizza Delivery

A. Before You Read. (Answers will vary.)

1. Do you like pizza?
2. Where do you eat pizza?
3. What toppings do you like on your pizza?

Clerk:	Hello, Buona Pizza. May I take your order?
Customer:	Hello, I'd like to order a large pizza.
Clerk:	What toppings do you want on it?
Customer:	Pepperoni and green pepper.
Clerk:	OK. A large pizza with pepperoni and green peppers. That's $8.50. What's your address?
Customer:	1516 Central Avenue.
Clerk:	What's your phone number?
Customer:	555-6644.
Clerk:	OK. Thank you.
Customer:	How long will it take?
Clerk:	Thirty minutes. It's Friday, and we're always busy on Fridays.
Customer:	OK. Thank you. Good-bye.
Clerk:	Thank you for calling Buona Pizza.

B. Complete.

1. What size pizza did the customer order? _____ Large _____
2. How many toppings did the customer order? _____ Two _____
3. What toppings did the customer order? _____ Pepperoni and green peppers _____
4. It's 7:00. What time will the pizza arrive? _____ 7:30 _____

Writing Our Stories: Home Cooking

A. Read.

I live with my parents. My mother is a good cook, and we always eat dinner together. We are from Italy, and we like fresh Italian food. My mother shops in the afternoon. She usually buys cheese, pasta, bread, meat, and fresh vegetables. For dinner, we always have pasta, a little meat, and a vegetable. We always have salad. We all drink water with our meal. Everything is delicious!

B. Complete the sentences or circle the answers. (Answers will vary.)

1. I live _____.

2. _____ _____ a good cook.

3. We **always / sometimes / never** eat meals together.

4. I am from _____.

5. _____ _____ at _____.
   shop/shops   supermarket

6. For dinner, I have _____.

7. I drink _____.

8. For dessert, I have _____.

C. In your notebook, write about meals at your home.
(Answers will vary.)

Writing Note

Use commas in a list of three or more people, places or things: cheese, pasta, bread, and meat.

Writing Our Stories: Home Cooking

A. Read.

Read the story aloud to students. Ask them to point out any sentences they don't understand. Explain what the sentences mean.

B. Complete the sentences or circle the answers.

Ask students to look at the sentences in the story for ideas about how to complete the sentences in this exercise.

C. In your notebook, write about meals at your home.

• Students should use the information from Exercise B as they complete this activity.

• Students can use the story at the top of the page as a model for their writing. Show how they can adapt sentences to fit their own needs. For example, *For dinner we always have pasta* can become *For dinner we sometimes have vegetables and rice.*

Teacher Note

You might start Exercise C by writing about meals at your own home. Such a personal approach will be very interesting and motivating to students, and will provide a model for their own writing.

Practicing on Your Own

A. Complete.

Students will come up with a wide variety of responses. Encourage them to include food items not yet studied in class.

Suggestion

Review the answers orally in class. Write any sentences containing new words on the board. For example: *I like waffles for breakfast.* Suggest that students copy the new words in their notebooks.

B. Put this conversation in order.

Have students complete this activity on their own. Review the correct answers with the class.

Suggestion

Have pairs of students practice the completed conversation together.

Practicing on Your Own

A. Complete. (Answers will vary.)

1. I like _____ for breakfast.

2. I sometimes eat _____ for breakfast.

3. I always drink _____ at breakfast time.

4. I never eat _____ for breakfast.

5. I like _____ or _____ for lunch.

6. I sometimes eat _____ or _____ for dinner.

7. I sometimes eat _____ for dessert.

8. I don't like _____ .

B. Put this conversation in order. Then, write the conversation.

_6_	**Customer:**	I'll have a large soda.
_2_	**Customer:**	Yes, I am.
_3_	**Waitress:**	What'll you have?
_1_	**Waitress:**	Are you ready to order?
_5_	**Waitress:**	Anything to drink?
_4_	**Customer:**	I'll have a small cheese pizza.

Waitress: _Are you ready to order?_

Customer: _Yes, I am._

Waitress: _What'll you have?_

Customer: _I'll have a small cheese pizza._

Waitress: _Anything to drink?_

Customer: _I'll have a large soda._

166 UNIT 11

Looking at Numbers

A. What is the total for each bill? How much tip will you leave?

Hill's Diner

Scrambled Eggs	$3.00
Juice	.75
Coffee	.75
Total	$4.50

(Tip should be 68¢ to
90¢ for good service.)

Mario's Italian Restaurant

2 salads	$8.00
Spaghetti	9.50
Chicken	12.50
2 coffees	2.50
Total	$32.50

(Tip should be $4.88 to
$6.50 for good service.)

Grammar Summary

1. Present tense	
I **like** chicken.	
I **don't like** fish.	
He **likes** mangoes.	
He **doesn't like** bananas.	
2. Adverbs of frequency	
I **always** drink water.	She **always** eats a small breakfast.
I **sometimes** drink coffee.	She **sometimes** eats a big lunch.
I **never** drink soda.	She **never** eats a big dinner.
3. *Will / 'll*	
I'll have the chicken.	**We'll** have a pizza.
He'll have the fish.	**They'll** have hamburgers.
She'll have the turkey.	

☀Looking at Numbers

A. What is the total for each bill?

• Talk about tips. Then ask: *How much tip will they leave for each bill?*

• Have students work in pairs. Ask one pair to do the math on the board and show how they got their answer.

Grammar Summary

• Review the summary with the class. Invite students to say other statements that might appear in each of the three sections of the summary.

• See the Grammar Summary Expansion on page 239 for a more complete explanation of these grammar points.

Unit 12
Finding an Apartment

Discuss the person next to the unit number. Ask:

- *Who is standing next to the number 12?* (A man)
- *What is he doing?* (He's holding up a giant key.)

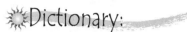

Dictionary:

Adjectives, Inside the Apartment, Apartment Problems

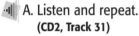 **A. Listen and repeat.**
(CD2, Track 31)

> Play the audio or read the words for the *Adjectives* and *Inside the Apartment* sections of pages 168 and 169. Have students point to each word or phrase as they hear it. Do the activity again, this time pausing for students to repeat each word or phrase.

Suggestion

Ask questions about students' own apartments using language from previous units. For example:

- *Is your apartment on a big street?*
- *Are your neighbors noisy?*
- *Do you like your apartment?*
- *How old is your refrigerator?*
- *How much is your electricity bill?*

12 Finding an Apartment

Dictionary: Adjectives, Inside the Apartment, Apartment Problems

 A. Listen and repeat.

Adjectives

| sunny | dark | clean | dirty |

| quiet | noisy | near / close to | far from |

Inside the Apartment

faucet   freezer refrigerator   heater / radiator

stove oven   lights   electricity

lock

air conditioner

ceiling

Apartment Problems

The faucet is leaking.

The paint is peeling.

The air conditioner isn't working.

The stove isn't working.

The lights aren't working.

The freezer is broken.

The lock is broken.

The heat is off.

The electricity is off.

The window is stuck.

There's a mouse.

There are cockroaches.

🔊 **A. Listen and repeat.**
(CD2, Track 31 *continued*)

Now focus on the *Apartment Problems* section on page 169. Play the audio or read the words and have students point to the words or sentences as they hear them. Do the activity again, this time pausing for students to repeat the words or sentences.

Suggestion

Help students make statements about particular problems they are having with their apartments. Write each statement on the board and ask students to repeat. For example:

- *The living room window is broken.*
- *The stove isn't working.*

Students may want to copy some of the sentences into their notebooks.

Active Grammar:
Present Continuous

A. Listen and circle.
(CD2, Track 32)

Point out the floor plan and give students a chance to ask questions about it. Then play the audio as they listen and look at the illustration. Play the audio again and have students circle their answers. Play the audio a third time so students can check their answers.

B. Sit in a group of three or four students.

Review the sample language in the box. Then have students talk about the floor plan in small groups. Set a time limit, perhaps five minutes. Then call on individual students to make *There is . . .* and *There are . . .* statements about the apartment.

C. Listen and write.
(CD2, Track 33)

Play the audio as many times as necessary.

D. Check and discuss.

Have a class discussion about how students found their apartments. Brainstorm other good ways to find a place to live. Finally, have the class vote on the best way to find an apartment.

Active Grammar: Present Continuous

A. Listen and circle.

1. (Yes, there is.)   No, there isn't.
2. Yes, there are.   (No, there aren't.)
3. (Yes, there are.)   No, there aren't.
4. (Yes, there is.)   No, there isn't.
5. (Yes, there is.)   No, there isn't.
6. (Yes, there is.)   No, there isn't.
7. Yes, there is.   (No, there isn't.)

B. Sit in a group of three or four students. Talk about the apartment.

> **There is / There are**
> There is a large kitchen.
> There are two bedrooms.

C. Listen and write.

1. The ___paint___ is peeling.
2. The ___ceiling___ is leaking.
3. A ___window___ is stuck.
4. The ___heat___ is off.
5. The ___neighbors___ are noisy.
6. The ___electricity___ is off.
7. There is a ___mouse___ in the apartment.

D. Check (✓) and discuss: How did you find your apartment? (Answers will vary.)

☐ I asked a friend.
☐ I looked in the newspaper.
☐ I saw a sign on a building.

What's the best way to find an apartment?

Audio Script

A. Listen and circle.
(CD2, Track 32)

1. Is there a kitchen in the house?
2. Are there three bedrooms in the house?
3. Are there many windows?
4. Is there only one bathroom?
5. Is there a garage?
6. Is there a closet near the door?
7. Is there a washer/dryer in the house?

C. Listen and write.
(CD2, Track 33)

1. The **paint** is peeling.
2. The **ceiling** is leaking.
3. A **window** is stuck.
4. The **heat** is off.
5. The **neighbors** are noisy.
6. The **electricity** is off.
7. There is a **mouse** in the apartment.

Reading the Classified Ads

A. Listen and repeat.

air conditioner	elevator	parking
apartment	furnished	pets
basement	included	security deposit
bath	large	transportation
bathroom	location	utilities
bedroom	modern	washer/dryer
carpeting		

Pets

B. Read and complete with a partner.

What does *apt.* mean?

apt.	
a/c	
BR	
bsmt.	
lge.	
loc.	
mod.	
elev.	
incl.	
sec. dep.	
utils.	

1. Apt. means _____apartment_____.
2. A/C means _____air conditioner_____.
3. BR means _____bedroom_____.
4. Bsmt. means _____basement_____.
5. Lge. means _____large_____.
6. Loc. means _____location_____.
7. Mod. means _____modern_____.
8. Elev. means _____elevator_____.
9. Incl. means _____included_____.
10. Sec. dep. means _____security deposit_____.
11. Utils. means _____utilities_____.

C. Pronunciation. Listen. How many syllables do you hear?

1. elevator __4__
2. utility __4__
3. utilities __4__
4. apartment __3__
5. neighborhood __3__
6. transportation __4__
7. superintendent __5__
8. electricity __5__
9. air conditioner __5__
10. neighbor __2__
11. basement __2__
12. included __3__

Practice the words above with a partner.

Reading the Classified Ads

A. Listen and repeat.
(CD2, Track 34)

Play the audio or read the list of words. Have students point to each word as they hear it. Do the activity again, this time pausing for students to repeat each word. Discuss the meaning of any words students aren't sure of.

B. Read and complete with a partner.

Point out that the full forms of the abbreviations are found in the box in Exercise A. Have students complete the activity in pairs.

C. Pronunciation.
(CD2, Track 35)

• Write one or two of the words on the board, placing slashes between the syllable divisions. For example:

el / e / va / tor
u / til / i / ty

• Play the audio several times so that students can check their work.

Practice the words above with a partner.

Have pairs practice saying the words to each other.

E. Read and complete.

Review the ad with the class before having students fill in their answers individually. Go over the answers with the class.

F. Read and circle.

Read each ad aloud and answer any questions students may have. Then ask students to circle the correct answers on their own. Have students check their answers with a partner.

Suggestion

Bring actual classified ads from a local paper. Ask students to work in groups, circling all the words and abbreviations they have learned so far. Then call on students to make statements like the ones in Exercise F.

G. Write a classified ad for your house or apartment.

First work with the whole class to write a classified ad on large poster paper or on the board. Then have students write their own ads.

H. Match.

Have students complete the exercise on their own, then check their answers with a partner.

E. Read and complete.

For Rent
Lge. 1 BR, w/ nice kitchen, sunny, elev. building w/ new windows, quiet, new carpet, no pets, utils. include, near trans., sec. dep., $625/mo.

1. The apartment is ___large___.
2. It's ___sunny___.
3. There are ___new windows___.
4. It has ___one bedroom___.
5. There is a ___new carpet___.
6. The rent is ___$625 a month___.

F. Read and (circle.)

2 BR sunny apt., lge., new carpeting, utils. incl., 1 1/2 bath, no pets, sec. dep.: $940

1. Yes (No) The apartment has three bedrooms.
2. (Yes) No Utilities are included.
3. Yes (No) You can have a pet.

3 lge. rooms, heat, hot water incl. Excellent loc., parking: $650

4. (Yes) No The rooms are large.
5. Yes (No) Electricity is included.
6. (Yes) No The apartment is in a good location.

Family house, 3 BR, 2 baths, liv. rm., hot water incl., parking, small pets ok, near transportation: $1700

7. Yes (No) The house has a dining room.
8. Yes (No) All utilities are included.
9. Yes (No) All pets are okay in this house.

G. Write a classified ad for your house or apartment. (Answers will vary.)

H. Match.

1. How many bedrooms are there?   a. It's $540 a month.
2. Where is the apartment?   b. No. No pets are allowed.
3. Can I have a dog?   c. Yes, a bus stop is on the corner.
4. Is it near transportation?   d. There are two bedrooms.
5. How much is the rent?   e. It's on Hope Street, near the bank.

172 Unit 12

Audio Script

(Audio Script for page 173, Exercise A begins here.)

A. Listen. Match the conversation and the problem. Then circle the time.
(CD2, Track 36)

Conversation 1
A: Hello, Mr. Williams. This is Mrs. Lopez in Apt. 3C.
B: Hello, Mrs. Lopez.
A: Could you come right away? It's 100 degrees in here. My air conditioner isn't working.
B: Your air conditioner isn't working?
A: That's right.
B: I'll be there right away.

Conversation 2
A: Hello, Mr. Williams. This is Miss DeVico in Apt. 5F.
B: Hello, Miss DeVico.
A: Aghh! Please come right away! There's a mouse in my kitchen.
B: A mouse in the kitchen?
A: Yes! Aghhh! Hurry up!
B: I'm coming right now.

Conversation 3
A: Hello, Mr. Williams. This is Mr. Martins in Apt. 14D.
B: Hello, Mr. Martins.

(Continued on next page.)

Calling the Super

super = superintendent

 A. Listen. Match the conversation and the problem. Then (circle) the time.

Problem		When will the super be here?		
a.	__6__ The lock is broken.	(Right away)	Later today	Tomorrow
b.	__3__ The faucet is leaking.	Right away	Later today	(Tomorrow)
c.	__4__ The stove isn't working.	Right away	(Later today)	Tomorrow
d.	__1__ The air conditioner isn't working.	(Right away)	Later today	Tomorrow
e.	__2__ There's a mouse in the kitchen.	(Right away)	Later today	Tomorrow
f.	__5__ There's a leak in the ceiling.	Right away	(Later today)	Tomorrow

B. Pair practice. Describe the problem to the super.

What's the problem?

The sink is leaking.

The window is stuck.

The faucet is leaking.

The heater is broken.

The electricity is off.

The stove isn't working.

There are cockroaches.

☼ Calling the Super

Note: Text for the Audio Script begins on page 172.

 A. Listen. (CD2, Track 36)

• Have students cover the second half of the exercise and focus only on the first column. Read aloud the six problems. Make sure students understand the problems. Then play the audio at least twice as students match each conversation with one of the problems.

• Now have students focus on the second half of the exercise. Explain that *right away* means *very soon* or *in a few minutes.* Play the audio again and have students circle their answers.

B. Pair practice.

Read the sample dialogue and ask students to point to the related picture. Then have pairs take turns asking and answering questions about the problems shown in the pictures. For example:

Student 1: *What's the problem?*
Student 2: *The window won't open.*

Student 1 then points to the picture Student 2 just described.

Audio Script

(Audio Script for page 173, Exercise A begins on page 172.)

A: The kitchen faucet has a small leak. Can you come look at it?
B: The faucet is leaking? Mr. Martins, I'm very busy today.
A: When can you come fix it?
B: I'll be there tomorrow.

Conversation 4
A: Hello, Mr. Williams. This is Mrs. Walker in 12B.
B: Hello, Mrs. Walker. How are you today?
A: I'm very upset. I'm trying to cook dinner, and the stove isn't working.
B: The stove isn't working?

A: That's right. When can you come fix it?
B: I'm a little busy right now, but I'll be there later.

Conversation 5
A: Hello, Mr. Williams. This is Mr. Young in 24A.
B: Hello, Mr. Young.
A: Mr. Williams, I think there's a leak in my ceiling. There's water on the floor.
B: Is it a big leak?
A: I don't think so. There's only a little water on the floor.
B: OK, I'll be there later this afternoon.

Conversation 6
A: Hi, Mr. Williams. This is Miss Dorisme in 10D.
B: Hello, Miss Dorisme. How are you?
A: Not well. I can't lock my door. I think the lock is broken.
B: I'll be there right away.

Working Together: Your Apartment

A. Interview two students about their apartments.

Have students work in groups of three. Ask students to interview their partners about their apartments.

B. Complete about the interview.

Point out that sentences 1 through 5 relate to Partner 1's responses and that sentences 6 through 10 relate to Partner 2's answers. Have students complete the sentences on their own.

C. Talk about the apartments with your partners.

Role-play some possible questions and answers with the class. For example:

Teacher: *Do you like your apartment?*
Student: *No, I don't.*
Teacher: *Is there an elevator in the building?*
Student: *No, there isn't.*
Teacher: *Is there one bedroom in the apartment?*
Student: *No, there are two bedrooms.*

Working Together: Your Apartment

A. Interview two students about their apartments. (Answers will vary.)

Questions	Partner 1: _____		Partner 2: _____	
1. Is your apartment sunny?	Yes	No	Yes	No
2. Are there two bedrooms in your apartment?	Yes	No	Yes	No
3. Is your kitchen large?	Yes	No	Yes	No
4. Is your apartment near transportation?	Yes	No	Yes	No
5. Is your apartment noisy?	Yes	No	Yes	No
6. Is your apartment close to school?	Yes	No	Yes	No
7. Is there an elevator in your building?	Yes	No	Yes	No
8. Is your neighborhood safe at night?	Yes	No	Yes	No

B. Complete about the interview. (Answers may vary.)

1. _____'s apartment **is / isn't** sunny.
   _{Partner 1}
2. **His / Her** apartment has _____ bedrooms.
3. **His / Her** kitchen **is / isn't** large.
4. **His / Her** apartment **is / isn't** near transportation.
5. **His / Her** apartment _____.
6. _____'s apartment **is / isn't** noisy.
   _{Partner 2}
7. **His / Her** apartment has _____ bedrooms.
8. **His / Her** apartment **is / isn't** close to school.
9. **His / Her** neighborhood **is / isn't** safe at night.
10. **His / Her** apartment _____.

C. Talk about the apartments with your partners. Do they like their apartments? Why or why not?

D. Read and practice.

A: Hello, I'm calling about the one-bedroom apartment.

B: Well, it's a nice apartment, and it's sunny.

A: Does the rent include utilities?

B: It includes heat and hot water.

A: Is the apartment near transportation?

B: Yes, it's near the bus stop.

A: Is there an elevator in the building?

B: No, there isn't.

A: When can I see the apartment?

B: You can see it tomorrow morning.

Culture Note
In the United States, people often have to make appointments to look at an apartment.

E. Complete with a partner. (Answers will vary.)

A: Hello, I'm calling about the _____ apartment.

B: Well, it's a _____ apartment, and it's _____.

A: Does the rent include utilities?

B: It includes _____.

A: Is the apartment near _____?

B: _____.

A: Is there _____ in the building?

B: _____.

A: When can I see the apartment?

B: You can see it _____.

F. Act out your conversation.

D. Read and practice.

• Have students practice saying the sentences to themselves. Review the conversation by having each sentence read aloud by a different student. Correct pronunciation as necessary.

• Ask students to practice in pairs. Call on a few pairs to present the conversation to the class.

E. Complete with a partner.

Ask students to use original information to fill in the blanks. Demonstrate some ways to personalize the conversation. For example:

A: *I'm calling about the* three-bedroom *apartment.*

B: *Well, it's a* big *apartment, and it's* quiet*.*

A: *Does the rent include utilities?*

B: *It includes* heat*.*

F. Act out your conversation.

Invite pairs of students to present their conversation to the class.

The Big Picture: My Neighborhood

The Big Picture: My Neighborhood

Suggestion

On the board, write questions with prepositions. For example:

• *Is the bank next to the laundromat?*
• *What is next to the library?*
• *What is across the street from the library?*
• *Is the bus stop between the library and the post office?*

Ask students to work in groups to answer the questions. Then go over the answers with the whole class.

A. Listen. (CD2, Track 37)

• Discuss the picture with students. Say the names of the various buildings and other places and have students point to them. Then play the audio.
• Ask some *Yes/No* questions to check comprehension. For example:

> *Does Anna live in a two-bedroom apartment?*
> *Is she a teacher?*
> *Is there an elevator in her building?*
> *Are there pets in the building?*

B. Read and circle.

Have students complete this activity on their own and check their answers with a partner.

A. Listen.

B. Read and circle.

1. The apartment is on the fourth floor.	Yes	(No)
2. The bedroom is small.	(Yes)	No
3. Ana has a cat.	Yes	(No)
4. Ana likes her neighborhood.	(Yes)	No
5. The telephone company is next to her apartment building.	Yes	(No)
6. Ana works at the post office.	Yes	(No)
7. Ana takes the bus to work.	Yes	(No)
8. Ana likes her neighbors.	(Yes)	No

176 UNIT 12

Audio Script

The Big Picture: My Neighborhood

A. Listen. (CD2, Track 37)

Hi, I'm Ana Lee. This is my apartment and my neighborhood. I live in a one-bedroom apartment on the third floor. There's no elevator, so I walk up and down the stairs. I have a small bedroom, but it's very sunny. I have a small bathroom, a living room, and a kitchen. I would like to have a pet, but I can't have any pets in my building.

I like my neighborhood. It's quiet, safe, and convenient. I'm near everything. The park is across the street, so I walk in the park every morning. I shop at the market, and I can pay my phone bill at the telephone company. Best of all, I can walk to work because I teach at the elementary school down the street. Finally, I have great neighbors. Mr. and Mrs. Robinson live next door, and my friend Kevin lives in the apartment on the other side. My neighbors are quiet, and they're very friendly.

C. Read and complete.

1. There is a _____bedroom_____ in the apartment.
2. There is a _____kitchen_____ in the apartment.
3. There are _____windows_____ in the apartment.
4. There isn't an _____elevator_____ in the building.
5. There aren't any _____pets_____ in the building.
6. There's a _____bank_____ down the street.
7. There is a _____parking lot_____ next to the building.
8. The _____neighbors_____ are quiet and friendly.

bank
✓ bedroom
elevator
kitchen
neighbors
parking lot
pets
windows

D. Complete.

1. The laundromat is _____next to_____ Ana's building.
2. The park is _____across from_____ Ana's building.
3. The bus stop is _____across from_____ Ana's building.
4. The bus stop is _____between_____ the post office and the library.
5. The market is _____across from_____ the school.
6. The parking lot is _____next to_____ Ana's building.
7. The bank is _____next to_____ the telephone company.
8. The laundromat is _____between_____ Ana's building and the market.

across from
between
next to

E. Pair practice. Where does she . . . ?

buy fruit
cash her check
get books
pay the telephone bill
wash her clothes
work

Where does she work?

She works at the school.

school   laundromat   supermarket

bookstore   telephone company   bank

C. Read and complete.

Have students complete this exercise on their own. If necessary, play the audio for Exercise A again.

D. Complete.

Point out the three prepositions in the box that students can use to fill in the blanks. Review the answers by having different students read aloud one answer and point to the part of the picture that proves their answer is correct.

E. Pair practice.

• Ask two students to read the sample dialogue.
• Point out the box to the left with words for the questions, and the tags at the bottom with words for the answers.
• Ask pairs of students to take turns asking and answering the questions as you and the other students check their work.

Reading: Walter the Exterminator

A. Before You Read.

• Invite several different students to answer the four questions.

• Ask students to read the story to themselves. When they finish, invite them to ask about anything they don't understand. You can use the illustrations at the top right to clarify the meaning of these words: *cockroach, mice (mouse), ants, spray,* and *poison.* Invite students to add their comments about the reading.

Suggestion

Write some irregular plural nouns students already know on the board. For example: *man/men, child/children.* Explain that the plural of *mouse* is irregular, too (*mouse/mice*).

B. Underline and number the answers in the reading.

Point out the numbered sentence in the story. Tell students to mark the answer to each question the same way.

Reading: Walter the Exterminator

A. Before You Read. (Answers will vary.)

1. Do you live in an apartment or a house?
2. What is an exterminator?
3. Do you ever need an exterminator?
4. How do you say *cockroach* in your language?

If you live in an apartment or a house, sometimes you need an exterminator. The exterminator goes into a house, apartment, or office building when there is a problem with ants, mice, or roaches.

Walter is an exterminator. He has a pest control business and 26 years of experience. ①He and his four employees work in private homes. ②His wife does the office work. ③Walter gets ten to twelve calls per day. He likes his job. ④He likes to talk to the different customers. He especially likes to eliminate pests. ⑤Walter's most common calls are about mice and ants. When Walter gets a call, he goes to the home. For many insects, he sprays insecticide in small spaces. For mice, he puts out traps or poison. ⑥When there are no more pests in the house, Walter is happy. Then he goes to the next home to find the next pest.

B. Underline and number the answers in the reading. (Answers are numbered and underlined above.)

1. Where does Walter work?
2. Who does the office work for Walter?
3. How many calls does he get per day?
4. Why does Walter like his job?
5. What is the most common problem for Walter's customers?
6. How does Walter feel when there are no more pests in the house?

Writing Our Stories:
My Apartment

A. Read.

My name is José. I live in a sunny one-bedroom apartment with my brother. We live on the first floor. Our building has three floors. Our building doesn't have an elevator. My brother sleeps on the pull-out sofa in the living room. We have a small kitchen and a living room. The rent is a little expensive, but our apartment is in a safe neighborhood, and our neighbors are very friendly. We need a bigger apartment with two bedrooms. We also need more space for our computer.

B. Check (✓) the true sentences about your apartment or house. (Answers will vary.)

☐ 1. My apartment is sunny.
☐ 2. My apartment has two bedrooms.
☐ 3. My kitchen is large.
☐ 4. I have a living room.
☐ 5. My building has an elevator.
☐ 6. My apartment is in a safe neighborhood.
☐ 7. My rent is cheap.
☐ 8. My neighbors are friendly.

C. In your notebook, write about your apartment or house.

Writing Note
Check your punctuation. Begin each sentence with a capital letter. End each sentence with a period.

Writing Our Stories:
My Apartment

A. Read.

Read the story aloud to students or have them read it silently. Answer any questions they may have.

B. Check the true sentences about your apartment or house.

Remind students to answer the questions about their own homes, not about José's home.

C. In your notebook, write about your apartment or house.

• Remind students that they can use the information from Exercise B as they complete this activity.

• The story in Exercise A can be used as a model for this writing assignment. Show students how they can adapt sentences to fit their own needs. For example, *We also need more space for our computer* can become *We also need more space for our two dogs.*

Suggestion

Make class copies of ten incorrect sentences you find in students' writing assignments, leaving space for rewriting below each sentence. Distribute the copies to the class. Have students correct the errors in these sentences. Ask different students to write one corrected sentence on the board. Go over the errors and corrections with the class.

Practicing on Your Own

A. Read and complete.

Ask students to look at the picture and complete the sentences.

B. Look at the map of a neighborhood.

Have students fill in the blanks on their own. Check the answers with the whole class.

Suggestion

Students can write a similar set of questions to use for conversation practice with a partner. As one student asks the questions, the other student gives answers that are true for his or her neighborhood. For example:

Student 1: *Is there a post office near your building?*
Student 2: *No, there isn't.*
Student 2: *Is there a parking lot next to your building?*
Student 2: *Yes, there is.*

Practicing on Your Own

A. Read and complete.

1. The lock is ___broken___.
2. There is a ___mouse___ in the hallway.
3. The air ___conditioner___ ___isn't___ ___working___.
4. The paint ___is___ ___peeling___.
5. The apartment is ___sunny___.
6. There ___are___ two ___pets___ in the apartment.
7. The apartment isn't ___big___.

B. Look at the map of a neighborhood. Complete each question and answer.

1. ___Is___ ___there___ a bus stop near the apartment?   Yes, there ___is___.
2. ___Is___ there a bank ___in___ the neighborhood?   No, there ___isn't___.
3. Is the laundromat ___next___ ___to___ the library?   No, it ___isn't___.
4. Is ___there___ a bookstore in the neighborhood?   Yes, ___there___ ___is___.
5. Is the apartment building ___across___ ___from___ the park?   Yes, ___it___ ___is___.
6. ___Are___ there any parking lots in the neighborhood?   Yes, ___there___ ___are___.

Looking at Forms: The Bottom Part of a Lease

A. Complete. (Answers will vary.)

Lease

_____	_____	_____
Last Name	First Name	MI
_____	_____	_____
Spouse's Last Name	First Name	MI

Number of Occupants _____ *
*No more than 5 occupants in one apartment

_____	_____	_____
Place of Employment	City	State

_____ Year of Employment   Occupation _____

References

_____ (____) _____
Name of Reference (Not a relative)   Tel.

_____ _____ _____
Name of Bank   Address   Account Number

_____ _____ _____ _____
Signature of tenant   Date   Signature of spouse   Date

Grammar Summary

▶ **1. Present continuous**

The faucet **is leaking.**

The air conditioner **isn't working.**

The lights **aren't working.**

▶ **2. There is / There are**

There is a large kitchen.

Is there a large kitchen?   Yes, **there is.**

There are two bedrooms.

Are there three bedrooms?   No, **there aren't.**

▶ **3. Adjectives**

The freezer is **broken.**   The window is **stuck.**

☀Looking at Forms: The Bottom Part of a Lease

A. Complete.

• Ask students questions about their leases and the process involved in getting their apartment. For example:

> *Do you live in an apartment?*
> *Did you sign a lease?*
> *Where is your lease?*
> *Did you need a reference?*
> *Did you pay a security deposit?*

• Ask students to read through the form and circle any words they don't understand. Use simple explanations and examples to clarify the meaning of these terms. For example:

An occupant *or* tenant *is someone who lives in an apartment or house. There are three occupants in my apartment—my wife and I, and our son. We are the tenants in Apartment 3-L.*

A reference *is someone who knows you well. This person will say that you are an honest person. I will use my boss as a reference.*

• Ask students to fill in the form as if they were signing a lease on the apartment they are in right now.

Grammar Summary

• Review the summary with the class. Invite students to say other statements, questions, and answers that might appear in each of the three sections of the summary.

• See the Grammar Summary Expansion on page 240 for a more complete explanation of these grammar points.

Unit 13
Applying for a Job

Discuss the people next to the unit number. Ask:

• *Who is standing next to the number 13?* (Two men)
• *What are they doing?* (One man is giving the other a "high five" because he just got a new job.)

☀ Dictionary:
Hotel Occupations

A. Listen and repeat.
(CD2, Track 38)

• Talk about what is happening in the pictures. Ask:

> *Where is this person?*
> *What is he/she doing?*
> *What is he/she wearing?*

• Have students listen as you play the audio or read the words and point to each picture.
• Play the audio again, pausing after each word to allow students to repeat.
• Point to different pictures at random and call on students to name the occupations.

---

13 Applying for a Job
Dictionary: Hotel Occupations

A. Listen and repeat.

Hotel Occupations

desk clerk

babysitter

busboy

cook

electrician

housekeeper

landscaper

laundry worker

manager

plumber

security guard

waiter / waitress

van driver /
airport shuttle driver

Active Grammar: Present Tense

A. Match.

_g_	**1.** an airport shuttle driver	**a.**	cleans and clears tables
_d_	**2.** a desk clerk	**b.**	washes and dries sheets and towels
_h_	**3.** a babysitter	**c.**	serves food
_c_	**4.** a waitress	**d.**	takes reservations
_i_	**5.** a cook	**e.**	repairs bathrooms
_b_	**6.** a laundry worker	**f.**	is the supervisor
_j_	**7.** a housekeeper	**g.**	drives a van
_f_	**8.** a manager	**h.**	takes care of children
_e_	**9.** a plumber	**i.**	prepares food
_a_	**10.** a busboy	**j.**	cleans and vacuums rooms

B. Complete with a partner. (Answers may vary.)

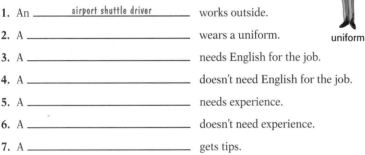

uniform

1. An _____airport shuttle driver_____ works outside.

2. A _____ wears a uniform.

3. A _____ needs English for the job.

4. A _____ doesn't need English for the job.

5. A _____ needs experience.

6. A _____ doesn't need experience.

7. A _____ gets tips.

8. A _____ has a boring job.

9. A _____ has an interesting job.

A. Match

Have students complete the matching activity on their own. Review the answers by calling on one student to read the complete statement. For example: *An airport shuttle driver drives a van.*

B. Complete with a partner.

• Point out the picture and the word *uniform* next to this exercise. Ask: *Who has to wear a uniform on the job?* (a cook, a security guard, a police officer, etc.)

• Have students complete the sentences with a partner. Several of the sentences have more than one correct answer. Review the answers with the class, allowing all possible correct answers for each item.

Suggestion

Ask students to circle all the *-s* endings on the present tense verbs on this page.

C. Complete the sentences about your present job.

• Ask students if any of them have jobs that haven't been mentioned yet. List these jobs on the board. Say the name of each job and ask the class to repeat. Then give a simple description of the duties of each job. For example:

Cashier. A cashier takes your money and gives you change.
Salesperson. A salesperson sells things in a store.

• Have students complete the sentences individually. Ask several different students to read their answers to the class.

D. Pair practice.

• Say the short answers in the box and ask students to repeat.
• Read the sample dialogue with a student. Then ask pairs of students to practice asking and answering the questions. Move around the room checking students' responses and their use of the short answers.

C. Complete the sentences about your present job. (Answers will vary.)

1. I am a(n) _____.

2. I _____ an interesting job.
   have / don't have

3. I _____ English at work.
   speak / don't speak

4. I _____ a uniform.
   wear / don't wear

5. I _____ tips.
   get / don't get

6. My job _____ experience.
   needs / doesn't need

D. Pair practice. (Answers may vary.)

Does a cook clean and clear tables?

No, he doesn't.

1. Does a cook wear a uniform?
2. Does a manager get tips?
3. Does a manager repair bathrooms?
4. Does a waitress serve food?
5. Does a housekeeper prepare food?
6. Does a babysitter take reservations?
7. Does a desk clerk stand all day?
8. Does an airport shuttle driver drive a van?

Yes, she does.   Yes, he does.
No, she doesn't.   No, he doesn't.

184   UNIT 13

Job Skills and Experience

A. Listen to each person talk about his or her job experience. Write the number of the speaker under each picture.

_4_

_1_

_2_

_3_

B. Check (✓) your job skills. (Answers will vary.)

☐ **1.** I can speak a little English.
☐ **2.** I can speak English well.
☐ **3.** I can clean a room.
☐ **4.** I can operate a riding lawn mower.
☐ **5.** I can make drinks.
☐ **6.** I can cook different kinds of food.
☐ **7.** I can drive a car.
☐ **8.** I can drive a stick shift.
☐ **9.** I can use a computer.
☐ **10.** I can drive a truck.

riding lawn mower

stick shift

What else can you do? (Answers will vary.)

I can _____.

I can _____.

Audio Script

A. Listen to each person talk about his or her job experience. Write the number of the speaker under each picture.
(CD2, Track 39)

1. I work in a large hotel. I can use a computer and register guests. I talk to people every day.
2. I work in the hotel kitchen. I can cook Mexican food and Italian food.
3. I work in the basement. I can operate a large washing machine and dryer. I can wash and fold towels and sheets.

4. I have a lot of experience. I can repair an air conditioner, a fan, or your lights. I work in many different rooms in the hotel.

A. Listen to each person talk about his or her job experience.
(CD2, Track 39)

- Point out the blank line under each picture. Play the first conversation and point out the number 1 under the picture of the desk clerk.
- Play the audio all the way through three times. The first time, have students just listen. The second time, ask them to write the correct number under each picture. The third time, have students check their work.

B. Check your job skills.

- Point out the riding lawn mower and the stick shift at the right of the exercise. Say the words and ask students to repeat.
- Ask students to read through the statements and circle any words they don't understand. Ask students to tell you the words they don't understand, and list these on the board. Define each word in simple terms and use it in a sample sentence. For example: _"Operate" means "use a machine." I can operate a washing machine._
- Have students check their answers individually.

What else can you do?

Ask students to write some other things they can do. Move around the room offering help as needed. Write some of the students' sentences on the board. Explain what each sentence means. For example:

- _Laura can sew. She can make clothes._
- _Carlos can operate a fork lift. He can use a small truck to lift heavy boxes._

If necessary, make simple drawings on the board to illustrate meanings.

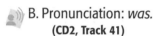 **Job Experience**

Suggestion

Review the occupations on page 182 before introducing Exercise A.

 A. Listen and complete.
(CD2, Track 40)

• Tell students that they will hear three different conversations. Explain that their task is to fill in the missing words in the conversation in their books.

• Before playing the audio, ask students to read through the three paragraphs and circle any words they don't know. Students might need help with *certificate, four-star, community college, samba,* or *salsa.* Write the new words on the board. Encourage students to explain what the words mean or explain the words yourself.

B. Pronunciation: *was.*
(CD2, Track 41)

• Point to the marks that show how the words are linked in spoken English. Contrast how the sentences sound when the words are not linked and when they are linked. For example:

> *I / am / a / cook.* versus
> *I ama cook.*
> *I / was / a / cook.* versus
> *I wasa cook.*

• Play the audio and have students listen to and repeat the sentences several times.

 Job Experience

Now: I am
Past: I was

 A. Listen and complete.

1. In my country, Colombia, I was a ___Spanish___ ___teacher___ in a high school. Now I am a ___van___ ___driver___ at a hotel. I am studying for my teaching certificate. I want to teach Spanish to high school students.

2. In my country, Poland, I was a ___manager___ in a four-star hotel. Now I am a ___desk clerk___ in a small hotel. I can make reservations and use a computer. I am preparing for a management job.

3. In my country, Brazil, I was a ___dance___ ___teacher___. Now I am a ___waitress___ in a hotel. I am studying English and dance at a community college. I can do the samba, salsa, and teach many dances. I want to get a degree.

 B. Pronunciation: *was.* Listen and repeat.

1. I am a cook.	I was a cook.
2. I am a mechanic.	I was a mechanic.
3. He is a landscaper.	He was a landscaper.
4. She is a housewife.	She was a housewife.
5. He is a teacher.	He was a teacher.
6. She is a manager.	She was a manager.
7. I am a plumber.	I was a plumber.
8. He is a security guard.	He was a security guard.

186 UNIT 13

Audio Script

A. Listen and complete.
(CD2, Track 40)

1. In my country, Colombia, I was a Spanish teacher in a high school. Now I am a van driver at a hotel. I am studying for my teaching certificate. I want to teach Spanish to high school students.

2. In my country, Poland, I was a manager in a four-star hotel. Now I am a desk clerk in a small hotel. I can make reservations and use a computer. I am preparing for a management job.

3. In my country, Brazil, I was a dance teacher. Now I am a waitress in a hotel. I am studying English and dance at a community college. I can do the samba, salsa, and teach many dances. I want to get a degree.

C. Listen and (circle) Now or Past.

1. Now (Past)
2. (Now) Past
3. Now (Past)
4. Now (Past)
5. (Now) Past
6. (Now) Past
7. Now (Past)
8. (Now) Past

D. Read.

Work Experience			
From	To	Employer	Position
1996	present	The Flamingo	assistant cook
1992	1996	Tio Pepe	head cook

Alex: I'm applying for a job as a cook.

Manager: Do you have any experience?

Alex: Yes, I am an assistant cook at the Flamingo in Tampa.

Manager: Any other experience?

Alex: I was the head cook at Tio Pepe in Mexico City from 1992 to 1996.

Manager: Do have you any references?

Alex: Yes, I do. You can call the head cook at the Flamingo, and I have a letter from the manager at Tio Pepe.

Culture Note
A reference is a person who knows about your work experience. It is not a friend or a relative.

E. Practice the conversation with a partner.

Audio Script

C. Listen and circle *Now* or *Past.* (CD2, Track 42)

1. I was an electrician in my country.
2. I am a desk clerk at a small motel.
3. I was the head cook at a Polish restaurant.
4. I was a housewife and stayed home with my children.
5. I am a van driver, and I drive passengers to the airport.
6. I am a babysitter for a family.
7. I was a security guard in a bank.
8. I am a waitress in a Colombian restaurant.

C. Listen and circle *Now* or *Past.* (CD2, Track 42)

• Explain that students will hear some sentences about the present (now) and some about the past. Ask:

> *What verb will you hear after the word "I" in the "now" sentences?* (Am)
>
> *What verb will you hear after the word "I" in the "past" sentences?* (Was)

• Play the audio and have students circle their answers.

D. Read.

• Ask students to read the information in the chart. Then ask questions to check students' comprehension. For example:

> *Where is Alex working now?* (The Flamingo)
> *What does he do?* (He is an assistant cook.)
> *Where did Alex work before?* (at Tio Pepe)
> *What was he?* (He was the head cook.)
> *When did he work there?* (From 1992 to 1996)

• Have students read the conversation to themselves. Answer any questions they may have. Call on students to read aloud one line each. Correct pronunciation as necessary.

E. Practice the conversation with a partner.

Have pairs of students practice the conversation. Invite some pairs to present their conversations to the class.

F. Complete with your work experience.

Explain to students that they can use the chart in Exercise D as a model. Remind them to put their current job (or their latest experience) at the top and their less recent experience at the bottom.

G. Tell a partner about your work experience.

Ask a student to put their answers for Exercise F on the board. Prompt that student to tell about his/her work experience. Model language as needed. For example: *I am a cashier at Bingo's. I was a waiter at Letty's from 2000 to 2002.*

☼ Job Ads

A. Read these job ads.

• Ask students to read the ads and circle the jobs on their own. Review the answers with the class.

• Ask students to underline any words they don't understand in the ads. Write these words and phrases on the board and define them in simple terms.

Suggestion

Ask the class other questions about the ads. For example:

• *Which jobs need experience?*
• *Which jobs ask for references?*

B. Sit with a partner.

Tell students to use the ads in Exercise A as models for their own ad. Have some students read their ads aloud.

F. Complete with your work experience. (Answers will vary.)

Work Experience			
From	To	Employer	Position

G. Tell a partner about your work experience.

Job Ads

A. Read these job ads. Circle the jobs.

Help Wanted
Bellhop
Desk Clerk
Western Hotel
137 Kennedy Street
Apply in person.

Job Openings
Housekeepers
Laundry Workers
No Experience.
Will train on job.
Call the Carlton Hotel.
555-6777

Position Available
Cook
Experience Required
Paradise Hotel
Call 644-8899
Ask for Mr. Thomas.

Immediate Opening
Waiters and
Waitresses for
3-star New York Hotel
Restaurant
Experience required.
Apply in person.

Help Wanted
Landscaper
Experience with large
machines
Call Ms. Smith
At 433-1199.

Openings
Babysitter
2 references
Oceanside Hotel
Apply in person.

B. Sit with a partner. Write an ad for a job. (Answers will vary.)

Help Wanted

_____

_____

_____

C. Read these classified ads from a newspaper. Check (✓) the information below.

FT= full time
PT = part time

Culture Note
A maintenance mechanic works in an office building or a hotel. The mechanic repairs anything that is not working.

COOK FT 2 years experience required. Excellent pay w/ benefits. Call Thurs. – Sat. 11:00 A.M. – 4:00 P.M. 555-2126

A

FRONT DESK CLERK for hotel PT Eve shift 3 P.M. – 11 P.M. Will train. Apply in person. Plaza Hotel. Seaside.

B

LANDSCAPER Immediate FT opening for landscape crew. Valid license required. $9.00/hour. Benefits, vacation. Call today. 555-9328

C

MAINTENANCE MECHANIC FT Must have painting, plumbing, and electrical skills. Salary based on experience. Good benefits. Sunrise Resort. 555-4334

D

		A	B	C	D
1.	This job is full time.	✓	☐	✓	✓
2.	This job pays $9.00 an hour.	☐	☐	✓	☐
3.	This job has benefits.	✓	☐	✓	✓
4.	This job requires a driver's license.	☐	☐	✓	☐
5.	This job requires experience.	✓	☐	☐	☐
6.	This job is from 3:00 P.M. to 11:00 P.M.	☐	✓	☐	☐
7.	You can apply in person for this job.	☐	✓	☐	☐
8.	You need to call about this job.	✓	☐	✓	✓
9.	I would like to apply for this job.	☐	☐	☐	☐ (Answers will vary.)

- Point out the Culture Note telling what a *mechanic* does. Ask what kind of things a mechanic fixes. (cars, lawn mowers, and other broken machines)
- Read each ad aloud as students listen. Go over the sample answers in item 1. Ask students to point to the part of the ads that shows the job is full time. (the abbreviation FT)
- Have students read the ads to themselves and check as many of the answers as they can. Review the answers with the class. For any incorrect answers, ask students to go back and locate the part of the ad that gives that target information.

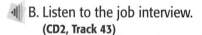

A Job Application

A. Read the information in Luis's application.

Ask students to read the job application to themselves. Answer any questions they may have.

Suggestion

For oral practice, you can have students make statements about the information on the application form. For example:

- *His name is Luis Moreno.*
- *His address is 397 Marina Way, Largo, Florida.*
- *His date of birth is June 15, 1980.*
- *He is a cashier at Frank's Fried Chicken.*

B. Listen to the job interview.
(CD2, Track 43)

- Before you play the audio, ask students to read through the statements.
- Play the audio once and have students just listen. Play the audio at least two more times as students circle their answers and check their work. Review the correct answers with the class.

Suggestion

For each *No* answer, help students use the words in the exercise to make a true statement. For example, item 2 can be changed to: *He has experience as a cashier.*

A Job Application

A. Read the information in Luis's application.

The Sunrise Hotel

Position	valet

Name	Moreno	Luis	A.
	Last	First	Middle

Address	397	Marina Way	Largo	FL
	Number	Street	City	State

Social Security No. 333-55-0012   Date of birth 6 / 15 / 80

Telephone 555-6000

Work Experience			
From	To	Employer	Position
1999	present	Frank's Fried Chicken	cashier

Signature of applicant ___ *Luis Moreno* ___

B. Listen to the job interview. (Circle) *Yes* or *No*.

(Yes) No   **1.** Luis is interviewing for a job as a valet.

Yes (No)   **2.** He has experience as a valet.

(Yes) No   **3.** Luis has a clean driver's license.

Yes (No)   **4.** Luis had an accident last year.

(Yes) No   **5.** Luis can start tomorrow.

(Yes) No   **6.** This job is part time.

Yes (No)   **7.** The salary is $8.00 an hour.

(Yes) No   **8.** Luis will get tips.

Yes (No)   **9.** Luis can wear sneakers.

a valet

190   UNIT 13

Audio Script

B. Listen to the job interview. Circle *Yes* or *No*. (CD2, Track 43)

Luis: I'm applying for the job as a valet.

Manager: Do you have any experience?

Luis: No, but I was a cashier at Frank's Fried Chicken.

Manager: Do you have a clean driver's license? Any tickets?

Luis: My license is clean. No tickets. No accidents.

Manager: We need to check your driver's license. When can you start?

Luis: Tomorrow.

Manager: The job is part time. Wednesday and Thursday, 5:00 to 10:00. Friday, Saturday, and Sunday, we're very busy. The hours are 5:00 to 12:00. The pay is $3 an hour plus tips.

Luis: That's good.

Manager: Wear black slacks and black shoes. We'll give you a red jacket.

Luis: Thank you very much.

Working Together

 A. Pair work. Read and practice with a partner.

Culture Note
Arrive five to ten minutes early for a job interview.

A: I'm applying for a job as a security guard.

B: Do you have any experience?

A: Yes. I was a security guard at a bank in Atlantic City.

B: When?

A: From 1997 to 2002.

B: We have an opening on the second shift, from 3:00 P.M. to 11:00 P.M.

A: What is the salary?

B: The salary is $7.50 an hour.

A: Good.

B: When can you start?

A: I can start tomorrow.

Culture Note
Many jobs have two or three shifts.

First shift:
7:00 A.M. to 3:00 P.M.

Second shift:
3:00 P.M. to 11:00 P.M.

Third shift:
11:00 P.M. to 7:00 A.M.

B. Write a conversation with a partner. One student is the manager. The other student is applying for a job.

C. Check (✓) and discuss: How did you find your job?

☐ A friend told me about the job.

☐ My relative works at the same place.

☐ I saw a Help Wanted sign at the company.

☐ I read about the job in the newspaper.

☐ I stopped at the factory and spoke to the manager.

☐ _____(Answers will vary.)_____

What's a good way to find a job? (Answers will vary.)

☀Working Together

Suggestion

Discuss the two Culture Notes. Find out the time people arrive for appointments in the students' home cultures. Look at the three work shifts. Ask students to tell what shifts they work now or have worked in the past.

A. Pair work.

Read the dialogue to the class. Answer any questions students may have. Then have students practice the dialogue in pairs.

B. Write a conversation with a partner.

• Ask students to use the sentences in Exercise A as models for their own conversations. Encourage students to use as many true facts as possible about one of the partners' job.

• Invite pairs to present their conversation to the class. Write on the board any lines that the class doesn't understand or that contain mistakes. Have students go to the board and correct the errors. Then use simple language to explain sentences that need clarification.

C. Check and discuss.

Ask students to read through the statements and raise their hands if they don't understand something. Explain as necessary. Then have students complete the exercise individually. Write some of the original answers on the board and discuss.

What's a good way to find a job?

Have a class discussion about good ways to find a job.

The Big Picture:
The Sunrise Hotel

Suggestion

Ask students to describe the picture. You might use questions like these to get started:

- *Where do these people work?*
- *What is his/her job?*
- *What is he/she doing?*
- *What's this?*
- *What are these people doing?*

A. Listen and circle.
(CD2, Track 44)

- Play the audio as students just look at the pictures. Play the audio at least two more times as students circle and then check their answers.
- Review all the answers by reading the statements one by one and calling on different students to answer. Play the audio once more so students can listen for information relating to any answers they missed.

A. Listen and circle.

1. Ricardo is the day manager of the Sunrise Hotel.   Yes   (No)
2. The hotel has more than 200 rooms.   (Yes)   No
3. The hotel has about 100 employees.   (Yes)   No
4. The van driver parks cars.   Yes   (No)
5. The hotel has three shifts.   (Yes)   No
6. Night employees make more money than day employees.   (Yes)   No
7. Everyone works full time.   Yes   (No)
8. The salary is high.   Yes   (No)
9. Many employees like the hours.   (Yes)   No
10. The hotel has many job openings.   (Yes)   No

Audio Script

The Big Picture:
The Sunrise Hotel

A. Listen and circle. (CD2, Track 44)

My name is Ricardo Lopez. This is the Sunrise Hotel, and I'm the evening manager. The Sunrise Hotel is a big hotel, and it has more than 200 rooms. There's a restaurant, a bar, two swimming pools, and tennis courts. Many tourists like to stay here.

The hotel has about 100 employees. We have desk clerks, housekeepers, bellhops, landscapers, and restaurant employees.

Then, we have a van driver. He drives the guests from the hotel to the airport.

We need people for all three shifts. People who work at night make one dollar more an hour than day employees. Some employees work full time, and we also have many part-time employees.

We are always looking for employees. The salary is low, and the employees work hard. Many employees leave us when they find a job with a better salary. But some people like the hours, and the workers like the tips. We have a friendly hotel here. Are you looking for a job? We have several job openings.

B. Listen. Who is the manager speaking to?

1. He's speaking to the _____housekeeper_____ .
2. He's speaking to the _____valet_____ .
3. He's speaking to the _____waitress_____ .
4. He's speaking to the _____desk clerk_____ .
5. He's speaking to the _____laundry worker_____ .
6. He's speaking to the _____electrician_____ .
7. He's speaking to the _____van driver_____ .

van driver
waitress
laundry worker
✓housekeeper
desk clerk
electrician
valet

C. Complete.

is   earns   works   likes

1. Shelley _works_ at the Sunrise Hotel. She _is_ a desk clerk. She _works_ from 11:00 to 7:00. She _likes_ the hours because she can be home with her children in the daytime. She _earns_ $10.00 an hour.

2. Chin-Kun _works_ at the Sunrise Hotel. He _is_ a desk clerk. He _works_ from 4:00 to 1:00 on Friday, Saturday, and Sunday. Chin-Kun _is_ a teacher during the week. He _earns_ extra money on weekends at the hotel.

3. Kasia _is_ a part-time waitress in the restaurant at the Sunrise Hotel. She _earns_ $4.00 an hour plus tips. She _likes_ the hours, but she doesn't like the pay. She _works_ from 10:30 to 3:30 four days a week.

4. Fernando _works_ part time as a busboy in the restaurant at the Sunrise Hotel. He _earns_ $3.00 an hour. He _works_ from 6:00 to 10:30 on weekends. He _likes_ the hours because he _is_ a college student, and he can take classes during the week.

Applying for a Job   **193**

B. Listen. (CD2, Track 45)

Point out the answers students can choose from in the box. Then play the audio and ask students to just listen. Play the audio a second time and have students fill in their answers. Play the audio a third time so they can confirm their answers.

C. Complete.

Have students complete the exercise on their own, then check their answers with a partner.

Audio Script

B. Listen. Who is the manager speaking to?
(CD2, Track 45)

1. Please clean rooms 371 and 374.
2. Could you park the cars for these guests, please?
3. Table 4 needs more water and the dessert menu.
4. How many empty rooms do we have for Saturday?
5. Some of these towels are not clean. What kind of detergent are you using?
6. The air conditioner isn't working in room 424. Could you check it?
7. Three guests need to get to the airport.

Reading: The Ice Hotel

A. Before You Read.

- Invite students to comment on the pictures that accompany the reading. Rephrase any incomplete or incorrect responses and expand on them. For example:

  S: *It's a building in ice.*
  T: *That's right. It's a building made of ice. It's an ice hotel.*

- Discuss the two prereading questions. Tell students to use the map to help them answer the question: *Where is Sweden?* (Sweden is near Denmark. It's between Norway and Finland.)
- Ask students to read through the story without worrying about words they don't understand.

B. Circle *T* for true and *F* for false.

- Have students do the exercise on their own.
- Review the answers by having students go back to the story and point out the sentence or sentences that give the answer to each item.

Suggestion

After students finish Exercise B, invite them to comment on the story. Ask: *Would you like to stay at this hotel. Why or why not?*

Reading: The Ice Hotel

A. Before You Read.

1. Where is Sweden? It's in northern Europe.
2. What's the weather in Sweden? It's cold, rainy, and snowy in the winter.

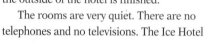

There's an unusual hotel in Jukkäsjarvi, Sweden. It's open only from the middle of December to late April. The name of the hotel is the Ice Hotel. The hotel is made completely of ice and snow. Every year, more and more visitors want to stay at this very cold hotel.

In the first year, the Ice Hotel had only one room. Now the hotel has 37 rooms and 6,500 overnight guests every year. The hotel has a reception desk, a main hall, a cinema, and hotel rooms. There's an ice church for weddings, too!

In early October, artists and workers prepare the hotel. They use special snow equipment to prepare snow and ice. In November, builders bring ice from a very clean river. In December, the outside of the hotel is finished.

The rooms are very quiet. There are no telephones and no televisions. The Ice Hotel visitors can use computers to send e-mail messages to friends and family.

In late April, the last guests leave the hotel. The weather becomes warmer, and the beautiful Ice Hotel begins to melt. In June, the Ice Hotel is a water hotel.

B. Circle *T* for true or *F* for false.

T	(F)	1. There are many ice hotels in Sweden.
T	(F)	2. The hotel is open for nine months a year.
(T)	F	3. The hotel has 6,500 overnight guests a year.
T	(F)	4. The hotel has a cinema, a church, and an exercise room.
T	(F)	5. Builders begin preparing the hotel in April.
(T)	F	6. The ice comes from a clean river.
T	(F)	7. The hotel closes in December.

Writing Our Stories:
On the Job

A. Read.

I am a desk clerk at a small motel near a busy highway. The motel has 50 rooms. I like my job. I check people into the motel, and I check people out of the motel. I don't wear a uniform. I use a computer to type names and addresses. I like my boss. He is helpful. I like my hours, too. I work five days a week. My days off are Monday and Tuesday. I work from 3:00 P.M. to 11:00 P.M. I have a dinner break from 7:00 to 7:30. My salary is low, but the work is easy, and I like to talk to people. I don't work overtime. I have two sick days and one week of vacation.

B. Check (✓) the true sentences about your job. (Answers will vary.)

_____ I have medical benefits.	_____ My hours are good.
_____ I have benefits for my family.	_____ I work a shift.
_____ I work overtime.	_____ I like my hours.
_____ I like my job.	_____ My co-workers are friendly.

C. In your notebook, write about your job.

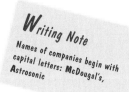

Writing Note
Names of companies begin with capital letters: McDougal's, Astrosonic

---

☀ Writing Our Stories:
On the Job

A. Read.

Ask students to read the story once all the way through. Ask:

What does this person do?
Why does he like his job?
How many hours does he work?
What benefits does he get?

B. Check the true sentences about your job.

Ask students to complete this exercise on their own.

C. In your notebook, write about your job.

• Remind students that they can use the information from Exercise B as they complete this activity.
• Explain to students that they should use the story in Exercise A as a model for their writing. Show students how they can adapt sentences to fit their own needs. For example: *I use a computer to type names and addresses* can become *I use a van to take people to the airport.*
• Ask several students to read what they have written about their jobs to the class. Encourage other students to ask questions.

Suggestion

For the next class, make copies of some sentences from the students' writing, leaving out regular present tense verbs and the verb *be*. Have students fill in these missing words.

Practicing on Your Own

A. Complete with *is* or *was*.

Instruct students to fill in the blanks on their own.

Suggestion

Have students use new information to write a story similar to the ones in Exercise A.

B. Answer.

Ask students to answer the questions using information about their own jobs.

C. Complete.

• Point out that each question may have more than one set of correct answers. For example, item 1 could be *Tony likes his job because it is interesting* or *Tony doesn't like his job because it is boring.*

• Ask students to read their responses to item 5 aloud to the class.

Practicing on Your Own

A. Complete with *is* or *was*.

1. Michelle ____is____ a manager at the Sunrise Hotel. She has other experience as a manager. She ____was____ a manager in a large hotel from 1997 to 1999.

2. Rima has experience as a cook. She ____was____ a cook in an Italian restaurant from 1996 to 2000. Now she ____is____ the head cook at an Italian restaurant in Boston.

3. Frank ____is____ an experienced electrician. He ____was____ an electrician in his country from 1994 to 1999. Now he ____is____ the supervisor of electricians at the Sunrise Hotel.

B. Answer. (Answers will vary.)

1. Do you work at a hotel? _____

2. Do you work at night? _____

3. Do you wear a uniform? _____

4. Do you get tips? _____

5. Do you earn a good salary? _____

| Yes, I do. |
| No, I don't. |

C. Complete. (Answers will vary.)

| likes | doesn't like |

| friendly |
| low |
| good |
| interesting |
| boring |
| helpful |

1. Tony _____ his job because it is _____.

2. Henry _____ his co-workers because they are _____.

3. Julia _____ her job because the hours are _____.

4. Yumiko _____ her job because the salary is _____.

5. I **like / don't like** my job because it is _____.

Looking at Numbers

A. Figure it out!

1. Martin is a desk clerk. He makes $10.00 an hour. He works 40 hours a week. What is his weekly salary? **$400**

2. Tom is a plumber. He works 40 hours a week and makes $20.00 an hour. How much does he earn per week? **$800**

3. Myra works part time as a housekeeper. She earns $8.00 an hour. She works 15 hours a week. What is her weekly salary? **$120**

4. Tina is an airport shuttle driver. She makes $4.00 an hour. She works 10 hours a day, 5 days a week. She usually makes $70 a day in tips. How much does she make per day? **$110**

Grammar Summary

1. **Present tense**	
I **wear** a uniform.	I **don't wear** a uniform.
I **have** an interesting job.	I **don't have** an interesting job.
He **wears** a uniform.	He **doesn't wear** a uniform.
She **has** medical benefits.	She **doesn't have** medical benefits.

2. *Yes/No questions*		
Do you **like** your job?	Yes, I **do.**	No, I **don't.**
Does she **like** her job?	Yes, she **does.**	No, she **doesn't.**

3. **Past** *be*	
I **am** a cook at the Flamingo.	(now)
I **was** a cook at Tio Pepe.	(past)
He **is** a plumber at a hotel.	(now)
He **was** a plumber at a motel.	(past)

4. *Can*	
I **can drive** a van.	**Can** you **use** a computer?
He **can repair** equipment.	**Can** he **speak** English?
She **can cook** Italian food.	

Looking at Numbers

A. Figure it out!

Have students complete the activity individually or in pairs. Check the answers with the whole class. If there is a difference of opinion about any answer, ask a student to put the mathematical work on the board.

Grammar Summary

• Review the summary with the class. Invite students to say other statements, questions, and answers that might appear in each of the four sections of the summary.

• See the Grammar Summary Expansion on page 241 for a more complete explanation of these grammar points.

Unit 14
A Visit to the Doctor

Discuss the person next to the unit number. Ask:

• *Who is standing next to the number 14?* (A doctor)

• *What is he wearing?* (He's wearing a green shirt and black pants. He has a stethoscope around his neck.)

☀Dictionary:
Parts of the Body,
Health Problems,
Remedies

A. Listen and repeat.
(CD2, Track 46)

• Ask students to look at the pictures in the *Parts of the Body* section as you play the audio or say the words aloud.

• Play the audio again, pausing after each word to allow students to repeat.

Suggestion

Name different parts of the body and ask students to point to these parts on their own bodies.

14 A Visit to the Doctor

Dictionary: Parts of the Body, Health Problems, Remedies

A. Listen and repeat.

Parts of the Body

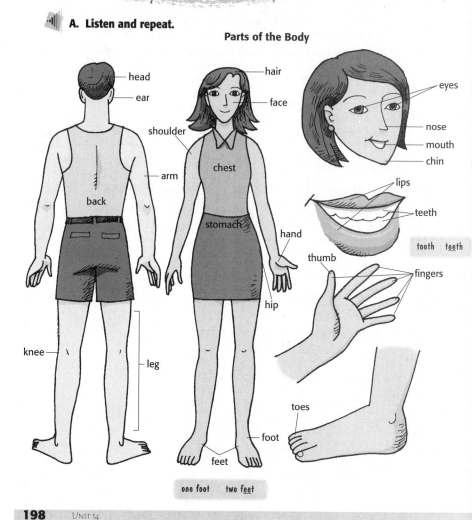

head
ear
shoulder
arm
back
knee
leg

hair
face
chest
stomach
hand
hip
foot
feet

one foot   two feet

eyes
nose
mouth
chin
lips
teeth

tooth   teeth

thumb
fingers
toes

Health Problems

allergy	asthma	burn	cold
chicken pox	cough	fever	headache
sore throat	stomachache	toothache	She's sneezing.

Remedies

aspirin	ibuprofen	ice pack	heating pad
inhaler	lotion	dentist	doctor

A. Listen and repeat.
(CD2, Track 47)

- Ask students to look at the pictures in the *Health Problems* and *Remedies* sections as you play the audio or say the words aloud.
- Play the audio again, pausing after each word to allow students to repeat.
- Answer any questions students may have using simple English sentences. For example:

S: *He has an allergy, right?*
T: *Yes. Maybe he has an allergy to flowers.*

- Invite students to comment on the pictures. Restate any ungrammatical comments in simple English. For example:

S: *Inhaler asthma?*
T: *That's right. He's using an inhaler for his asthma.*

☀Active Grammar:
Have / Has

A. Complete.

Have students complete the labeling activity on their own. Remind them that they can look back at the *Parts of the Body* dictionary on page 198 if they can't remember the names of any items.

Suggestion

Play a game of Simon Says. Have students stand by their seats. Explain that when you say the words *Simon Says* before a command, they should follow the command. If you do not say the words *Simon Says,* they should remain still. For example:

T: *Touch your neck.*
SS: (Students should stand still.)
T: *Simon says touch your neck.*
SS: (Students should touch their necks.)

You may wish to invite students to take turns leading the game.

Active Grammar: *Have / Has*

A. Complete.

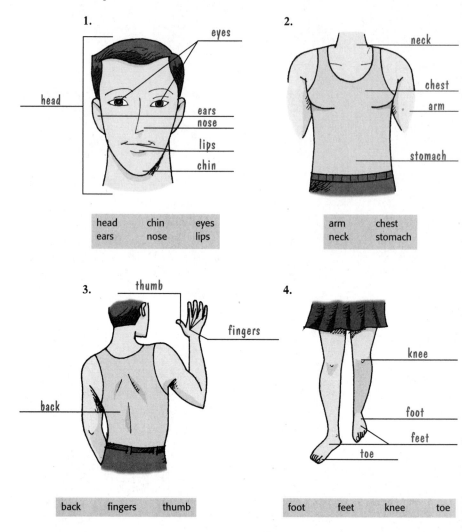

1.

eyes
head
ears
nose
lips
chin

| head | chin | eyes |
| ears | nose | lips |

2.

neck
chest
arm
stomach

| arm | chest |
| neck | stomach |

3.

thumb
fingers
back

| back | fingers | thumb |

4.

knee
foot
feet
toe

| foot | feet | knee | toe |

Where does it hurt?

1. Her __head__ hurts.   2. Her __back__ hurts.   3. Her __stomach__ hurts.

4. His __ear__ hurts.   5. His __foot__ hurts.   6. His __tooth__ hurts.

B. Listen again and write.

C. Listen and repeat.

hurt = ache

| backache | earache | headache | stomachache | toothache |

D. Complete.

1. His tooth hurts.   He has a _____toothache_____.
2. Her back hurts.   She has a _____backache_____.
3. My head hurts.   I have a _____headache_____.
4. His stomach hurts.   He has a _____stomachache_____.
5. My ear hurts.   I have an _____earache_____.

A Visit to the Doctor   **201**

Audio Script

A. Listen and repeat.
   (CD2, Track 48)
1. Her head hurts.
2. Her back hurts.
3. Her stomach hurts.
4. His ear hurts.
5. His foot hurts.
6. His tooth hurts.

☀ Where does it hurt?

A. Listen and repeat.
(CD2, Track 48)
Ask students to listen as you point to the pictures and play the audio. Then play the audio again, pausing after each sentence to allow students to repeat.

B. Listen again and write.
(CD2, Track 48)
Ask students to name the part of the body that is the focus of each picture. Draw attention to the jagged pain lines if necessary. Then play the audio again and have students fill in the missing words.

C. Listen and repeat.
(CD2, Track 49)
Point to the words as you play the audio or read the words aloud. Repeat the activity several times if students need more pronunciation practice.

Suggestion

Write the words *stomach, back,* and *ache* on the board. Ask a student to circle the letters that make the /k/ sound in each word. Point out that the k sound can be made with the letters *ch* or *che*, as well as with the letter *k*.

D. Complete.
Ask students to use the words in Exercise C to fill in the blanks. Have different students read the answers aloud. Correct pronunciation as necessary.

☀ Health Problems

A. Match.

Ask students to match each picture with one of the sentences. Tell students that they should look for the health problem that the person (or people) in each picture has, then look for the sentence that describes that problem.

Suggestion

Introduce *has* and *have*. Point to the box at the top right-hand corner and ask different students to read the sentences aloud. Then have students look at the pictures in the *Health Problems* section of page 199 and make sentences about each using the verb *have*. For example: *He has an allergy*.

Health Problems

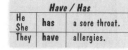

Have / Has		
He She	has	a sore throat.
They	have	allergies.

A. Match.

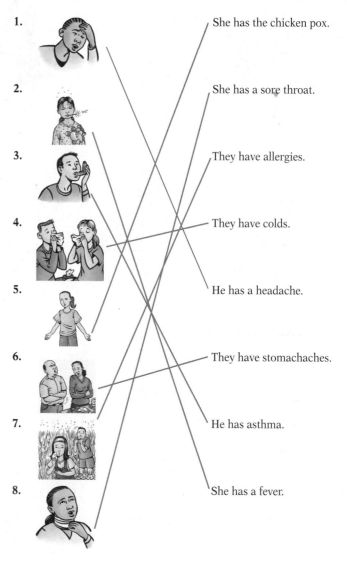

1.   She has the chicken pox.

2.   She has a sore throat.

3.   They have allergies.

4.   They have colds.

5.   He has a headache.

6.   They have stomachaches.

7.   He has asthma.

8.   She has a fever.

Household Remedies

·ıll A. Listen and repeat.

1.
2.
3.
4.

5.
6.
7.
8.

B. Read and number.

__5__ take aspirin   __8__ drink liquids   __6__ stay in bed

__2__ call the doctor   __4__ put on lotion   __7__ use a heating pad

__1__ use an ice pack   __3__ use an inhaler

C. Complete. What are they going to do?

(Answers may vary. Sample responses below.)

> I am going to call the doctor.
> He is going to call the doctor.
> She is going to . . .
> They are going to . . .

call the dentist	stay in bed
call the doctor	✓take aspirin
drink some soda	take ibuprofen
drink hot tea	take some medicine
use an inhaler	use a heating pad

1. She has a headache. She is going to _____ take aspirin _____.

2. They have sore throats. They are going to __drink hot tea.__

3. I have a backache. I'm going to __use a heating pad.__

4. She has a toothache. She's going to __call the dentist.__

5. My son has asthma. He __is going to use the inhaler.__

6. They have bad colds. They __are going to stay in bed.__

7. I have a fever. I __am going to take ibuprofen.__

☀ Household Remedies

·ıll A. Listen and repeat.
(CD2, Track 50)

- Ask questions about the pictures. For example:

T: *What's this?*
S1: *It's an ice pack.*
T: *When do you use an ice pack?*
S1: *When I hit my head.*

- Have students listen as you play the audio and point to the pictures. The second time through, have students repeat the sentences. Play the audio again if necessary.
- Point to pictures at random and call on different students to say the appropriate sentence.

B. Read and number.

Have students write the number of the appropriate picture in front of each instruction. Have them check their answers with a partner.

C. Complete.

Review the meaning of the phrases in the box to the right.

- Point out the grammar box to the left. Tell students that *going to* shows future meaning.
- Have students complete the sentences on their own. Review the answers by calling on individual students to read the statements.

Audio Script

A. Listen and repeat.
(CD2, Track 50)

1. Use an ice pack.
2. Call the doctor.
3. Use an inhaler.
4. Put on lotion.
5. Take some aspirin.
6. Stay in bed.
7. Use a heating pad.
8. Drink liquids.

☀ Reading Labels

Suggestion

Before doing Exercise A, introduce the meaning of *must* and *must not*. Explain: *We say* must *when it is necessary or very important to do something. For example, drivers must stop at a red light.* Repeat this kind of explanation for *must not*: *We say* must not *when it is necessary or very important to not do something. For example, drivers must not drive through a red light.*

Teacher Note

Point out the blue box that defines *once a day.* Since *once* means *eleven* in Spanish, it is important to remind Spanish speakers that this does not mean *eleven capsules a day.*

A. Read the directions.

Ask students to circle the answers in pairs. Then check the answers by reading each set of instructions aloud and calling on different students to read their answers.

Suggestion

Ask students to bring actual medicines from home. Go over the instructions on the outside of the packages and ask questions about what students *must do* and *must not do.*

Suggestion

Discuss where prescriptions can be filled in your community. You may also wish to outline with students the steps they will have to go through to get a prescription filled:

• See a doctor.
• Get the prescription.
• Take the perscription to a drug store.
• Give it to the pharmacist.
• Give their name, address, phone number, and health insurance number to the pharmacist.
• Sign their name in a book when they receive the prescription.

Reading Labels

A. Read the directions. Circle *must* or *must not*.

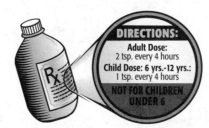

My Community
Three drugstores in my area:
1. _(Answers will vary.)_
2. _____
3. _____

1. Adults **(must)** / **must not** take two teaspoons every four hours.
2. Adults **must** / **(must not)** take four teaspoons every two hours.
3. Children under six **must** / **(must not)** take this medicine.

> **Directions:**
> Adults: Take 2 capsules every 4–6 hours.
> Do not give to children.
> Do not use with alcohol.

4. An adult **(must)** / **must not** take this medicine every four to six hours.
5. Parents **must** / **(must not)** give this medicine to children.
6. A patient **must** / **(must not)** drink alcohol and take this medicine.

> **Directions:**
> Take 1 capsule once a day.
> Take with food or milk.

`once a day = one time a day`

7. A patient **(must)** / **must not** take one capsule once a day.
8. Patients **(must)** / **must not** take this medicine with food or milk.

Culture Note
To get a prescription, you must see a doctor.

Working Together: Who's your doctor?

A. Complete. (Answers will vary.)

My doctor is _____ .

My children's pediatrician is _____ .

My dentist is _____ .

My hospital is _____ .

My pharmacy is _____ .

Culture Note
Many doctors think that women and men forty years of age and older should have a full medical checkup (examination) once a year.

B. Match.

1. A pediatrician — checks my eyes.
2. An allergist — takes care of my children.
3. An obstetrician/gynecologist — helps me talk about my problems.
4. An optometrist — checks my skin.
5. A psychologist — takes care of women.
6. A dermatologist — helps me control my allergies.

C. Pair practice. Ask and answer questions about these health problems.

(Answers may vary.)

What do you do for a headache?

I take aspirin.

headache

a fever

an allergy

a bad cold

backache

chicken pox

a stomachache

a bad cough

call the dentist
call the doctor
drink soda
drink hot tea
put on lotion
stay in bed
take asprin
take ibuprofen
take some medicine
use a heating pad

Working Together: Who's your doctor?

Suggestion

Before introducing Exercise A, provide local telephone books and show students how to locate the sections in the Yellow Pages that list doctors, dentists, hospitals, and pharmacies.

A. Complete.

Have students complete this information on their own.

B. Match.

• Read the list of specialists aloud and ask students to repeat. Correct pronunciation as necessary.

• Discuss what each kind of specialist does and complete the matching exercise with the whole class.

C. Pair practice.

• Say the list of instructions in the box at the right and ask students to repeat. Then read the sample dialogue with a student.

• Ask pairs of students to practice asking and answering questions about health problems and remedies. Move around the room providing assistance as needed.

Suggestion

Ask students to tell their classmates about remedies from their home cultures. For example, in some Asian countries people eat a special type of green orange to help cure a cold.

☀ Making an Appointment

A. Read.

Read the dialogue to students or have them read it on their own. Answer any questions they may have.

Suggestion

Have pairs of students read the dialogue. Make sure that students in each pair switch roles to get practice with both parts. Move around the room helping with pronunciation.

B. Complete the conversation with a partner.

• Before writing the answers in their books, have students work in pairs to practice the activity orally with several different sets of names, family members, and health problems.
• Have students complete Exercise B using Exercise A as a model. Move around the room checking students' work.

C. Act out the conversation.

Have students practice acting out the conversation in pairs. Invite several pairs to perform their conversation for the class.

Making an Appointment

A. Read.

Receptionist: Hello, Dr. Walsh's office.

Patient: Hello, this is Mrs. Moreno.

Receptionist: Hello, Mrs. Moreno. How can I help you today?

Patient: My daughter is sick.

Receptionist: What's the problem?

Patient: She has a high fever and a sore throat.

Receptionist: Can you come in today at 2:00?

Patient: Yes, I can.

Receptionist: OK, Mrs. Moreno. See you at 2:00.

B. Complete the conversation with a partner. (Answers will vary.)

Receptionist: Hello, Dr. _____'s office.

Patient: Hello, this is _____.

Receptionist: Hello, _____. How can I help you today?

Patient: _____

Receptionist: What's the problem?

Patient: _____

Receptionist: Can you come in today at _____?

Patient: _____

Receptionist: OK, _____. See you at _____.

C. Act out the conversation.

Looking at Forms: Patient Information Form

A. Complete. (Answers will vary.)

Culture Note
When you visit a doctor's office for the first time, you will have to fill out an information form or a medical information form.

Patient Information Form

Last Name _____ First Name _____ MI _____

Address _____

City _____ State _____

Zip Code _____

Home Telephone: _____ – _____ – _____

Work Telephone: _____ – _____ – _____

Employer _____

Insurance Company _____

Policy Number _____

Do you have any allergies to medication?   Yes   No

Explain _____

What is your problem today?

_____

_____

Looking at Forms: Patient Information Form

A. Complete.

• Discuss new vocabulary on this form, such as: *insurance company, policy number,* and *medication.* Write this new vocabulary on the board and ask students to give specific examples of each.

• Have students complete the forms with their own information.

The Big Picture:
In the Waiting Room

Suggestion

Ask students to describe the picture. You might use questions like these to get started:

- *Where are these people?*
- *Where is the doctor?*
- *Who is this?*
- *What is he/she doing?*
- *What is this person's problem?*
- *What is Mrs. Jacob's job?*

A. Listen. (CD2, Track 51)

Point to the picture and play the audio. Answer any questions students may have. Play the audio once or twice more.

B. Read and answer.

- Ask students to read the questions and locate the people mentioned in the picture.
- Check the answers by reading the questions one by one and calling on different students to answer. Note that there is more than one answer to the question *Who is sick?*

The Big Picture: In the Waiting Room

A. Listen.

B. Read and answer.

tetanus shot

1. Who is getting a checkup? Mr. Green.
2. Who has an allergy? Miss Gonzalez.
3. Who has a burn? Julia.
4. Who has a bad cough? Mrs. Lee.
5. Who is working in the office? Dr. Johnson and Mrs. Jacob.
6. Who is sick? Many patients.
7. Who has a headache? Mr. Patel.
8. Who is getting a tetanus shot? Andy
9. Who is a new patient? Mrs. Jackson

208 UNIT 14

Audio Script

The Big Picture:
In the Waiting Room

A. Listen. (CD2, Track 51)

Dr. Johnson's waiting room is very busy. It's early spring, and many patients are sick. Mrs. Jacob is Dr. Johnson's nurse. She's talking to Mrs. Jackson. She's a new patient, so she's going to fill out a patient information form. Mrs. Lee is reading a magazine. She has a bad cough. The doctor is going to listen to her chest. Mr. Green is 75 years old, and he's in good health. He's in the office for his checkup. He has a checkup once a year. Mrs. Rios and her daughter, Julia, are in the office, too. Julia's crying because she has a bad burn on her finger. She burned her finger on the stove. Mr. Patel is holding his head. His head hurts. He has a bad headache. Miss Gonzalez is sneezing and coughing. She has allergies, and she needs a prescription from Dr. Johnson. Mr. Henderson is talking to his son, Andy. Andy cut his arm and he needs a tetanus shot. He's scared because he doesn't like shots.

C. Read and circle.

1. Mrs. Jacob is the doctor.   Yes (No)
2. Mrs. Lee has a headache.   Yes (No)
3. Mr. Green has a cold.   Yes (No)
4. Mrs. Rios has allergies.   Yes (No)
5. Julia's finger hurts.   (Yes) No
6. Mr. Patel has a bad back.   Yes (No)
7. Mrs. Jackson is a new patient.   (Yes) No
8. Miss Gonzalez's throat hurts.   Yes (No)
9. Andy has a stomachache.   Yes (No)

D. Complete.

1. Mrs. Lee has a _____ bad cough _____.
2. Mr. Green needs a _____ checkup _____.
3. Mr. Patel's _____ head _____ hurts.
4. Miss Gonzalez has _____ allergies _____.
5. She needs a _____ prescription _____.
6. Andy needs a _____ tetanus shot _____.

allergies
checkup
✓bad cough
head
prescription
tetanus shot

E. Read and circle.

1. Why is the waiting room busy? It's busy because . . .

   a. it's late.   **b.** the doctor is away.   **(c.)** many people are sick.

2. What is Mrs. Jackson going to fill out?

   a. a prescription   **(b.)** a patient information form   **c.** an application

3. What is Mrs. Lee doing?

   (a.) She's coughing.   **b.** She's talking to the nurse.   **c.** She's sneezing.

4. Miss Gonzalez needs a prescription for _____.

   (a.) allergies   **b.** asthma   **c.** a cold

5. How does Andy feel?

   a. sick   **b.** happy   **(c.)** scared

C. Read and circle.

Ask students to circle the answers on their own. Remind them to look back at the picture on page 208 if they are not sure of an answer. Then have students check their work with a partner.

D. Complete.

Point out the possible answers in the box to the right. Then have students complete the sentences individually. Go over the answers with the class.

E. Read and circle.

Complete this activity with the whole class. After deciding on the right answer together, discuss the meanings of the wrong answers. Help students with any confusing terms. For example, say: The doctor is away *means the doctor is not in the office. Maybe he's at the hospital. Maybe he's on vacation.*

Reading: A Good Night's Sleep.

A. Before You Read.

Ask about the woman in the picture:

Where is she? (She's in bed.)
What is she doing? (She's sleeping.)
Is she sick? (No, she isn't.)

• Ask: *How many hours of sleep do you need?* Point out the chart. Ask students to answer the question for themselves.

• Ask students to read the instructions on getting a good night's sleep. Answer any questions students may have. Then read the instructions to the class.

Suggestion

Take a poll to see how many hours students sleep at night. Find out who feels they need more sleep.

B. Read and answer.

• Read through the three questions with students. Rephrase in simple English any sentences students don't understand. For example: *He can't concentrate in school* can be rephrased as *He thinks about other things in school.*

• Discuss the questions with the class. There may be several correct answers to each question. Accept all suggestions from the list in the reading as well as other reasonable ideas students offer.

Reading: A Good Night's Sleep

A. Before You Read. Look at the chart. How many hours of sleep do you need?

Age	Hours of sleep per night
Adults	7–8 hours
Teenagers	8–9 hours
Children	10–12 hours

Is it difficult for you to fall asleep? Sometimes your body is tired, but your mind is still working. Here are some ideas for a good night's sleep:

1. Try to go to bed and get up at the same time every day.

2. Take a warm shower or bath before you go to bed.

3. Relax before you close your eyes. Watch TV, read a book, or listen to soft music.

4. Don't eat late at night.

5. Make your room quiet and comfortable. Turn off the light and close the curtains.

6. Drink a cup of warm milk before you go to bed. Don't drink coffee, tea, or alcohol. The caffeine in the drinks will keep you awake.

Everyone has trouble sleeping once in a while. If you have trouble sleeping for more than one month, see your doctor.

B. Read and answer.   (Answers will vary.)

1. Joseph is 16 years old. He goes to school, plays soccer after school, works from 6:00 to 9:00, and then does his homework until 12:00 A.M. He can't concentrate in school. What can he do?

2. Maribel has many family problems. When she goes to bed, she thinks about her children, her husband, and her sisters. She can't sleep. What can she do?

3. Mr. Andaba works from 3:00 to 11:00. When he gets home, he eats dinner. He goes to bed at 1:00, but he doesn't sleep well. What can he do?

Writing Our Stories:
My Lifestyle

A. Read.

I am 70 years old. I am a senior citizen. I think I am in good health. I am very active. I am retired, but I volunteer three days a week at the elementary school. I help the children read. I go to the park five days a week. I walk two miles every morning. I go to the doctor every year for a checkup, and I see my dentist twice a year. I am a healthy person.

B. Complete these sentences about your lifestyle. (Answers will vary.)

1. I **am / am not** healthy.

2. I **always / sometimes / never** exercise.

3. I exercise _____ time(s) a week.

4. I get a checkup **every year / every other year**.

5. I visit the dentist **once a year / twice a year**.

6. I need to ☐ exercise more.
   ☐ **lose weight / gain weight.**
   ☐ visit the **doctor / dentist.**

Writing Note
Check the plural nouns in your story. Most plural nouns end in s: days, miles. Some plural nouns are irregular: children.

C. In your notebook, write about your health.

A Visit to the Doctor **211**

☀Writing Our Stories:
My Lifestyle

Suggestion

Ask students: *How old do you think the man in the picture is? How do you think he feels?* (happy, healthy, strong)

A. Read

• Read the story aloud. Use simple definitions and sample sentences to clarify vocabulary as necessary. For example:

Retire: *When a person stops working at age 60 or 70 they "retire."*
Volunteer: *When someone works for no pay, they "volunteer." Some people volunteer at hospitals or schools.*

• Ask students to reread the story on their own. Answer any questions they may have.

B. Complete these sentences about your lifestyle.

Ask students to complete the sentences by circling, filling in, and checking information that is true about themselves. If necessary, explain that *every other year* means *every second year*.

C. In your notebook, write about your health.

Remind students that they can use the reading in Exercise A as a guide for this writing practice. Show how they can adapt sentences to fit their own needs. For example, *I walk two miles every morning* can become *I ride my bicycle every evening*.

Practicing on Your Own

A. Describe the picture.

Ask students to complete the activity individually, then check their answers with a partner.

B. Complete the sentences.

Have students complete the sentences individually. Review the answers orally with the class. Write on the board and discuss any new remedies that students mention.

C. Read the directions.

Review the correct answers with the class.

Practicing on Your Own

A. Describe the picture. (Answers may vary. Sample responses below.)

Mr. Carter   Caroline   Ms. Brown   **EMERGENCY ROOM**   Mr. Rios   Mr. Lee

1. Mr. Carter _'s knee hurts_
2. Caroline _'s finger hurts_
3. Ms. Brown _has a bad headache_
4. Mr. Rios _has a backache_
5. Mr. Lee _'s stomach hurts_   .

B. Complete the sentences. (Answers will vary.)

1. When I have a cold, I take _____
2. When I need a doctor, I call _____
3. When I have a headache, I _____
4. When my tooth hurts, I _____
5. When I have a sore throat, I _____

C. Read the directions. (Circle) **must** or **must not.**

> Take 2 capsules a day, 1 in the morning and 1 before bed.
> Do not take with milk or juice.
> Take with water.

1. The patient **must** / (**must not**) take this medicine three times a day.
2. The patient (**must**) / **must not** take this medicine with water.

Looking at Numbers: Reading a Thermometer

A. Read the temperature.

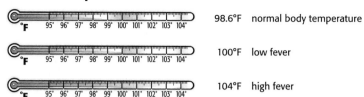

98.6°F normal body temperature

100°F low fever

104°F high fever

B. Write the temperature. Circle *normal*, *low*, or *high fever*.

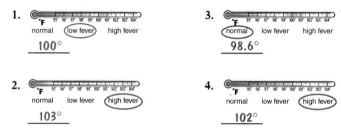

1. normal (low fever) high fever
   100°

3. (normal) low fever high fever
   98.6°

2. normal low fever (high fever)
   103°

4. normal low fever (high fever)
   102°

Grammar Summary

▶ **1. Have / Has**	▶ **2. My _____ hurt(s).**
I **have** a fever.	My back **hurts.**
You **have** a headache.	Your knee **hurts.**
We **have** sore throats.	Our feet **hurt.**
He **has** a stomachache.	His arm **hurts.**
She **has** asthma.	Her neck **hurts.**
They **have** colds.	Their stomachs **hurt.**

▶ **3. When I . . . , I . . .**

When I have a headache, **I** take aspirin.
When they have colds, **they** drink lots of liquids.

▶ **4. Must / Must not**

An adult **must take** two teaspoons of this medicine.
A child **must not take** this medicine.

☀Looking at Numbers: Reading a Thermometer

A. Read the temperature.

Have students study the thermometers and the words next to each one. Answer any questions students may have.

Suggestion

For students who are used to using Celsius temperatures, write these equivalents on the board.

98.6°F = 36.6°C
100°F = 37.8°C
104°F = 40.0°C

B. Write the temperature.

Have students circle and write the answers on their own. Review the correct answers with the class.

Grammar Summary

• Review the summary with the class. Invite students to say other statements that might appear in each of the sections of the summary.

• See the Grammar Summary Expansion on page 242 for a more complete explanation of these grammar points.

Unit 15
School

Discuss the people next to the unit number. Ask:

• *Who is standing next to the number 15?* (A woman and a little girl)

• *What are they doing?* (The woman and child are looking at the little girl's schoolwork together.)

☀ Dictionary:
Classroom Activities, School Subjects

 Dictionary: Classroom Activities, School Subjects

A. Listen and repeat.
(CD2, Track 52)

• Ask students to look at the pictures in the *Classroom Activities* section as you play the audio or say the words and phrases aloud.

• Play the audio again, pausing after each word or phrase to allow students to repeat.

• Say the words and phrases in random order and ask students to point to the correct picture.

• Have students sit in pairs and take turns saying words and pointing to the correct picture.

Suggestion

To review present continuous, point at the pictures and ask students to make sentence, telling what the children are doing. For example: *He's coloring. She's cutting out pictures.*

A. Listen and repeat.

Classroom Activities

 color

 cut out pictures

 do puzzles

 draw

 paint a picture

 play an instrument

 raise his hand

 sing

 sit in a circle

 take a test

 work in groups

 work on the computer

School Subjects

art

foreign language

geography

handwriting

math

music

physical education

science

social studies

spelling

Active Grammar: Present Continuous

A. Listen and complete.

1. Luisa _____ is playing _____ a game.

2. Cesar _____ is raising _____ his hand.

3. Yury _____ is drawing _____ a picture.

4. Irina and Marie _____ are reading _____ a story.

5. Paul and Michelle _____ are watching _____ a video.

draw
✓play
raise
take
watch
work
read

A. Listen and repeat.
(CD2, Track 52 *continued*)

• Ask students to look at the pictures in the *School Subjects* section as you play the audio or say the words aloud.

• Play the audio again, pausing after each word to have students repeat.

Active Grammar: Present Continuous

A. Listen and complete.
(CD2, Track 53)

Tell students that they will hear seven sentences. Explain that their task is to fill in the missing present continuous verb forms in the sentences in their books. Point out the verb choices in the box at the right.

(Continued on page 216)

Audio Script

A. Listen and complete.
(CD2, Track 53)

1. Luisa **is playing** a game.
2. Cesar **is raising** his hand.
3. Yury **is drawing** a picture.
4. Irina and Marie **are reading** a story.
5. Paul and Michelle **are watching** a video.
6. Anita **is taking** a test.
7. Young Su **is working** in a group.

B. Match the school subject with the picture.

Ask students to complete the matching activity on their own. Then have students check their answers with a partner.

Suggestion

Introduce other common names for some of these subjects. Write the names on the board and have students practice pronouncing them. For example:

Math—Arithmetic
Physical Education—Gym

6. Anita _____ is taking _____ a test.

7. Young Su _____ is working _____ in a group.

B. Match the school subject with the picture.

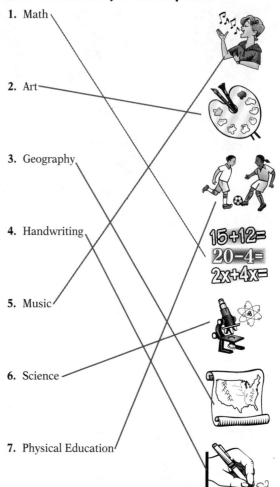

1. Math

2. Art

3. Geography

4. Handwriting

5. Music

6. Science

7. Physical Education

C. Pair practice. Ask and answer questions about school activities.

color	raise his hand
sing	talk to the teacher
draw a picture	work on the computer
play an instrument	write a report

What is he doing?

He's drawing a picture.

1.

2.

3.

4.

5.

6.

7.

8.

D. Describe your class. Circle Yes or No. (Answers may vary.)

1. We watch videos.   Yes   No
2. We read books.   Yes   No
3. We read newspapers in English.   Yes   No
4. We sing songs in English.   Yes   No
5. We take tests.   Yes   No
6. We work on computers.   Yes   No
7. We draw pictures.   Yes   No
8. We _____.

School   **217**

C. Pair practice.

- Read the sample dialogue with a student. Then have students complete the activity in pairs.
- To check the answers, call on a different pair of students to present each dialogue to the class.

D. Describe your class.

Ask students to complete the activity on their own. Then discuss the answers with the whole class. Ask students to tell you the sentences they created for item 8. Write several of these sentences on the board and have students repeat them.

☀ Ordinal Numbers: Grades

 A. Listen and repeat.
(CD2, Track 54)

- Ask students to look at the numbers and words as you play the audio or read the words. Point out that the word forms for ordinal numbers (such as *first*) and the number plus abbreviation of ordinal numbers (such as *1st*) are pronounced exactly the same way.
- Play the audio again and have students repeat. You may do this step several times.

Suggestion

- Ask twelve students to stand in a row and tell which position in the row they occupy. For example: *I'm first. I'm second,* etc.
- Call out the name of a student in the row and call on another student to tell where this person is in the row. For example:

T: *Yoko.*
S1: *She's third.*
T: *Pablo.*
S1: *He's ninth.*

- Have students change places and do the activity again. Rotate students until everyone has had a chance to be in the row.

Suggestion

Point out the Culture Note and tell students that schools for children in the United States are organized by grades. Ask students about schools in their town or city. Ask: *Is there an elementary or a middle school? A junior high school? What grades are in each school?*

B. Complete.

Have students fill in the blanks with ordinal numbers.

Ordinal Numbers: Grades

A. Listen and repeat.

Culture Note
Children start kindergarten when they are five or six years old.

kindergarten	1 first 1st	2 second 2nd	3 third 3rd	4 fourth 4th	5 fifth 5th
6 sixth 6th	7 seventh 7th	8 eighth 8th	9 ninth 9th	10 tenth 10th	11 eleventh 11th	12 twelfth 12th

Culture Note
Middle school = Grades 6, 7, and 8
Junior high school = Grades 7 and 8
Do you have a middle school or a junior high school in your town?

B. Complete.

Elementary School

1	2	3	4	5
first	second	third	fourth	fifth

Middle School

6	7	8
sixth	seventh	eighth

High School

9	10	11	12
ninth	tenth	eleventh	twelfth

C. Pronunciation: Ordinal numbers. Listen and repeat.

a. 1 1st	**e.** 5 5th	**i.** 9 9th
b. 2 2nd	**f.** 6 6th	**j.** 10 10th
c. 3 3rd	**g.** 7 7th	**k.** 11 11th
d. 4 4th	**h.** 8 8th	**l.** 12 12th

D. Listen and (circle.)

a. (3) 3rd	**d.** (10) 10th	**g.** 8 (8th)
b. 12 (12th)	**e.** 7 (7th)	**h.** 6 (6th)
c. 4 (4th)	**f.** (11) 11th	**i.** (9) 9th

E. Listen and (circle.)

1. elementary (middle) high school
2. (elementary) middle high school
3. elementary middle (high school)
4. (elementary) middle high school
5. elementary middle (high school)
6. elementary (middle) high school

F. Complete. (Answers may vary.)

1. My ____daughter____ is in the ____third____ grade in ____elementary____ school.

2. My _____ is in the _____ grade in _____ school.

3. My _____ is in the _____ grade in _____ school.

> brother
> sister
> son
> daughter
> grandson
> granddaughter
> friend

School   **219**

C. Pronunciation: Ordinal numbers. (CD2, Track 55)

The first time through, play the audio or read the cardinal number/ordinal number pairs as students just listen. The second time through, have students repeat. Do the activity several times.

Suggestion

Some students may benefit from focused practice of the pronunciation of the -st and -th endings. It may be beneficial to first practice the sounds in isolation (-st, -th), and then practice them in word context (first, fourth).

D. Listen and circle. (CD2, Track 56)

Ask students to listen and circle the cardinal or ordinal number they hear.

E. Listen and circle. (CD2, Track 57)

Have students listen to the ordinal numbers for various grades and then circle the type of school in which the grade is found.

F. Complete.

Ask students to complete the sentences with information about their family members, friends, or the children of friends. Invite several students to read their sentences to the class.

Audio Script

C. Pronunciation: Ordinal numbers. Listen and repeat. (CD2, Track 55)

a. one	first
b. two	second
c. three	third
d. four	fourth
e. five	fifth
f. six	sixth
g. seven	seventh
h. eight	eighth
i. nine	ninth
j. ten	tenth
k. eleven	eleventh
l. twelve	twelfth

D. Listen and circle. (CD2, Track 56)

a. three	**d.** ten	**g.** eighth
b. twelfth	**e.** seventh	**h.** sixth
c. fourth	**f.** eleven	**i.** nine

E. Listen and circle. (CD2, Track 57)

1. seventh grade
2. fourth grade
3. tenth grade
4. kindergarten
5. eleventh grade
6. eighth grade

Report Card

A. Listen and complete.
(CD2, Track 58)

Play the audio and ask students to complete the sentences. Play the audio as many times as students require, then check the answers with the class. As you check each answer, ask students for suggestions for how Paula's behavior could be improved. For example, for item 1 students might suggest: *She should raise her hand.*

B. Complete with a partner.

Have students complete the sentences in pairs.

Report Card

A. Listen and complete.

doesn't follow	doesn't pay	doesn't get along
doesn't do	doesn't raise	

☑ **Her behavior needs improvement.**

1. Paula ___doesn't raise___ her hand to answer questions.

2. She ___doesn't pay___ attention.

3. She ___doesn't get along___ with her classmates.

4. She ___doesn't do___ her homework.

5. She ___doesn't follow___ directions.

B. Complete with a partner.

Present Tense
He follow**s** directions.
He work**s** in a group.

☑ **Excellent behavior**

1. Victor ___raises___ his hand to answer questions.

2. He always ___does___ his homework.

3. He ___gets along___ very well with his classmates.

4. He ___pays attention___ to the teacher.

Audio Script

A. Listen and complete.
(CD2, Track 58)

1. Paula **doesn't raise** her hand to answer questions.
2. She **doesn't pay** attention.
3. She **doesn't get along** with her classmates.
4. She **doesn't do** her homework.
5. She **doesn't follow** directions.

C. Read the report card.

Pupil	Rani Singh	School	Emerson School
Teacher	Mrs. Lawson	Principal	Mr. Hobbie

Pupil Progress Report   Grade 4

A = Excellent   B = Very Good   C = Satisfactory   D = Poor   F = Not Passing

Subjects	1	2	3	4	Social Skills	1	2	3	4
Math	A	A	A		Follows school rules	B	A	B	
Art	A	B	B		Pays attention to teacher	A	B	A	
Handwriting	C	B	A		Works and plays well with others	C	B	A	
Music	B	B	B		**Work**				
Physical Education	C	B	B		Takes care of books	B	B	B	
Spelling	B	A	A		Follows directions	A	B	A	
Social Studies	C	B	C		Does homework well and on time	B	B	A	
Science	A	A	A		Asks for help	C	C	B	

Culture Note

Most public schools give report cards to the students four times a year. The parents must sign the report card and return it to school.

D. Answer.

1. What are two of Rani's best subjects?
   Math, Science
2. What subject is more difficult for Rani?
   Social Studies
3. Does Rani work and play well with others?
   Yes
4. Is Rani a good student? Why or why not?
   (Answers may vary.)

C. Read the report card.

- Discuss the different sections of the report card with the class and explain anything students don't understand. Point out the columns numbered 1 through 4. Explain that students get marks or grades from the teacher four times a year and these columns represent the four *marking periods* of the school year.
- Have students read the report card. Answer any remaining questions.

Suggestion

Ask questions about the report card. For example:

- *What is the student's name?*
- *What is the teacher's name?*
- *What grade is Rani in?*
- *What does "A" mean?*
- *What is his/her grade in math?*

D. Answer.

Discuss the answers to these questions with the whole class.

Working Together

A. Complete the information about your child's education or the education of a child you know well.

• Have students complete the information, then share what they have written in small groups. Move among the groups, offering help as needed.
• Invite some students to read their information to the class.

B. Complete about the child in Exercise A.

Have students complete these sentences about the child in Exercise A. Then ask students to read their sentences to a partner.

Working Together

A. Complete the information about your child's education or the education of a child you know well. Compare with a group of three or four classmates.

1. The name of my _____'s school is _____.
2. My _____ is in _____ grade.
3. The school is in _____.
   city
4. The school is on _____. (Answers will vary.)
   street
5. The teacher is _____.
6. The principal is _____.

B. Complete about the child in Exercise A. (Answers will vary.)

1. _____ **likes / doesn't like** the school.
   name of the child
2. _____ **likes / doesn't like** the teacher.
   name of the child
3. I **like / don't like** the teacher.
4. _____ **is / isn't** learning to play an instrument.
   He/She
5. _____ **is / isn't** learning how to use a computer.
   He/She
6. _____ **is / isn't** studying science.
   He/She
7. _____ **is / isn't** learning another language.
   He/She
8. _____ **is / isn't** in a club at the school.
   He/She
9. _____

Helping a Child Succeed in School

A. Read.

Read to her.

Help her with her homework.

Give her a quiet place to study.

B. Read this list of ways to help a child in school.

1. Take her to the library.
2. Talk with her teacher regularly.
3. Go on field trips with her class.
4. Encourage her to play a musical instrument.
5. Encourage her to play a sport or to join a school club.

C. In your notebook, write two more ways to help a child in school.

School **223**

☀ Helping a Child Succeed in School

A. Read.

Ask students to look at the pictures and read the sentences under each picture. Answer any questions students may have.

Suggestion

Take an informal poll of the parents in your class. Ask: *Do you read to your child? Do you help with your child's homework? Do you give your child a quiet place to study?* Write the total number of parents who do each of these things on the board. Ask why each activity is important. (Reading to a child will help the child learn to read and to love reading. Getting help with homework shows that you care about the child's work. Having a quiet place to study makes it easier for the child to learn.)

B. Read this list of ways to help a child in school.

Ask students to read through the list and circle any words or phrases they don't understand. Use simple explanations and examples to teach these words. For example:

• Regularly *means every week or every two weeks.*
• Field trips *are class visits to places like museums, zoos, or concerts.*
• A school club *is a group that meets after school. School clubs focus on certain activities, such as playing chess, putting on plays, and writing the school newspaper.*

C. In your notebook, write two more ways to help a child in school.

Students can use the information from Exercise B to start thinking about answers to this question. You might wish to brainstorm ideas with the whole class before having students write their own answers.

☀The Big Picture:
In the Classroom

A. Listen. (CD2, Track 59)

- Invite students to talk about the picture. Ask:

  What grade do you think this is?
  About how old are the students?
  What subject do you think they are studying?
  What is this student doing?

- Play the audio and have students just listen. Then ask what they heard on the audio that was different from what was suggested in class before the audio was played.

B. Listen again and label the people.

- Say the names in the box and ask students to repeat.
- Play the audio again and have students label the people in the pictures. Play the audio as many times as students require.
- Go over the correct answers with the class.

C. Read and circle.

Have students circle their answers. You may wish to play the audio one last time so students can check their work.

The Big Picture: In the Classroom

A. Listen.

Marta Vicky Ricky Mr. Wash.

Ernest Glori.

Nancy Steve Mei

B. Listen again and label the people.

Ricky	Marta	Gloria	Nancy	Mr. Washington
Vicky	Ernest	Mei	Steve	

C. Read and circle.

1. Yes **No** This is a sixth-grade class.
2. Yes **No** Mr. Washington is using the computers.
3. **Yes** No Ernest is drawing a map.
4. Yes **No** Ricky is raising his hand.
5. Yes **No** Mei is painting a picture.

224 UNIT 15

Audio Script

☀The Big Picture:
In the Classroom

A. Listen. (CD2, Track 59)

This is Mr. Washington's fifth-grade social studies class. It is almost the end of the school year, so everyone is busy. Almost all of the students are working in groups. They are doing their final projects for the class. Ricky and Vicky are working on computers. Mr. Washington is helping them. Marta is also working on a computer. She has a question, so she is raising her hand. Ernest and Nancy are drawing a map. Gloria and Mei are cutting out pictures. Steve isn't sitting with a group because he doesn't like to work in groups. He likes to work alone. He is reading a book about science and writing a report. It is a very noisy classroom, but the students are working hard.

6. (Yes) No   Steve is reading alone.

7. Yes (No)   Steve likes to work in groups.

8. Yes (No)   All of the students are working in groups.

D. Complete. Some of the sentences are negative.

do	help	raise	work
draw	read	sit	

1. The students ____are doing____ final projects.

2. Mr. Washington ____is helping____ the students.

3. Most of the students ____are working____ in groups.

4. Students ____are working____ on computers.

5. Ernest and Nancy ____are drawing____ a map.

6. Marta has a question, so she ____is raising____ her hand.

7. Steve ____isn't sitting____ with other students. He's working alone.

8. Gloria and Mei ____aren't working____ on the computer, but Ricky and Vicky are.

E. Pair practice. Ask and answer questions about your English class.

Do you take tests in your class?

Do you work in groups in your class?

Yes, I do.

No, I don't.

Present Tense
Do you . . . ?
Yes, I do.
No, I don't.

practice pronunciation

raise your hand

study U.S. geography

practice handwriting

draw pictures

work on computers

D. Complete.

Point to the list of verbs in the box. Ask questions about the spelling of these verbs in the present continuous form:

T: *How do you spell sitting?*

S: *S-I-T-T-I-N-G.*

T: *That's right. Double the final consonant.*

T: *How do you spell raising?*

S: *R-A-I-S-I-N-G.*

T: *Yes, that's correct. Drop the final e.*

• Have students complete the exercise and check their answers with a partner. Then ask students to write their answers on the board.

E. Pair practice.

• Have a pair of students read the sample dialogue to the class. Point out the sample phrases students can use in their questions and answers. Encourage students to also use their own phrases.

• After students have had a chance to practice for a few minutes, invite pairs to present their dialogues to the class.

☀Reading: School Uniforms—Yes or No?

A. Before You Read.

• Discuss the questions with the class. Invite students to tell about the school uniforms in their home countries. Ask:

What do the uniforms look like?
Do the boys wear jackets?
What color?
Do the girls wear skirts?
How much does a student uniform cost?

• Ask students to read the story to themselves. When they finish, invite them to ask about anything they don't understand. Encourage students to comment on the reading.

B. Answer.

Point out the underlined and numbered answer to item 1 in the story. Tell students to mark the answers to questions 2 through 5 the same way.

C. List the five reasons why many schools have uniforms.

Have students work individually to scan the reading for the five reasons. Ask students to write the reasons in their books, then check their work with a partner.

Reading: School Uniforms—Yes or No?

A. Before You Read. (Answers will vary.)

1. Do your children or children you know wear uniforms?

2. What kinds of schools require school uniforms?

Culture Note
State and local taxes pay for public school education. Parents must pay for private school and religious school education.

① In the past, only students in U.S. private and religious schools wore uniforms to school. Today, many states are changing. Many public schools require students to wear uniforms to school. ② Some people like uniforms, but others don't.

There are many reasons to have school uniforms. One reason is to decrease theft. ③ In some schools, people steal expensive clothing. Students do not think about their expensive sneakers or designer jackets when they wear uniforms. A second reason is discipline. ④ Principals and teachers think students pay better attention when they wear uniforms. A third reason is safety. A security guard can easily see a stranger in the school. Another reason is for school spirit. When all the students are wearing uniforms, the students feel part of a group. Finally, for students who don't have much money, ⑤ uniforms are cheap.

Many students don't like school uniforms. They want to decide what to wear. What do you think? Do you think school uniforms are a good idea?

B. Answer. <u>Underline</u> and number the answers in the reading.

1. In the past, which students wore uniforms?
2. Does everyone like school uniforms?
3. Why do school uniforms help decrease theft?
4. Why do principals and teachers like school uniforms?
5. Are uniforms more expensive than regular clothes?

(Answers are numbered and underlined above.)

C. List the five reasons why many schools have uniforms. 1. To decrease theft. 2. For discipline. 3. For safety. 4. For school spirit. 5. Uniforms are cheap.

Writing Our Stories:
An Absence Note

A. Read.

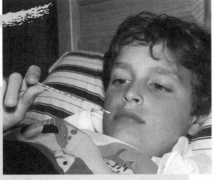

May 1, 2003

Dear Mrs. Woods,
    Please excuse Billy's absence from school on Monday and Tuesday. He could not come to school because he had a fever and cold. Please give him the homework.
                 Sincerely,
                 Mrs. Collins

B. Write an absence note. (Answers will vary.)

```
                                        _____
                                              Date

Dear _____,
        Name of teacher
    Please excuse _____
_____.  _____ could not come to
school because _____.
Please _____.
                            Sincerely,
                                    _____
```

Writing Note
Circle the commas in this letter. Where do you use a comma?

Writing Our Stories:
An Absence Note

A. Read.

Read the letter aloud to students or have them read it silently. Answer any questions they may have.

B. Write an absence note.

- Ask:

  Who has a child in school? When your child is absent, do you need to call the school? When your child returns to school, do you need to send an absence note?

- Ask students to complete this activity using information from their own lives, if possible.
- The letter in Exercise A can serve as a model for this writing assignment. Show how students can adapt sentences to fit their own needs. For example: *He could not come to school because he had a fever and a cold* can become *She cold not come to school because she had a stomachache.*

Suggestion

After students have finished their letters, have several of them write one sentence from their letter on the board. Correct any spelling or grammar errors. Remind students to watch for these errors in their own writing.

☀Practicing on Your Own

A. Write the answers about your class and your teacher.

Point out the short answers in the box and have students complete the activity on their own.

B. Read and complete.

Point out the words in the box that students can use for answers.

Suggestion

Write these idiomatic expressions on the board.

- *pay attention*
- *do (your) homework*
- *get along with (someone)*
- *follow directions*

Invite students to make up original sentences using each expression.

Practicing on Your Own

Yes, I do.	No, I don't.
Yes, she does.	No, she doesn't.
Yes, he does.	No, he doesn't.
Yes, we do.	No, we don't.
Yes, they do.	No, they don't.

A. Write the answers about your class and your teacher. (Answers will vary.)

1. Do you always do your homework? _____
2. Does your teacher give homework every day? _____
3. Do you and your classmates get along? _____
4. Do you try to speak English in every class? _____
5. Do you play games in class? _____
6. Do your classmates speak your native language? _____
7. Does your teacher help you after class? _____
8. Does your teacher write on the blackboard? _____

B. Read and complete.

Jason is a poor student. His behavior needs improvement.

Patty is a good student. Her behavior is excellent.

doesn't do	doesn't pay	doesn't get along
does	pays	gets along
	follows	doesn't follow

1. Jason ___doesn't___ ___pay___ attention in class.
2. Patty ___does___ her homework every day.
3. Patty ___follows___ the teacher's directions.
4. Jason ___doesn't___ ___do___ his homework.
5. Patty ___gets___ ___along___ well with the other students.
6. Jason ___doesn't___ ___get___ ___along___ with the other students.

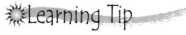

Learning Tip

> I raise my hand in class.
> I try to talk and answer questions.
> It's OK if I make a mistake.

☐ I like this idea.
☐ I don't like this idea.
☐ I'm going to try this idea.
(Answers will vary.)

Grammar Summary

▶ **1. Present tense**

| He **pays** attention. | She **doesn't pay** attention. |
| He **raises** his hand. | She **doesn't raise** her hand. |

▶ **2. Present-tense *yes/no* questions**

| **Do** you **have** computers? | Yes, I **do.** |
| **Do** you **take** tests? | No, I **don't.** |

▶ **3. Present continuous**

He **is drawing** a picture.

She **is working** on a computer.

They **are sitting** in a circle.

Learning Tip

Discuss the learning tip with students. Ask:

- *Do you raise your hand in class?*
- *Do you try to talk and answer questions?*
- *Do you believe it's OK to make a mistake?*

Teacher Note

In some countries and cultures students are expected to answer questions only if they can give perfectly correct answers. Partial or incorrect answers are not acceptable in these cultures. It may be necessary to explain to your students that one of the best ways to learn is to start with an incomplete or even an incorrect response.

Grammar Summary

- Review the summary with the class. Invite students to say other statements, questions, and answers that might appear in each of the three sections of the summary.
- See the Grammar Summary Expansion on page 243 of the Teacher's Guide for a more complete explanation of these grammar points.

Grammar Summary Expansion

1. Statements: *Be*

Full Forms			Contractions	
Subject	*be*		**Subject** + *be*	
I	**am**	from Cuba.	I**'m**	from Cuba.
You	**are**	a teacher.	You**'re**	a teacher.
He	**is**	a student.	He**'s**	a student.
She	**is**	from Haiti.	She**'s**	from Haiti.
We	**are**	from Mexico.	We**'re**	from Mexico.
They	**are**	from Egypt.	They**'re**	from Egypt.

Notes

- We often use contractions when we speak.
- We usually use full forms in writing.
- We sometimes use contractions in writing.
- Some uses of the verb *be* are:
  —to name things: *This is a pen.*
  —to describe a person's origin: *I am from Russia.*
  —to describe location: *The book is on the table*
  —to tell age: *I am 18 years old.*

2. Possessive adjectives

Possessive adjective	Noun	
My	name	is Vito.
Your	ID number	is 442455.
His	teacher	is Mr. Lee.
Her	telephone number	is 833-8899.
Our	last name	is Garcia.
Their	last name	is Smith.

Notes

- A possessive adjective always comes before a noun.
- A possessive adjective shows who owns something.
- A possessive adjective takes the place of a noun + an apostrophe.
  *Hiro's teacher is Mr. Lee = **His** teacher is Mr. Lee.*

3. *Wh-* questions

What/Where	*be*	
What	is	your telephone number?
What	are	your teachers' names?
Where	is	Rita from?
Where	are	you from?

Notes

- Questions with *What* ask questions about things.
- Questions with *Where* ask about places or the location of objects.

1. *Yes/No questions*

Questions			Short Answers		
Be	Subject		*Yes/No*	Subject	*be*
Is	this	your pen?	Yes,	it	**is.**
Is	this	a clock?	No,	it	**isn't.**

Notes

- The answer to a *Yes/No* question is usually a short answer.
- Short answers always use a pronoun, not a noun.
  Yes, it is. NOT: ~~Yes, your pen is.~~
- We never use a contraction with a *yes* answer.
  Yes, it is. NOT: ~~Yes, it's.~~

2. Singular and plural nouns

Regular		Irregular	
Singular	Plural	Singular	Plural
clock	clock**s**	man	m**en**
chair	chair**s**	woman	w**o**men
door	door**s**	child	child**ren**

Notes

- Most nouns have plural forms that end in *-s*.
- The United States is a singular noun.
  The United States is a big country.
- Some other common irregular plural forms are: *person/people* and *foot/feet*.
- Some nouns have only a plural form: *clothes, glasses, pants*.

3. *There is/There are*

There	*be*	
There	**is**	a pencil on the desk.
There	**are**	ten desks in our classroom.

Notes

- We use *there* instead of *it* to point things out.
  There is a book on the table. NOT: ~~It is a book on the table.~~
- A sentence beginning with *there* often shows location.
- We use *there* only the first time we mention something.
  There *is a clock in the room.* ***It*** *is over the door.*

1. *How old* questions

How old questions			Answers	
How old	*be*	Subject	Subject + *be*	Number
How old	is	he?	He is	15.
How old	is	Rosa?	She's	29.

Note

Questions with *How old* ask about age.

2. Adjectives

Adjectives in sentences with *be*			Adjectives in sentences with *have/has*			
Subject	*be*	Adjective	Subject	*have/has*	Adjective	Noun
Rita	is	**thin.**	She	has	**long**	hair.
Grandmother	is	**tall.**	He	has	**brown**	eyes.

Notes

- Adjectives describe people, places, or things.
- In sentences with *be*, we put the adjective after the verb.
- In sentences with *have*, we put the adjective before the noun it describes.
- Adjectives are never plural.
  I have three red pens. NOT: ~~I have three reds pens.~~

3. Short questions and answers

Questions			Short Answers		
Be	Subject		*Yes/No*	Subject	*be* (*not*)
Is	she	young?	Yes,	she	**is.**
Is	he	heavy?	No,	he	**isn't.**
Is	my hair	wavy?	No,	it	**isn't.**

Notes

- These *Yes/No* questions end with an adjective.
- For more information about *Yes/No* questions, see Unit 2, Item 1.

1. Prepositions

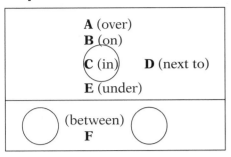

Notes

- Prepositions tell where things are.
- Prepositions usually appear in a prepositional phrase.
- The following prepositional phrases describe the objects in the picture.
  The A is **over the** *circle.*
  The B is **on** *the circle.*
  The C is **in** *the circle.*
  The D is **next to** *the circle.*
  The E is **under** *the circle.*
  The F is **between** *the two circles.*

2. *Where* questions

Where questions			Answers with a prepositional phrase		
Where	*Be*	Subject	Subject + *be*	Preposition	Location
Where	is	the desk?	It's	next to	the window.
Where	are	the books?	They're	on	the table.

Notes

- Questions with *Where* ask about the location of objects.
- *Where* questions are often answered with a prepositional phrase.

3. *Yes/No* questions

Questions			Short Answers		
Be	Subject	Prepositional phrase	*Yes/No*	Subject	*be*
Is	the bed	in the bedroom?	Yes,	it	**is.**
			No,	it	**isn't.**
Are	the sofas	in the kitchen?	Yes,	they	**are.**
			No,	they	**aren't.**

Note

For more information about *Yes/No* questions, see Unit 2, Item 1.

1. Present continuous statements

Full Forms				Contractions		
Subject	*be*	*-ing* form		**Subject + *be***	*-ing* form	
I	**am**	**reading.**		I**'m**	**reading.**	
You	**are**	**driving.**		You**'re**	**driving.**	
He	**is**	**sleeping.**		He**'s**	**sleeping**	
She	**is**	**studying.**		She**'s**	**studying.**	
We	**are**	**cleaning**	the house.	We**'re**	**cleaning**	the house.
They	**are**	**doing**	their homework.	They**'re**	**doing**	their homework.

Notes

- The present continuous tense is used to talk about an action that is happening right now.
- Some verbs are not usually used in the present continuous. These verbs include *see, hear, know, be, like,* and *want*. These verbs are usually used with the simple present rather than the present continuous.

2. *Yes/No* questions

Questions				Short Answers	
Be	Subject	*-ing* form			
Am	I	sleeping?		Yes, you **are.**	No, you**'re not.**
Are	you	studying	English?	Yes, I **am.**	No, I**'m not.**
Is	he	reading	a book?	Yes, he **is.**	No, he **isn't.**
Is	she	drinking?		Yes, she **is.**	No, she **isn't.**
Are	we	watching	TV?	Yes, we **are.**	No, we **aren't.**
Are	they	helping	Mother?	Yes, they **are.**	No, they **aren't.**

Note

For more information about *Yes/No* questions, see Unit 2, Item 1.

3. *Wh-* questions

Questions				Answers		
Wh- word	*be*	Subject	*-ing* form	**Subject + *be***	*-ing form*	
What	am	I	wearing?	You're	wearing	a dress.
What	are	you	doing?	I'm	cooking	dinner.
What	is	he	eating?	He's	listening	to music.
Where	is	she	going?	She's	going	to the car.
What	are	we	buying?	We're	buying	books.
What	are	they	studying?	They're	studying	English.

Note

For more information about *Wh-* questions, see Unit 1, Item 3 and Unit 4, Item 2.

1. *Want/Wants*

Subject	*want*	Infinitive	
I	**want**	to go	to the movies.
He	**wants**	to visit	Mexico.

Notes

- Statements with *want* + infinitive describe things people wish to do.
- *Want* can also appear without the infinitive:
  I want some coffee.
- *Like* and *need* can also be followed by an infinitive:
  I like to swim. (I enjoy swimming.)
  I need to study. (It is necessary for me to study.)

2. *Yes/No* questions

Questions			Short Answers		
Be	Subject		*Yes/No*	Subject	*be*
Is	the city	old?	Yes,	it	**is.**
Is	New York	small?	No,	it	**isn't.**
Are	the people	friendly?	Yes,	they	**are.**
Are	restaurants	expensive?	No,	they	**aren't.**

Note

For more information about *Yes/No* questions, see Unit 2, Item 1.

3. *Or* questions

Questions					Short Answers	
Be	Subject		*or*			
Is	Boston	large	**or**	small?	It's	large.
Are	refrigerators	expensive	**or**	cheap?	They're	expensive.

Notes

- An *or* question gives the listener two choices.
- The two choices in an *or* question are often opposites.
- The answer to an *or* question usually contains one of the choices given.

1. Prepositions

Prepositional Phrase			
Subject	*be*	Preposition	Location
The post office	is	**across from**	the library.
The Statue of Liberty	is	**in**	New York City.
The hospital	is	**on**	Main Street.

Notes

- These prepositions consist of more than one word: *on the corner of, in front of, next to, across from.*
- The meaning of *in* and *on* are different when locating objects on a map. (*in* a city, *in* a state; *on* a street.)

2. *Who* questions

Questions			Short Answers	
Who	Present Continuous		Subject	*be*
Who	is cooking	dinner?	I	am
Who	is talking?		You	are.
Who	is parking	the car?	He	is.
Who	is watching	the children?	Linda	is.
Who	is eating	lunch?	We	are.
Who	is drinking	coffee?	They	are.

Notes

- The word *who* asks questions about people.
- Use *is* (never *are*) to ask a present continuous *who* question. *Who is coming to class today?* NOT: ~~*Who are coming to class today?*~~
- *Who is* is often abbreviated by *Who's* especially in speech: *Who's studying?*

3. *Can* statements

Subject	*can*	Base form	
I	**can**	borrow	books from the library.
You	**can**	drive	a car.

Note

Can never takes an -*s* ending with *he, she,* or *it*.
He can ride a bicycle. NOT: ~~*He cans ride a bicycle.*~~

Unit 8

How much questions

How much	*be*		Subject + *be*	Price
How much	is	the cell phone?	It's	$189.00
How much	are	the headphones?	They're	$39.95

Notes

- *How much* questions ask about price.
- *How much?* is a shorter version of the question. It is used in conversation when the item asked about is known.

Unit 9

1. Present tense

Subject	Verb	
I	sell	clothes.
You	fill	prescriptions.
He	cut**s**	hair.
She	take**s**	pictures.
We	prepare	food.
They	take	orders.

Notes

- The simple present tense describes regular activities and repeated actions.
  I get up at 8:00.
- This tense also shows that something is true all the time.
  I like pizza.
- Simple present verbs following *I, you, we,* and *they* don't have an *-s* ending.
- Simple present verbs following *he, she,* and *it* have an *-s* ending.

2. *Yes/No* questions

Questions				Short Answers	
Do/Does	Subject	Base form			
Do	I	take	orders?	Yes, you **do.**	No, you **don't.**
Do	you	prepare	food?	Yes, I **do.**	No, I **don't.**
Does	he	help	customers?	Yes, he **does.**	No, he **doesn't.**
Does	she	cut	hair?	Yes, she **does.**	No, she **doesn't.**
Do	we	watch	customers?	Yes, we **do.**	No, we **don't.**
Do	they	help	customers?	Yes, they **do.**	No, they **don't.**

Notes

- Simple present tense *Yes/No* questions use the base form of the verb.
- Simple present tense short answers use *do* or *does.*

3. *Wh-* questions

Questions				Answers	
Wh- word	*do/does*	Subject	Base form	Subject	Verb
Where	do	you	work?	I	work at Mim's.
What	does	he	do?	He	takes pictures.

4. Prepositions: *at, from . . . to*

	Preposition	Time		
She leaves the house	**at**	9:00.		

	Preposition	Time	Preposition	Time
She works	**from**	9:30	**to**	4:30.

Notes

- The preposition *at* tells a specific time.
- The preposition *from . . . to* gives a time range or a beginning and an ending.

1. Present continuous

Subject	be	-ing form	
I	**am**	**wearing**	jeans.
You	**are**	**wearing**	a blouse.
He	**is**	**wearing**	a tie.
She	**is**	**wearing**	a dress.
We	**are**	**wearing**	hats.
They	**are**	**wearing**	T-shirts.

Note

For more information about the present continuous, see Unit 5, Item 1.

2. *How much* questions

Questions			Answers	
How much	*be*		Subject + *be*	Price
How much	is	the dress?	It's	$49.00.
How much	are	the shoes?	They're	$29.95.

Note

For more information about *How much* questions, see Unit 8, Item 1.

3. Short *Yes/No* questions and answers

Questions				Short Answers		
Be	Subject	Weather word	Place	*Yes/No*	Subject	*be*
Is	it	rainy	in Seattle?	Yes,	it	**is.**
Is	it	cold	in Miami?	No,	it	**isn't.**

Note

For more information about *Yes/No* questions, see Unit 2, Item 1.

1. Present tense

Affirmative Statements			Negative Statements			
Subject	Verb		Subject	*do/does + not*	Base form	
I	**eat**	toast.	I	**don't**	**eat**	bagels.
You	**live**	with your sister.	You	**don't**	**live**	with your parents.
He	**likes**	cake.	He	**doesn't**	**like**	ice cream.
She	**drinks**	tea.	She	**doesn't**	**drink**	coffee.
We	**shop**	on Saturday.	We	**don't**	**shop**	on Sunday.
They	**drink**	coffee.	They	**don't**	**drink**	tea.

Notes

- We use *don't* + base form to make negative statements with *I, we, you,* and *they.*
- We use *doesn't* + base form to make negative statements with *he, she,* and *it.*
- For more information about the present tense, see Unit 9, Item 1.

2. Adverbs of frequency

Subject	Adverb of frequency	Verb	
I	**always**	eat	breakfast.
He	**sometimes**	drinks	soda.
She	**never**	eats	fish.

Notes

- Adverbs of frequency tell how often something happens.
- Adverbs of frequency come before all verbs except the verb *to be.*
- Adverbs of frequency come after the verb *to be.*
  I'm always busy.
- Some frequency adverbs can come at the beginning of a sentence.
  Sometimes, he is busy.

3. *Will/ 'll*

Subject + *will/('ll)*	*have*	Food item
I'll	have	the steak.
He'll	have	an iced tea.
She'll	have	ice cream.

Notes

- When ordering food in a restaurant, we often use subject + *will ('ll)* + *have* + a food item.
- In this situation, *will* is not really used to talk about the future; it is a set expression used to order food from a waiter or waitress.

1. Present continuous

Affirmative Statements				Negative Statements		
Subject	*be*	*-ing* form of verb		Subject	*be + not*	*-ing* form of verb
I	**am**	**eating.**		I	**'m not**	**sleeping.**
You	**are**	**studying.**		You	**aren't**	**driving.**
He	**is**	**reading.**		He	**isn't**	**talking.**
She	**is**	**cooking.**		She	**isn't**	**eating.**
The paint (It)	**is**	**peeling.**		The stove (It)	**isn't**	**working.**
We	**are**	**talking.**		We	**aren't**	**studying.**
The faucets (They)	**are**	**leaking.**		The lights (They)	**aren't**	**working.**

Note

For more information about the present continuous, see Unit 5, Item 1.

2. *There is/There are*

Questions				Short Answers		
Be	*there*			*Yes/No*	Subject	*be*
Is	**there**	a sink?		Yes,	**there**	**is.**
Is	**there**	a refrigerator?		No,	**there**	**isn't.**
Are	**there**	elevators?		Yes,	**there**	**are.**
Are	**there**	two bathrooms?		No,	**there**	**aren't.**

Note

For more information about *There is/There are*, see Unit 2, Item 3.

3. Adjectives

Subject	*be*	Adjective
The apartment	is	**cold.**
The lock	is	**broken.**

Note

For more information about Adjectives, see Unit 3, Item 2.

1. Present tense

Affirmative Statements			Negative Statements			
Subject	Verb		Subject	do/does + not	Base form	
I	**have**	a good job.	I	**don't**	**have**	a good job.
You	**wear**	a uniform.	You	**don't**	**wear**	a uniform.
He	**has**	experience.	He	**doesn't**	**have**	experience.
She	**wears**	glasses.	She	**doesn't**	**wear**	glasses.
We	**have**	new uniforms.	We	**don't**	**have**	new uniforms.
They	**have**	interesting jobs.	They	**don't**	**have**	interesting jobs.

Notes

- Both regular verbs and irregular verbs, like the verb *have*, form the negative by using *don't* or *doesn't* and the base form of the verb.
- *Have* is irregular because *-s* isn't added to the base form after *he* and *she*.
- For more information about the present tense, see Unit 9, item 1.

2. *Yes/No* questions

Questions				Short Answers	
Do/Does	Subject	Base form			
Do	you	**speak**	Spanish?	Yes, I **do.**	No, I **don't.**
Does	he/she	**get**	tips?	Yes, he **does.**	No, he **doesn't.**

Note

For more information about *Yes/No* Questions, see Unit 9, Item 2.

3. Past tense of *be*

Subject	*be*	
I	**was**	a housekeeper.
You	**were**	a bartender.
He	**was**	a plumber.
She	**was**	a landscaper.
We	**were**	waiters.
They	**were**	busboys.

Notes

- The past tense of *be* is used to talk about things that were true or happened in the past.
- The past form of *be* after *I, he* and *she* is *was*. After *you, we,* and *they* it is *were*.

4. *Can*

Statements				Questions			
Subject	*can*	Base form		Can	Subject	Base form	
I	**can**	**repair**	watches.	**Can**	you	**drive?**	
He	**can**	**use**	a computer.	**Can**	she	**speak**	two languages?

Note

For more information about *can*, see Unit 7, Item 3.

1. Have/Has

Subject	*have/has*	Noun
I	**have**	a headache.
You	**have**	a sore throat.
He	**has**	a fever.
She	**has**	a cough.
We	**have**	the flu.
They	**have**	a doctor's appointment.

Note

For more information about *have/has* see Unit 13, Item 1.

2. My _____ hurt(s).

Subject	Verb		Subject	Verb
My head	**hurts.**		Their stomachs	**hurt.**
His eye	**hurts.**		Our feet	**hurt.**

Notes

- When the subject is singular, *hurt* has an *-s* on the end.
- When the subject is plural, there is no *-s* on the end of *hurt*.

3. When I . . . , I . . .

	When clause				Main clause	
When	Subject	Verb		Subject	Verb	
When	**I**	have	a cold,	**I**	stay	in bed.
When	**she**	has	a backache,	**she**	uses	an icepack.

Notes

- These are factual conditionals. Factual conditionals tell what generally happens in certain situations.
- Simple present tense verbs are used in both the *when* clause and the main clause.
- When the *when* clause comes first, a comma is used before the main clause.
- When the main clause comes first, no comma is placed before the *when* clause.
  They stay in bed when they have a fever.

4. Must/Must not

Must

Subject	*must*	Base form	
You	**must**	**take**	your medicine every day.
She	**must**	**see**	a doctor today.

Must Not

Subject	*must not*	Base form	
You	**must not**	**take**	this medication. (You're allergic to it.)
He	**must not**	**go**	to work today. (He's too sick.)

Notes

- The word order is subject + *must (not)* + the base form of the verb.
- *Must* means that something is absolutely necessary.
- *Must not* means that you can't do something because it is dangerous, against the rules, or is bad for you.

1. Present tense

Affirmative Statements			Negative Statements			
Subject	Verb		Subject	*do/does + not*	Base form	
I	**listen**	to my teacher.	I	**don't**	**listen**	to my teacher.
You	**pay**	attention.	You	**don't**	**pay**	attention.
He	**likes**	his class.	He	**doesn't**	**like**	his class.
She	**writes**	stories.	She	**doesn't**	**write**	stories.
We	**raise**	our hands.	We	**don't**	**raise**	our hands.
They	**study**	English.	They	**don't**	**study**	English.

Note

For more information about the present tense, see Unit 9, Item 1.

2. Present-tense *Yes/No* questions

Questions				Short Answers	
Do/Does	Subject	Base form			
Do	I	**study**	English?	Yes, you **do.**	No, you **don't.**
Do	you	**walk**	To school?	Yes, I **do.**	No, I **don't.**
Does	he	**use**	a dictionary?	Yes, he **does.**	No, he **doesn't.**
Does	she	**raise**	her hand?	Yes, she **does.**	No, she **doesn't.**
Do	we	**take**	tests?	Yes, we **do.**	No, we **don't.**
Do	they	**read**	stories?	Yes, they **do.**	No, they **don't.**

Note

For more information about *Yes/No* questions, see Unit 9, Item 2.

3. Present continuous

Subject	*be*	*-ing* form of verb	Noun
I	**am**	**doing**	a puzzle.
You	**are**	**taking**	a test.
He	**is**	**raising**	his hand.
She	**is**	**drawing**	a picture.
We	**are**	**eating**	dinner.
They	**are**	**reading**	the newspaper.

Note

For more information about the present continuous, see Unit 5, Item 1.

Skills Index

Arithmetic
  Adding, 167
  Numbers, 2, 8
  Word problems, 151, 197
Culture Notes, 9, 32, 33, 63, 104, 106, 155, 156, 161, 175, 176, 187, 191, 204, 205, 207, 218, 221, 226
Dictionary, 2, 18, 32, 46–47, 60, 74–75, 90–91, 104, 120–121, 136–137, 142, 152–153, 182, 198–199, 214–215
Grammar
  a/an, 20, 139
  Abbreviations, 171
  Adjectives, 34–35, 40, 45, 74–75, 78, 79, 81, 86, 87, 88, 168, 181
    possessive, 64
  Adverbs of frequency, 167
  always/sometimes/never, 156
  be, 17
  can statements, 103
  Continuous statements, 73
  Contractions, 3, 7, 61, 82, 85, 88, 174, 180
  Final *s*, 128
  how much questions, 119, 151
  is/are, 24, 27, 30, 45, 58, 82, 85, 88, 118, 140, 174, 180
  Prepositions, 91, 92, 103, 125, 135
  Pronouns, 6, 7, 17, 39
  Punctuation, 29, 44
  of questions, 77, 85, 89
  Short questions and answers, 151
  Singular and plural nouns, 21–22, 31, 109
  Statements, 59
  Syllables, 171
  there is/there are, 30, 31, 181
  Verb tenses, 147
    Present, 123, 131, 135, 159, 167
    Present continuous, 151, 181
  want, 89
  where questions, 59
  who questions, 103
  Wh– questions, 17, 73, 135
  will/'ll, 167
  yes/no questions, 31, 59, 73, 89, 130, 132, 135
Graphs and Charts, 78, 159
Jobs
  Applications, 131, 182–197
  Schedules, 123–126, 128, 131, 134
Learning Tips, 17, 45, 59, 89, 135
Listening
  Adjectives, 74–75, 76
  Alphabet, 4

Checking for understanding, 7, 8, 11, 21, 22, 23, 24, 27, 40, 66, 73, 84, 98, 115, 127, 130, 131, 139, 145, 154, 157, 158, 162, 170, 179
Contractions, 61
Conversations, 16, 20, 54, 66
  Face–to–face, 93
  Telephone, 63
Map locations, 95
Numbers, 2, 8, 23, 105, 106
Place names, 11, 78, 79, 80
Pronouns, 3, 11
Stress on words, 139
Syllables, 108, 171
Times, 124
Vocabulary, 2, 18, 32
Maps
  City, 92–95, 102
  State, 83
  United States, 75, 77, 143
Reading
  Addresses, 52
  Advertisements, 56, 171, 172
  Aloud, 128
  Comprehension, 12, 14, 22, 23, 24, 42, 86, 116, 123, 126, 130, 132
  Conversation, 50, 141, 160
  Forms, 37, 119
  Letters, 53
  Library resources, 100
  Maps, 93–95, 102, 143, 180
  Paragraphs, 148
  Pronouns, 6
  Sentences, 48, 52
  Signs, 28
  Spelling, 5
  Telephone directories, 68
  Telephone numbers, 9
  Verbs, 62
  Vocabulary, 39
Sharing Our Stories, 13, 29, 43, 57, 69, 87, 101, 117, 133, 149, 165, 179
Speaking
  Ask and Answer, 5, 6, 10, 20, 25, 35, 41, 45, 49–50, 53, 55, 63, 67, 72, 77, 81–82, 88, 96, 140, 174
  Conversations, 63, 93, 127, 175
  Describing, 145
  Discussions, 42, 64, 93, 112, 121, 138, 144, 148, 161, 170, 174
  Explaining, 38
  Helpful expressions, 5, 10, 17

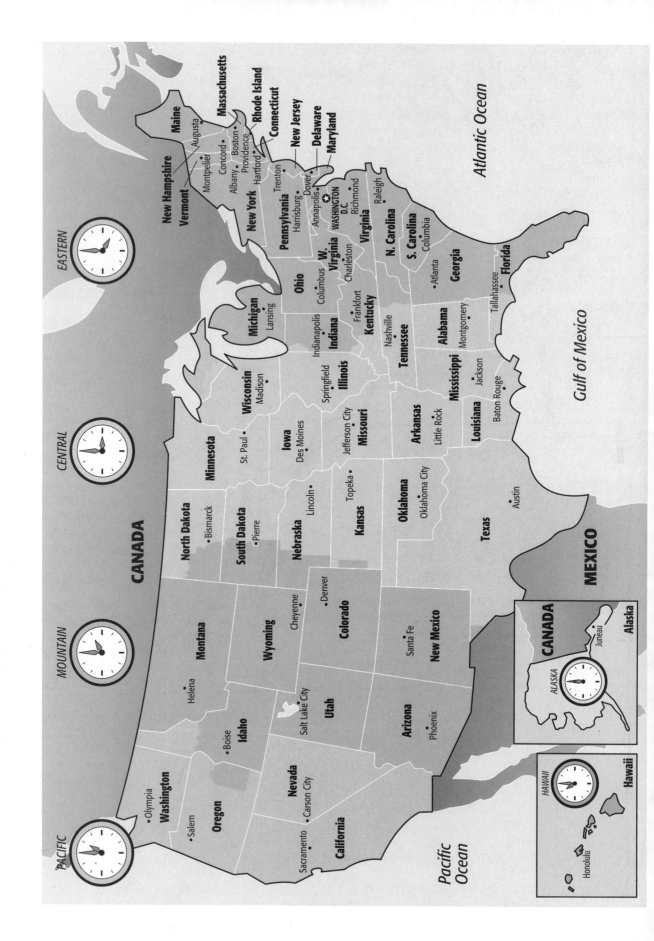

LBCC VOLUNTEER PROGRAM
Please return to W.E.B. 117